de Gruyter Studies in Organization 81

Korean Management

de Gruyter Studies in Organization

International Management, Organization and Policy Analysis

An international and interdisciplinary book series from de Gruyter presenting comprehensive research on aspects of international management, organization studies and comparative public policy.
It covers cross-cultural and cross-national studies of topics such as:
- management, organizations, public policy, and/or their inter-relation
- industry and regulatory policies
- business-government relations
- international organizations
- comparative institutional frameworks.

While each book in the series ideally has a comparative empirical focus, specific national studies of a general theoretical, substantive or regional interest which relate to the development of cross-cultural and comparative theory are also encouraged.

The series is designed to stimulate and encourage the exchange of ideas across linguistic, national and cultural traditions of analysis, between academic researchers, practitioners and policy makers, and between disciplinary specialists.
The volumes present theoretical work, empirical studies, translations and "state-of-the-art" surveys. The *international* aspects of the series are uppermost: there is a strong commitment to work which crosses and opens boundaries.

Kae H. Chung, Hak Chong Lee, Ku Hyun Jung

Korean Management

Global Strategy and Cultural Transformation

W DE G

Walter de Gruyter · Berlin · New York 1997

Kae H. Chung, Prof. Dr., Management Department, College of Business and Public Administration, Old Dominion University, Norfolk, USA

Hak Chong Lee, Prof. Dr., College of Business and Economics, Yonsei University, Seoul, Korea

Ku Hyun Jung, Prof. Dr., College of Business and Economics, Yonsei University, Seoul, Korea

With 12 tables and 7 figures.

⊗ Printed on acid-free paper which falls within the guidelines of the ANSI to ensure permanence and durability.

Library of Congress Cataloging-in-Publication Data

Chung, Kae H.
Korean Management : global strategy and cultural transformation / Kae H. Chung, Hak Chong Lee, Ku Hyun Jung.
XIV, 266 p. 23,0 × 15,5 cm. – (De Gruyter studies in organization ; 81)
Includes bibliographical references and index.
ISBN 3-11-014669-X (cloth : alk. paper). –
ISBN 3-11-014668-1 (pbk. : alk. paper)
1. Management – Korea (South) 2. Corporate culture – Korea (South) 3. Industries – Korea (South) I. Lee, Hak Chong. II. Jung, Ku Hyun. III. Title. IV. Series.
HD70.K6C48 1997
658′.0095195–dc21 97-22804
CIP

Die Deutsche Bibliothek – Cataloging-in-Publication Data

Chung, Kae H.:
Korean management : global strategy and cultural transformation / Kae H. Chung ; Hak Chong Lee ; Ku Hyun Jung. – Berlin ; New York : de Gruyter, 1997
(De Gruyter studies in organization ; 81)
ISBN 3-11-014668-1 brosch.
ISBN 3-11-014669-X Gb.
DBN: 95.059435.0 ⊗
SG: **17**

Printing: WB-Druck, Rieden am Forggensee. – Binding: Fuhrmann GmbH & Co. KG, Berlin. – Cover Design: Johannes Rother, Berlin.

Preface

Korea has achieved spectacular economic growth in the past three decades. The origin of its industrialization can be traced to the early 1960s when the military-dominated government established economic development as its primary goal and mobilized the nation's resources to achieve this end. The economy grew at an annual rate of nine percent. Its gross national product (GNP) per capita increased from less than $100 in 1962 to over $10,000 in 1995. Korea is now the world's 13th largest economy and the 10th largest trading nation. It became a member of OECD in 1996.

Several observers have attributed Korea's economic success to a number of factors: governmental economic policy, entrepreneurial business owners, a productive labor force, education-oriented Confucian culture, and favorable international trade. The government created, nurtured, and controlled big businesses to carry out its economic development policy. Individual entrepreneurs, commonly known as *Chaebols*, emerged and prospered as they followed the lead of the government in industrializing the nation. Confucian culture encouraged the population to be highly educated and dedicated to public service. Highly educated labor toiled under the "growth first, distribution later" policy to fuel the engine of economic growth. In addition, the international business environment was favorable to Korea's export drive.

Many of the factors that contributed to Korea's initial success have changed in the 1990s. The civilian-dominated government now keeps big businesses at arm's length. Today's businesses can no longer rely on government for financial support and monopolistic protection. Workers are no longer willing to toil under arduous working conditions with low pay. Dirty, hard, and dangerous jobs are now relegated to foreign workers. Wages are now the second highest in Asia. The Confucian virtue of loyalty and filial piety has been replaced by the materialistic pursuit of individual happiness and success. Korea's export drive based on cost leadership has been challenged by other newly developing nations such as China, India, Thailand, and Malaysia. These changes in the business environment present challenges to Korean firms. In the absence of governmental protection, Korean firms need to modify their managerial practices to become more competitive in their domestic and global markets. As protectionism becomes less common around the world, well-managed multinational firms are beginning to enter the Korean market and dominate its previously sheltered industries. In the global market too, only those firms that can compete with other developing and advanced nations in terms of product quality and price will survive. Are Korean firms prepared to meet these challenges?

If Korean firms can adapt to the new and challenging domestic and global environments, the Korean people will once again show the world that they can serve as a model for developing countries in their struggle to achieve economic development. Korean firms are already making some adjustments in response to environmental changes. They are restructuring far-flung enterprises in order to focus their energies on core technologies, are increasing R&D expenditures, are globalizing business operations (setting up research centers in Japan and U.S.A.), and are capitalizing on new opportunities (making inroads into China, Vietnam, and Russia). These efforts are modest but can be seen as the first step in upgrading Korea's capacity to engage in global industrial competition.

The purposes of this book are three-fold: First, this book reviews the transformation process of the Korean economy from an agrarian society to a dynamic industrial one. Various factors that involved in this process will be reviewed.

Second, the book examines the changing forces in Korea's business environment and the response of Korean businesses to these forces. Finally, the book provides some suggestions for Korean business executives and policy-makers in dealing with these changes.

Many books have been written about Korea's economic success in recent years. These books focused on Korea's economic success from the perspective of it being a state-led economy. But conditions have changed and a new perspective is needed. Political reform, coupled with the increasing complexity of managing a growing economy, has minimized the role of government. Consequently, the old paradigm of a state-led economy is no longer useful for studying the Korean economy and its managerial practices.

This book reflects on the change in the theoretical paradigm from a government-led economy to a more free-market economy. It also reflects on some changes needed in managerial practices in Korean firms. As the role of government in economic development is minimized, the role of individual managers in business affairs is increased. This is not to say that government becomes irrelevant in managing a nation's economy, but rather to point out that the role of government becomes limited when sustaining an advanced economy. This book takes the position that the role of government is crucial during the developmental stage of an economy and that the role of individual businesses becomes increasingly important as the economy expands.

A number of individuals and institutions contributed to the completion of this book. First, we thank the Korea Foundation for its financial support for this project. The Korea Research Foundation also supported this project. Second, Old Dominion University has contributed to this project by way of granting a research leave. Dean Taylor Sims, Old Dominion University, provided encouragement for completing the book. The Management Research Institute, Yonsei University, also provided us with partial support. Third, we thank Chairman Suk Rae Cho and Mr. Jai Whan Inn of Hyosung Group for providing us with valuable data. Ssangyong Human Resource Development Institute is also recognized for giving us opportunities to share our ideas. Its director, Mr. Hong Goon Yoon, provided continuous support for Korean Management Center at Old Dominion University. Finally, Bill Thompson, Hae Ryong Kim, and Rebecca White for their editorial comments. While these individuals and organizations have contributed to this book, any shortcomings are ours.

Kae H. Chung
Norfolk, Virginia
U.S.A.

Hack Chong Lee
Ku Hyun Chung
Seoul
Korea

Table of Contents

Chapter 1
Korean Industrial System: An Overview

1.1 Introduction

This book is about the Korean industrial system and how it helped to transform an underdeveloped economy into a major economic power. The Korean industrial system has been characterized by the concerted efforts of the government, business, labor, and the general public in industrializing the economy. These multi-faceted societal entities worked as if they were members of an industrial organization, often called *Korea, Inc.* This system is credited with the spectacular growth of the Korean economy in the past three decades. Since 1962, the Korean economy grew at an annual rate of nine percent. Korea is now the world's 13th largest economy and the 10th largest trading nation. In 1996, Korea became a member of the Organization for Economic Cooperation and Development (OECD).

The question now is whether or not the Korean industrial system will maintain its uniqueness and continue to propel the economy into a global economic power. What made Korea successful in the past will not necessarily make it successful in the future. When the economy was relatively small, it was possible for such a unified industrial system to emerge. As the economy has grown and become more complex, however, it has become increasingly difficult for the system to pursue the growth-oriented strategy and at the same time maintain a unity among various stakeholders. One problem is that, as the size of economic gains increases, so does the size of the relative share of these gains for various stakeholders. As the gap between relative shares of economic gains increases, so does the disunity between various stakeholders, making it difficult to maintain a national consensus regarding economic growth.

This chapter presents an overview of the process by which the Korean industrial system has emerged and contributed to Korea's economic success. In addition, it examines the changing nature of the Korean industrial system and how this change will affect its future economic growth. As an introduction to the book, this chapter outlines the issues that will be discussed later in other chapters. More specifically, this chapter first reviews those factors that have contributed to Korea's economic success in the past and then discusses various challenges and opportunities that lie ahead for the Korean economy.

1.2 Contextual Factors

A nation's economic performance is seen as an outcome of managing its industrial system. Management of an industrial system involves manipulating the system's internal factors within the context of external conditions. These internal factors are called *design factors* because they can be manipulated by managers to influence their performance. External conditions are called *contextual factors* because they provide the context within which managers operate. Contextual factors are usually not under the control of managers, but they nevertheless influence the system's performance. A number of contextual and design factors individually and jointly have contributed to Korea's economic success (Exhibit 1.1).

Scholars assert that certain contextual factors or preconditions must prevail in a society prior to its economic development (Weber, 1930; Nash, 1954; Kahl, 1959; McClelland, 1961; Spengler, 1961). In the case of Korea, the following contextual factors are cited as having a positive influence on its economic development: commitment to work, high achievement needs, education-oriented culture, leadership commitment, absence of retrogressive social elite, and favorable international business climate.

Exhibit 1.1: Contributing Factors to Korea's Economic Development

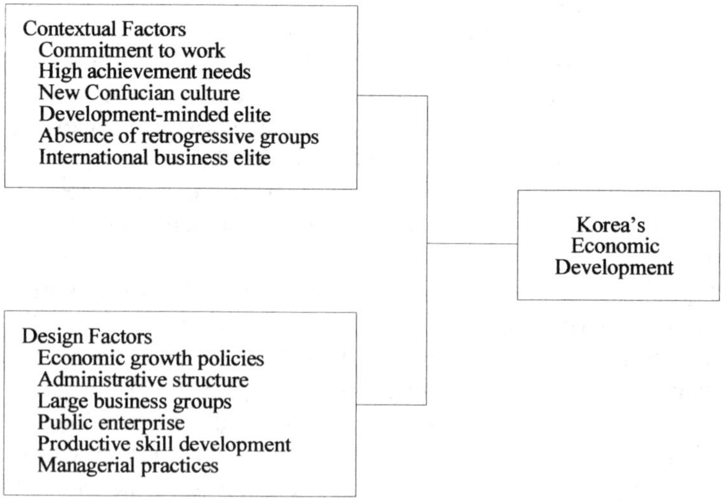

1.2.1 Commitment to Work

Max Weber (1930) asserted that the Protestant work ethic paved the way for industrialization in Western societies. In this value system, hard work is seen as a way of glorifying God, and its fruit or profit is considered a direct sign of God's blessing. In recent years, the meaning of work ethic has changed from a religious exaltation of work to an emphasis on work as a person's central life interest for satisfying a variety of human needs: biological, social, emotional, growth-oriented, and spiritual (Chung, 1977, pp. 241-244).

Although Koreans have not inherited the religious heritage of the Protestant work ethic, they nevertheless possess a strong work ethic to satisfy a variety of needs. Initially, Koreans toiled hard to survive in a resource-scarce and densely-populated country. Once they achieved their needs for food and shelter, other needs such as better pay, promotion, and personal growth emerged as reasons for hard work.

A study by Kim (1984) reported that, in 1967, 38.7 percent of the respondents surveyed in Korea said that they would work irrespective of economic necessity, and 57.6 percent would rather work on a job they consider worthwhile. Less than 2 percent would reject work totally. However, a similar study conducted in 1978 (Kim, 1992) reported that the percentage of people who would work irrespective of economic necessity had dropped to 10 percent and the percentage of people who would work only on meaningful tasks had dropped to 42.7 percent. Eighteen percent said they would work only if work had to be done. The decrease in commitment to work is not surprising because as people satisfy their basic needs, they are likely to work selectively or to spend more time on leisure activities.

The above findings have several implications for staffing people and designing work in the future. First, as Korean workers shy away from less meaningful work, firms need to depend on foreign workers. Foreign workers are now imported from countries such as China, Bangladesh, and the Philippines to do dirty, hard, and dangerous work in Korea. Second, some Korean firms outsource their production overseas to deal with labor shortages in Korea and to take advantage of low labor costs. Finally, some firms have abandoned labor-intensive operations in favor of high-tech and high value-added ones.

1.2.2 High Achievement Needs

McClelland (1961, 1962) believed that the people in a country must possess a desire to achieve a high standard of living (high achievement need) prior to the nation's economic success. According to him, an achieving society is full of individuals with high achievement needs. Individuals with high achievement needs are likely to set realistic goals for themselves, take moderate risks, and actively search for opportunities to succeed. A study by Kim (1984) found that Koreans possessed high achievement needs. Achievement needs, measured by "aggressiveness in materialistic pursuit," "frugality in consumption," and "materialistic outlook on life," were higher among Korean workers and managers than in their counterparts in North America and Japan. It is possible that Koreans are still striving to achieve a higher standard of living, while Japanese and Americans may have achieved theirs.

In contrast to the decline in commitment to work, the achievement orientation of Korean workers and managers increased slightly between 1966 and 1978 (Kim, 1992). The achievement orientation, measured by the desire to invest one's wealth and energy for the future, was high for both managers and workers. These findings suggest that Korean workers avoid dirty and hard work, but they strive to achieve worthwhile goals in their lives. To them, work must have a meaning other than simply serving as a means of survival.

What instills high achievement orientation in Koreans? For a start, Koreans need to be competitive to survive in a resource-poor land with a large population. They have to eliminate a large number of their peers in the process of entering good schools and gaining employment in major corporations or governmental agencies. Academic achievement is essential in these endeavors. Korea's Confucian culture also reinforces the desire to achieve. This point will be discussed in the following section.

1.2.3 New Confucian Culture

Confucianism places heavy emphasis on education and building harmonious relationships (Song, 1990; Chang and Chang, 1994). These two elements seem to have had conflicting effects on Korea's economic development. On one hand, Confucianism encouraged people to pursue careers that require higher education. But, on the other hand, it discouraged people to engage in commerce and manufacturing jobs that are the backbone of a nation's economic development. In the Confucian value system, scholars and government officials are at the top of the social strata, followed by farmers, engineers (artisans), merchants, and slave laborers. This value system is deeply rooted in Korean minds. In an occupational study in 1978, Kim (1993) found that survey respondents placed government officials, professors, and lawyers at the top of the social status scale. However, when these respondents were asked who contributed to the nation's economic development most, they rated engineers, technicians, and professors at the top.

The old Confucian view of commerce and manufacturing could have been an obstacle to Korea's industrial development. If most young people had viewed commerce and engineering negatively, talented people might not have entered into these wealth-generating occupations. Max Weber (1951) even argued that Confucianism hindered economic progress in Asian countries. But in reality, the anti-industrial element in Confucianism has been gradually moderated by the Western influences of capitalism, democracy, and Christianity. These Western values have been well received by Asians, especially by Koreans, who tend to be non-ideological in their search for economic well-being, freedom, and spiritual awareness.

In Asian countries such as Korea, Japan, Taiwan, Hong Kong, and Singapore, traditional Confucian values are modified by Western values to form new Confucian ethics (Tu, 1984). As the Western and Eastern ethics are both world-affirming value systems, they can be easily blended. As a result, new Confucian ethics have emerged as an amalgam of the education-minded and group-oriented values of the East and the pragmatic and economically-oriented values of the West. These new ethics are characterized by an emphasis on education, consensus formation, strong affirmation for commercialism, strong leadership of government, and growth-oriented economic goals, providing a dynamic force behind industrialization.

Another key element in Confucianism is its emphasis on building harmonious relationship (Chang and Chang, 1994; Song, 1990). Confucianism places a heavy emphasis on maintaining harmonious relationships between the king and his subjects, the father and his son, the husband and his wife, the young and the old, and between friends. These relationships are governed by appropriate rules:

(1) loyalty to the king;
(2) filial piety to parents;
(3) respect for elders;
(4) obedience to husband;
(5) trust between friends.

As one can see, these rules define obligations for the weaker parties in the Confucian context (children, sons, people, wives, and the young) towards their superiors (parents, father, husband, elders, and the king). The superiors are in return expected to protect their weaker members and bestow kindness upon their beneficiaries.

These authoritarian and paternalistic values played an important role in implementing government economic plans in Korea. Given the fact that the Korean economy has been led by the government, the Confucian ethic stressing authoritarianism permitted the government to focus its bureaucratic energies on its national priority--economic development (SaKong, 1993). At the same time, the emphasis on harmonious relationships produced receptive responses from the nation's entrepreneurs. Close personal relationships based on family, school, and regional ties helped to strengthen the relationship between businessmen and government officials. On the other hand, the authoritarian Confucian ethic fostered dependency of businesses on government and retarded the development of managerial skills in the private sector that are necessary for survival in an increasingly complex and globally interdependent business world.

1.2.4 Development-minded Elite

A nation's economic development, as Spengler (1961) asserted, depends on the transformation of the people, especially the elite. This requirement is more evident in a developing economy than in an advanced one. In an advanced economy, such as the U.S., the combination of the Protestant work ethic, free-market economy, and plentiful natural resources have contributed to the rise of individual entrepreneurs and private capital formation, making the nation's economic expansion possible. In this free market economy, the government played a passive role in the nation's business affairs. In the absence of natural resources and capital formation, however, the ruling elite in Korea stepped in to play an important role in capital formation and in acquiring raw materials for both the private and public sectors.

The presence of political elite alone, however, is not enough for a nation's economic development. There must be a pool of talented technocrats who carry out the political elite's intentions. In Korea, while the land is poorly endowed with natural resources, it has an abundant resource in its relatively well-educated and disciplined population. In the early 1960s, prior to Korea's economic takeoff, the level of formal education was judged to be as high as that of advanced nations (Kim, 1980; Jones and SaKong, 1980). At that time, Korea was believed to have the highest concentration of foreign-trained doctorates of any country in the world. In addition, Korean workers were judged to be highly industrious, manually dexterous, and highly trainable.

Though the Korean War in the early 1950s was a tragedy, it had a positive effect on the development of political and social elites. A nation's economic development can be seen as a major resource mobilization program, and the War prepared the Korean people to carry out such a resource mobilization effort. Young people were taken out of remote villages and put through rigorous training and military maneuvers, preparing them to function in an industrial society. At the same time, the war produced a cadre of political elites who were capable of mobilizing the nation's resources to undertake a series of economic developmental efforts.

1.2.5 Absence of Retrogressive Groups

An absence of socially powerful, retrogressive groups in Korea cleared the way for the nation to strive for economic development. Strong social groups with world-rejecting religion, communists, or conservative landlords, if they had existed, could have retarded Korea's effort for industrialization. In 1985, about 20 percent of Koreans classified themselves as Buddhists and about the same percentage as Christians (Economic Planning Board, 1987). As a world-rejecting religion, Buddhism might have had a negative effect on the Korean economy. In reality, however, Buddhism had neither a positive nor a negative effect on economic development. Except for a few monks who chose to reject worldly comfort, most Buddhists have accepted the worldly way of life and limited their religious practices to visiting temples on special occasions or participating in Buddha's birthday celebration.

In contrast, Christianity has had a visible effect on Korea's modernization (Song, 1990). Western-style schools and hospitals established by missionaries educated people to function in a modern society. Korean Christians also learned democratic processes in governing church activities. Organized Sunday services, regular Bible studies, and prayer meetings have taught Korean Christians to function in organized endeavors.

Korea avoided the effects that communism could have an economy by adopting a staunch anti-communist political stance while establishing an economy based on capitalist principles. After World War II, Korea was divided into the communist North and capitalist South. Communist North Koreans rejected business activities for profit because they viewed such activities as exploitation of the proletariat. South Korean capitalists, on the other hand, embraced the concept of profit as the fruit of their work. The end result has been that while the South Korean economy continued to expand, the northern economy stagnated. Given the fact that North Korea is richly endowed with minerals and inherited Korea's industrial base at the end of World War II, the devastating effect of communism on the economy is clearly evident. Few communist countries have ever succeeded in sustaining themselves as viable economic entities; North Korea is an example.

Korea was also free of conservative landlords. As a privileged class, they could have dominated economic power and resisted any economic developmental effort because such a development might have meant a sharing of power or wealth with others. Landlords in the Philippines are examples of the stultifying effect landlords can have on economic growth (Park and Green, 1994). During the period of American colonialization in the Philippines, before and during World War II, the agrarian elite remained as a strong social, economic, and political power. They managed the agrarian economy to produce and export agricultural products. These landlords, even after the war, maintained their power structure to resist any industrialization efforts for the fear of losing their power base. If industrialized, landlords would have lost their economic power to industrialists.

In contrast, the 36 years of Japanese occupation in Korea and the subsequent Japanese departure left no oligopolistic economic classes nor powerful landlords. In the post-war period, Korea undertook a series of land reforms that distributed the formerly Japanese-owned land to small tenant farmers. As a result, when the military-dominated government in the 1960s launched a series of economic development plans, there was no visible resistance. The apparent economic stagnation of the Philippines and the phenomenal growth in Korea offer a striking contrast in the post World War II economic development of these two countries.

1.2.6 International Business Climate

The international business climate in the 1960s was favorable to Korea. Since Korea was short of capital formation and technology to launch a series of economic development plans, it had to rely on the assistance of advanced nations and the international financial community. The U.S. was the major provider and lender of capital. Until early 1960s, foreign aids from the U.S. was the major source of foreign currency during the post-war period. Foreign aid was then replaced by loans. The U.S. also provided the market for Korean products, permitting Korea to pursue an export-driven economy.

The normalization of relationships between Korea and Japan in the mid-1960s opened the door for Japanese capital and technology to enter into Korea. Due to the geographical proximity and complementary nature of the two economies, Japanese inroads into Korea took initially the form of foreign direct investment; Japan then gradually became a provider of low to mid-range technology. In the 1960s, the Japanese invested in Korean manufacturing facilities to take advantage of low wages in Korea. They subsequently sold mid-range technologies--automobile manufacturing, steel making, and less-advanced consumer electronics.

Korea initially depended on these two economic partners--the U.S. and Japan--for its economic development. As Koreans gained experience in industrialization, they looked for opportunities elsewhere. The first such opportunity came in the mid-1970s during the worldwide energy crisis. As the oil-rich Middle Eastern countries began to spend money on construction, Koreans were there to capitalize on this construction boom. In the 1980s, as the cold war ended, Koreans rushed into the former Communist bloc countries--China, USSR, Hungary and others--looking for business opportunities.

Korea undoubtedly benefitted from the friendly international business community, which helped the Korean economy to emerge as a major global economic power. Korea is a relatively small country geographically, but as one of the world's ten largest trading nations, it is economically important enough to influence the global economy through its foreign trade. As the country emerges as a global economic power, its economic partners expect Korea to play a more responsible role in world business affairs. Trade partners demand that the Korean market to be opened to their products; developing nations expect Korea to lend aid to them. Other industrialized nations now hesitate to transfer their technology to Korea for the fear of a boomerang effect. In other words, the world business community has become less friendly toward Korea.

1.3 Design Factors

While contextual factors provided the Korean economy with opportunities for its industrialization, the following design factors were manipulated by Korean policy makers to produce desired outcomes. Export-oriented economic policies, government administrative structure, big businesses, public enterprises, productive labor force, and aggressive managerial systems were all contributing factors in Korea's industrialization.

1.3.1 Economic Growth Policies

In the early 1960s, the military-dominated government established economic growth and development as its primary goal and started to mobilize the nation's resources to achieve that end. The government undertook a series of five-year economic plans and carried them out with superb administrative skills. Government officials, under the leadership of General Park Chung Hee and later Chun Do Whan and Roh Tae Woo, applied administrative principles that were applied to military operations to manage the nation's economic affairs (Jones and SaKong, 1980). They adopted a management-by-objective (MBO) system in their developmental efforts. They set specific goals, planned and organized their activities to achieve these goals, executed them, and reviewed their progress.

Economic plans existed in Korea prior to the early 1960s, but they were ineffective because they had been designed in order to receive foreign aids rather than to develop the nation's industrial base. A series of five-year plans began in 1962. These were different from previous plans because they involved the full commitment of political leaders and had a clear developmental vision. From the inception of the first five-year plan, the government economic planners charted their economic development courses in a coherent manner. The first two five-year plans (1962-71) were designed to break the cycle of poverty, establish the foundation for self-sustaining economy, and modernize the nation's industrial structure. Investment priorities were given to build the nation's infrastructure (cement and fertilizer), produce import-substituting consumer goods, and build export-oriented light-manufacturing capacities. In the third and fourth five-year planning cycles (1972-81), the government made a major effort to build chemical and heavy industries in order to gain industrial competitiveness. Automobile, machinery, steel, shipbuilding, chemical, and petrochemical industries were the direct beneficiaries of the government's financial and legislative support. This was the period when Korea laid a firm foundation for its export-driven economy. This was also a period when Korea's big businesses emerged as a dominant force in the Korean economy and globally visible entities.

In the fifth and sixth five-year planning periods (1982-91), the focus was on improving the balance of payments by accelerating export-led growth and technology. Excessive investment in heavy and chemical industries and export-related imports during the third and fourth economic planning period resulted in high inflation, foreign debt, and trade deficit in the 1970s and early 1980s. In order to remedy this situation, the government slowed new investments and fiscal subsidies but expanded its export-related activities --intensive export promotion, export market diversification, and financial support for exporters. As a result, inflation slowed and a trade surplus began to appear.

1.3.2 Administrative Structure

In many underdeveloped countries, economic plans often fail, not because of a lack of sincerity or substance, but because of a lack of administrative mechanisms and skills. This was not the case with Korea. In order to implement its economic plans, the government established an administrative structure that guided, supported, and controlled the business activities of the private and public sectors of the economy. Although the government had been dominated by the military, its economically oriented ministries and agencies (such as Agriculture, Finance, Industry and Trade, and Science and Technology) were staffed by people with professional backgrounds, including professors, lawyers, and scientists. These leaders were given sufficient authority to shape and direct economic policies. Their activities were coordinated through the Economic Planning Board, composed of economically-oriented ministry officials and the Prime Minister, and were often directed by the President. The "visible hand" of the government frequently intervened in the operation of the market system and the activities of the private sector. The Korean economy was often called "Korea, Inc.," because it was managed as if it were a company, in which the President acted as the CEO (Chief Executive Officer), the ministry officials as planners and coordinators, and heads of private and public corporations as COOs (Chief Operating Officers).

The active participation of the government in managing the nation's business affairs has diminished in recent years. The new civilian-dominated government, which came into power in 1993, is taking a less active role in steering the nation's economy. As the economy grew substantially and became increasingly complex, the direct intervention of the government in the nation's business affairs is becoming less effective. As a result, the responsibility for managing business affairs is gradually relegated to the private sector.

1.3.3 Business Groups (*Chaebols*)

In the process of industrializing the Korean economy, the roles of government and business were clearly differentiated. The government was the planner and businesses were the implementer. The government used a selected group of enterprises as its instrument for economic development. Prior to the 1960s, Korean businesses were relatively small and poorly capitalized. The government, in an effort to industrialize the economy, had to raise capital for a selected group of successful and loyal entrepreneurs and nurture them with low-interest loans, preferential taxes, import-export licenses, and acquisitions of governmental properties at below-market prices (Shin, 1985).

As a result of this preferential treatment, a selected group of businesses were able to expand their business activities and accumulate enormous wealth. The government did little to restrain these businesses as long as they used their wealth to expand economic activities, create jobs and increase exports. These big businesses are commonly known as *Chaebols*. A *Chaebol* is a group of firms owned and controlled by an entrepreneur and his family members (Jones and SaKong, 1980; Lee and Lee, 1990).

Successful Korean *chaebols* gained their prominence in the 1970s when the government aggressively promoted heavy and chemical industries (SaKong, 1993). In order to promote these industries, well-established entrepreneurs were called in to launch new ventures in targeted industries. They were again provided with various subsidies and incentives. As a result, these enterprises became highly diversified and rapidly. Between 1973 and 1978, the 46 large *chaebols* grew at an average annual rate of 22.8 percent. This is compared to the nation's economic growth rate of 9.9 percent during the same period (SaKong, 1993, p. 61). The *Chaebols*' contribution to the nation's economy during this period was most noticeable in the manufacturing sector, which increased from 31.8 percent in 1973 to 43.0 in 1978.

1.3.4 Public Enterprise

While private enterprise served as the primary engine for Korea's economic growth, public enterprise laid the foundation on which the economy could expand. The government used the public sector primarily to build the infrastructure of the economy (such as banking, education, electricity, communications, and transportation). Korea Development Bank, Electric Power Corporation, Korea Broadcasting Systems, Korea Highway Corporation, and Korea Trade Promotion Corporation are examples. When the government perceived the critical need of building the economy's infrastructure, it did not hesitate to create such public enterprises and directly got involved in owning and managing them.

The importance of public enterprises in the nation's economy can be demonstrated by their activities and the strategic position they occupy. In 1972, the public sector accounted for 87 percent in financial transaction, 66 percent in electricity, 31 percent in mining, 30 percent in transportation and communication, and 15 percent in manufacturing (Jones, 1976, p. 76). The public sector grew at an annual rate of 10 percent between 1963 and 1977; its share in the nation's GDP averaged about 10 percent between 1963 and 1986 (SaKong, 1993, p. 31). These figures are as high as those in socialist economies such as India and Pakistan. Furthermore, the fact that public enterprises dominated the infrastructure of the economy indicates that they have played a vital role in the nation's economic development.

In many countries, public enterprises were known for their inefficiency. For this reason, the public often demanded privatization. The Korean case was different. From its inception, the growth-oriented government relied on a highly trained professional elite to plan, organize, execute, and monitor the nation's economic affairs at all levels of organizations (Caiden and Kim, 1991). Management of public enterprises was no exception. Trained managers were hired to run these enterprises and were held accountable for their performance as if they were managing private enterprises. Performance evaluation systems with an accompanying incentive bonus system were introduced in the early 1980s (SaKong, 1993). To maintain the objectivity of these evaluation systems, outside professionals were often summoned for the evaluation process.

1.3.5 Productive Labor Force

The labor force, too, played an important role in Korea's industrialization. While Korea is poorly endowed with natural resources, it has an abundant stock of relatively well-educated, disciplined human resources. More than 98 percent of those under the age of 55 can read and write. Student enrollment in secondary schools comprised more than 94 percent of their age group, the highest among developing countries. This figure is even higher than the average of 93 percent for 19 advanced nations (Song, 1990). Total expenditures for education amounted to 13.3 percent of GNP in 1984, including both private (6.9 percent) and public (6.4 percent) sources, compared to 5.7 percent in Japan, 6.7 percent in the U.S. (Kim, 1986).

Korean workers are not only well-educated but also relatively well-disciplined. The compulsory military training instills discipline, preparing the young populace to function effectively in a complex industrial society. Young people are taken out of remote villages and towns and sent through rigorous military training. Life in modern manufacturing plants demands worker discipline; the military services act as a training ground for Korean workers.

While the quality of the labor force is relatively high, wages had been relatively low until recently. Wages have risen substantially since the late 1980s when the labor movement was liberalized. In 1987, entry level male production workers received an average of $420 per month (Chang and Chang, 1994), about one-fifth of their counterparts' wages in the U.S. Under the government policy of “growth first, distribution later,”workers' wages were deliberately kept low. Workers were discouraged by the government from organizing themselves for better pay and improved working conditions. Whenever there was a dispute between labor and management concerning wage increases, the government intervened in favor of management. This practice stopped in the late 1980s as a part of the political reform process started in 1987. Currently, labor negotiations are left up to management and employees, and worker wages are new about $1,200 per month.

1.3.6 Managerial Practices

Korean managers and their managerial systems also contributed to the nation's economic development. To the casual observer, Korean managerial systems may appear similar to Japanese managerial systems. For a start, both Korea and Japan have business groups. Each business group is composed of a number of companies. Although these companies are independently listed in their respective stock exchanges, they more or less cooperate with each other as though they were parts of a major corporation. Another similarity is the formal hierarchical structure of Korean and Japanese firms. Hierarchical ranks such as section chief, department head, division head, and president of an organization are expressed by the same Chinese characters. Indeed, Korea has adopted numerous managerial systems and practices from Japan.

Although Japanese and Korean managers share many similarities, significant differences can be found between them. First, while Japanese managers rely on consensual decision making processes, Korean managers tend to make top-down managerial decisions. Top-down decisions stifle information flow within an organization, preventing effective cooperation. In the case of Korea, however, such decision processes have not deterred chief executives or managers from making effective decisions. Chief executives rely on the office of planning and control, which serves as a think tank for the CEO for information processing (Chang and Chang, 1994). A typical office of planning and control at the business group's headquarters serves as the nerve center of the entire organization. Its main functions are to provide relevant information for the decision-makers at the head office, as well as for individual companies, and to coordinate the activities of individual companies as well as those of the head office.

Second, Korean managers tend to be more individualistic than their counterparts in Japan (Kim, 1982). Individualistic thinking and behavior can prevent people from blindly following other people's bad ideas. The nature of individualism among Koreans, however, is different from that of Americans. While Americans pursue individualism outside the context of a group, Koreans pursue individualistic behavior within the context of a group (Chang and Chang, 1994). They are loyal to their group but do not hesitate to disagree with other members. This peculiar mixture of individualism and groupism can have a positive impact on managerial behavior by preventing "groupthink" and, at the same time, promoting group solidarity.

Finally, many Korean managers received the American style of managerial education and training, and these experiences serve them well in dealing with American managers. Most Korean men have served in the military where the American-style military training and services are provided. Also, most managerial practices during the military-dominated administration in Korea were adopted from the U.S. military management systems. The use of the office of planning and control is a case in point. Further, a high percentage of Korean management professors have received their formal educational training in the U.S.

In short, Korean managers have developed a unique style of management that is built on the merits of three distinctive cultural heritages: Korean, American, and Japanese. This uniqueness will serve Korean firms well as they expand globally. Flexibility and adaptability will be the key to success in the increasingly complex global economy. This challenge will be further elaborated on in the next section.

1.4 Managerial Challenges

Many of the factors that contributed to Korea's success in the past have changed in the 1990s. These changes present challenges and opportunities for Korean businesses. Some of these changes are discussed in the following sections: changing business-government relations, the changing nature of big businesses, demands for equitable income distribution, new world trade order, and north-south Korea relations.

1.4.1 Changing Business-Government Relations

The symbiotic relationship between business and government was inevitable in the initial stage of economic development. Since the private sector of the economy was weak in administrative structure and capital formation, the government played an active role in overcoming such weakness and steering the nation's economy. However, as the economy has grown in size and complexity, so has the task of managing it. As a result, the government's ability to steer the economy has become less effective. For example, the investment decisions made by the government during the 1970s in heavy and chemical industries created unbalanced economic growth, resulting in excess capacity, cut-throat competition, and serious financial burdens (SaKong,

1993, pp. 170-171). The demands for products in these industries were overestimated during times when the world market was experiencing oversupplies of these products.

The political reform process that started in 1987 brought about major changes in economic policy. No longer is the nation's economic policy dictated by the Office of the President, with the assistance of the Economic Planning Board (EPB) and the Ministry of Trade and Industry (MTI). The National Assembly, which used to rubberstamp the economic planning of the executive branch, now shares the responsibility of formulating the nation's economic plans. Moreover, the civilian-dominated administration under President Kim Young Sam keeps big businesses at an arm's length. President Kim made a pledge of not taking monetary donations from these businesses (Sohn, 1993a). Now the government has become just one of the many stakeholders that a business has to deal with in a pluralistic and complex society.

The new relationship between business and government will weaken the tight control of government on business. However, this new relationship does not mean that Korea is entering into a free market economy. Despite the announced policy of liberating the economy, the government still intervenes in the investment decisions of the private sector. For example, the government initially blocked Samsung Business Group from entering the automobile industry (Sohn, 1994). (This was reversed later.) It also prevented Hyundai from entering the steel industry (Kang, 1994). The government's objections were based on an argument that such a free entry would lead to excessive investment and cut-throat competition, which in turn would result in the waste of the nation's valuable resources. In short, the role of government has changed from protecting and nurturing big businesses to regulating them.

1.4.2 Managerial Reform

Korea's big businesses have grown under the protection of the government. Because these businesses were nurtured and protected by the government by providing low interest loans, favorable exchange rates, direct subsidies, and market entry protection, they have survived and expanded without much competitive pressure and without the skills of professional management. Moskowitz (1989), relying on Alfred Chandler's framework of studying the relationship between the development of large industries and the rise of professional management in the U.S., observed that in the case of Korea the rise of *chaebols* was not the outcome of professional management. The unique characteristic of Korea's economic growth has been the ownership of industrial assets in the hands of a few entrepreneurs and their families and the visible hand of government in allocating such assets.

As the nation's economic power is concentrated in the hands of a few individuals and families, issues have been raised regarding their legitimacy and efficiency (SaKong, 1993; *Business Korea*, 1993, pp. 18-20). The legitimacy issue is based on the perception that *chaebols* have accumulated huge wealth with governmental supports. The government's preferential treatment of *chaebols* is perceived to be have been carried out at the expense of taxpayers and non-*chaebol* businesses. Taxpayers have carried the burden of supporting the *chaebols*, and non-*chaebol* firms have been deprived of available resources. To the extent that big businesses expanded the nation's economy and created jobs for the populace, they took the credit. However, as these firms become too powerful, sometime negatively affecting economic well-being, people become resentful. A survey conducted by Jung (1994) revealed that *chaebols* have a serious image problem with the Korean people. Some of the negative images include beliefs that they engage in speculation on real estate, have excessive concentration of economic power, pursue octopus-style diversification, and portray lack of concern for the environment.

The issue of efficiency is related to the political nature of the nation's resource allocation. No one denies that *chaebols* have been the main instrument for Korea's economic success. At the early stages of industrialization, the government had to channel the nation's limited resources to a few loyal and successful entrepreneurs to achieve the needed economies of scale. However, dependency on government created inefficiency on the part of *chaebols* in two ways.

First, because *chaebols* were protected from competition by the government, they were able to expand into businesses unrelated to their core businesses. This lack of competition resulted in inefficiency in the economy by limiting the entry of other competitors or by not allowing potential competitors access to a level playing field. Second, since *chaebols* depended heavily on government for survival, they had to spend a considerable amount of their resources for political lobbying and bribes. It was speculated that Korean businesses spent as much as 0.8 percent of their sales or one-third of their profits for such purpose (Jung, 1989).

Additionally, the management style of Korean firms, which had served them well during the early stages of economic development, may not be suitable for managing organizations in an increasingly complex and dynamic global economy. Korean management has been generally characterized by authoritarian leadership and relation-oriented personnel management, practices reinforced by the Confucian culture (Chung and Lee, 1989, pp. 163-180; Chang and Chang, 1994). Authoritarian leadership is said to be effective when tasks are relatively simple and structured and people expect their leader to be authoritarian (Fielder, 1967). These two qualifications exemplify the management style during the early stages of economic development. As the economy matures and opens itself to the world economy, it requires the participation of large numbers of talented people. Relation-oriented personnel management based on family, school, and regional ties limits a wider participation of talented individuals.

Korean management is at a crossroad. In order to survive in an increasingly open and competitive global market, Korean firms need to transform their retrogressive managerial style into a more open and progressive one. Authoritarian leadership and relation-based personnel management must give way to participative leadership and competency-based personnel management. Samsung, the leading business group in Korea, already has taken a major step to revolutionalize its managerial culture (Sohn, 1993b; Chun, 1994). Job applicants are no longer required to identify the schools they attended, executives are required to be at production plants several times per week, and the group secretariat is banned from meddling in the personnel affairs of its subsidiaries. Additionally, staff training has been significantly expanded to include all levels of employees. Managerial reforms at Samsung are aimed at putting the company in the center of the world's first-class enterprises in the 21st century.

1.4.3 Income Distribution and Equity

In the past three decades, Korea has pursued an unbalanced economic growth policy that favored the manufacturing sector of the economy over the agricultural sector, large companies over small and medium-sized companies, and entrepreneurs over workers. As a result, the industrial sector expanded rapidly, but the preferred segments of the society gained proportionally higher incomes than did the others. The disparity between the rural farming sector and the urban industrial sector widened. Because the government favored large firms as its instrument for industrialization, small firms were deprived of funds. Wages were deliberately kept low to make Korean products competitive in the international market.

However, Korea's income distribution has been recognized as one of the most equitable among the newly developed nations. It is also comparable to the U.S. and Japan (Song, 1990). To narrow the income disparity between rural and urban households, the government launched the New Village Movement (*Saemaul Undong*) in 1971, which was aimed at improving the infrastructure (electricity, irrigation, and flood control) in the rural area and farm income (Moon, 1991). Additionally, a price support policy for agricultural products was adopted.

The government's industrial policy of picking winners made Korea a land of large firms (Hamilton and Orrù, 1989). Within this policy framework, small and medium-sized firms have been treated as second-class citizens in the nation's resource allocation. The Kim Young Sam administration has been keenly aware of the importance of small and medium-sized firms in the economy and the need for correcting the imbalance. The seventh five-year economic plan under President Kim pledged to support small and medium-size firms to enhance their competitiveness (*New Five-Year Economic Plan*, 1993, Republic of Korea, 1993).

The political reform process, started in 1987, changed the low wage strategy in the Korean economy. As a result of the diminishing role of government in the nation's labor relations, workers' wages have risen substantially in recent years. Hourly wages in the manufacturing sector went up by 500 percent between 1985 and 1995 (*The Economist*, 1996, p.77). Korean wages are the second highest in Asia after Japan. Due to increasing wages, Korean goods have become less competitive in the international market. Korea's export drive, based on cost leadership, has been challenged by newly developing countries such as China, India, Malaysia, and Thailand.

While the income distribution gap between urban and rural households and among industrial sectors has improved somewhat, the disparity between property-owners and non-owners has worsened in recent years. It was estimated that, as of 1989, about 3 percent of the population owned over 65 percent of total private land. Among landowners, the upper 5 and 10 percent owned 65.2 and 76.9 percent respectively (Kang, 1989; Hong, 1991; SaKong, 1993). Meanwhile, the price of land went up on the average of 24 percent annually between 1987 and 1990 (Hong, 1991). The increase in land price adversely affected home ownership for average wage earners. Home ownership in urban areas had declined to less than 50 percent by the late 1980s, while the price of apartments went up by 51.4 percent between 1985 and 1989 (Korea Research Institute for Human Settlements, 1991). It is estimated that in 1994 unearned incomes from properties were as high as 66.5 percent of Korea's GNP (*Hankook Ilbo*, October 18, 1994, p. 4).

The income disparity between property owners and non-owners offers serious challenges as well as opportunities to the Korean economy. As the price of land increases, so does the pressure for higher wages, rents, and consumer prices. As noted earlier, Korea is no longer a low-wage country; companies that once relied on low wages have moved out of the country or ceased to operate. As the percentage of unearned incomes from properties in GNP increases, the motivation of workers to work decreases. In the United States, where wages and salaries constitute a major source of household incomes, people are motivated to work. In Korea, where unearned incomes overshadow earned incomes, motivation to work will diminish.

The appreciation of land prices, on the other hand, presents a rare opportunity for the Korean economy. *Chaebols* are believed to own a large share of the private land. Proceeds from the sale of their land can be a major source of capital formation, which can be invested in plant and equipment, R&D, and on other wealth-producing activities. The government also can tap into the land price appreciation to improve the nation's infrastructure and the pool of scientific and technological expertise. Although land prices have gone up substantially, Korea's property tax revenue as a percentage of the GNP in 1989 was less than 0.5 percent, compared to 3.1 percent in 1988 for the U.S. and 3.4 percent in 1988 for Japan (SaKong, 1993). The Korean government in recent years has made serious efforts to increase property tax revenue and at the same time to curb speculation on and increases in land prices. Property owners are now required to register their properties on a "real name" basis. This system is to accurately trace real estate transactions and to reflect actual values of equity holdings in taxation.

1.4.4 New World Trade Order

In the absence of domestic capital formation and technological development, Korea heavily relied on foreign sources for its economic survival and development. President Syngman Rhee depended on foreign aids to sustain the economic life of Korea in the aftermath of World War II and during the Korean War. Industrial programs during this period were aimed at developing import substitution industries primarily in consumer goods, food and textiles. Subsequent leadership, under President Park Chung Hee, relied on foreign loans, technology, and trade to pursue Korea's export-oriented industrialization programs. These programs led Korea out of perpetual poverty to becoming a global economic power.

As Korea's economic power increases, so do trade disputes with other nations and difficulties associated with technology transfer. The U.S., which used to treat Korea with most favored nation status, now sees Korea as a fierce competitor, closing its market to Korean products while forcing the Korean market to open up to U.S. products. Likewise, the Japanese, who provided Korea with mid-range technology in the past, now withhold technology transfer for fear of a boomerang effect.

Another major development has been the successful conclusion of the multilateral trade agreements in 1994, commonly known as the Uruguay Round. These agreements call for a reduction in tariffs and trade barriers on a global basis. Under these agreements, Korea no longer can protect the inefficient agricultural and service sectors of its economy. As protection is removed worldwide, well-managed multinational firms can enter the Korean market and dominate its previously sheltered industries. In the global market too, only those firms that can compete with other firms on product quality and price will survive. This means Korean firms must to compete with Japanese, American, and other multinational firms on product quality, and newly-developing nations such as China and India on price.

All these changes in the global market mean that Korea has to become more competitive to survive and prosper in the global economy. The new world trade order calls for the survival of the fittest. To be competitive, Korea first needs to upgrade research and developmental activities to compete with Japan and the U.S. on industrial goods. Currently, Korea spends less than 2.5 percent of its GNP on R&D, compared to about 3 percent in Japan and the U.S. Second, Korean industries must control labor costs or outsource production overseas to maintain cost competitiveness. Korea so far has enjoyed a cost advantage over its competitors in industrial goods; losing such an advantage will be a disaster to the Korean economy. Finally, Korea does not have much choice but to open its market to others. Reciprocity is in order. Opening the market will probably increase the competitiveness of Korea's formerly inefficient agricultural and service industries.

1.4.5 North-South Korean Relations

Another major challenge that South Korea faces is dealing with North Korea. The two Koreas have been at odds with each other since the end of World War II. The Korean War started in 1950 and ended with a cease-fire in 1953. A threat of war still remains. However, several developments in recent years offer a glimmer of hope that the two Koreas can peacefully reunify or coexist, making economic cooperation seem possible: the defeat of worldwide communism, the death of Kim Il Sung, and the chronic shortage of foods.

The collapse of the former Soviet Union and of eastern European countries ended the Cold War between the capitalist West and the communist East (Kim, 1992). Furthermore, the Chinese have abandoned a pure form of communism and are now experimenting with capitalism within a socialistic framework. The collapse of communism in its former allies has left North Korea with a broken dream of creating a utopian society for the proletariat. As the country lost the support of its former communist allies and at the same time became isolated from the rest of the world, its economy has deteriorated substantially in recent years. Its economy has been shrinking since 1990, resulting in GNP per capita income of $957 in 1995, compared to more than $10,000 for South Korea (*Hankook Ilbo*, December 3, 1996, p. 10). In 1995, North Korea's GNP was less than five percent of South Korea's GNP (approximately $22 billion versus $450 billion respectively).

This economic foe has been further accentuated by the major flood in 1995 and 1996 that destroyed the farming land. Since then, the chronic shortage of foods has become a way of life in North Korea. A sudden increase in the number of defectors in recent years, including high-ranking government officials of North Korea, attests to the seriousness of the situation. Whether or not the deteriorating economic condition will lead to the collapse of North Korea is not certain, but it adds to the uncertain future of the communist regime. Faced with a threat of economic collapse, the North Koreans may have to develop economic ties with their southern brothers and with other capitalist countries.

The death of North Korean President Kim Il Sung has provided an opportunity for productive dialogue between the two Koreas. Unlike his father, Kim Il Sung, a victim of his own rigid communistic and self-reliance ideologies, the new North Korean leader, Kim Jong Il, is a pragmatist seeking courses of action that will enhance his own political survival (Institute for South-North Korea Studies, 1993). Kim Jong Il is likely to experiment with both hawkish (such as infiltrating of the South by a submarine) as well as dovish (the Najin-Sunbong economic development forum) strategies in dealing with South Korea. Based on these experimentations, he will decide on a survival strategy. If he perceives economic cooperation with South as a means of his own political survival, he will seek a dovish strategy. On the other hand, if he feels insecure in opening to South, he will choose the hawkish path.

Unlike his charismatic father, who could command respect from his people even in the midst of economic hardship, Kim Jong Il must produce economic comfort for the hungry population in order to sustain his political life. Consequently, Kim Jong Il is more likely than his father to modify North Korea's economic system to experiment with a Chinese style capitalism to improve the North Korean economy (Yoo, 1994). The acceptance of South Korean nuclear power plants and relief rice from their southern-brothers in recent years are such indications, although implementation of such cooperation is at times problematic. If Kim Jong Il revives his father's self-reliance ideology, the relationship between North and South will remain tenuous, causing continuous discomfort to all Koreans.

Is the reunification of two Koreas possible? What would be the effect of reunification on the Korean economy? Korean reunification is possible by three ways: a bloody war, an internal disintegration of North Korean society, or a gradual opening and modernization of the North Korean economy.

The first option would mean mutual destruction and is therefore unacceptable to both sides. But, there is a possibility that North Koreans take such an unacceptable path out of frustration. The second option is becoming increasingly plausible as the North Korean economy deteriorates, but it would be very costly for the southern brothers to bear. The cost of reunifications estimated to be from $500 billion to $980 billion (Darlin, 1994). South Koreans seem to prefer the third option because it presents the possibility for peaceful coexistence, economic cooperation, and eventual reunification. Economic cooperation can benefit both. Mineral rich North Korea with inexpensive labor and the technically advanced South Korea could jointly propel the economy at an astonishing rate. South Korean businesses see this possibility and are preparing for potential economic ties with North Korea (Klernan, 1992; Lee, H.C., 1994).

All these changes in business environments present formidable challenges to Korean firms. In an age of unlimited global competition, Korean firms need to change their managerial practices to become more competitive in their domestic and global markets. They have to be more productive to counteract rising production costs; they have to be more innovative to meet technological demands; and they have to be more globally oriented to become a viable free trader. Korean firms are making some adjustments in responding to these environmental changes. They have started to restructure far-flung enterprises to focus on core technologies, increase R&D expenditures, and capitalize on new opportunities abroad. These efforts are a modest beginning; more has to be done to make Korean firms competitive in the brave new world of industrial competition.

1.5 Summary

The Korean economy grew at an average growth rate of about 9 percent per year for the last three decades. A number of contextual and design factors jointly and independently contributed to Korea's economic success. Contextual factors are those preconditions that existed in Korea prior to its economic takeoff. These include Confucian culture, development-minded elite, lack of retrogressive social groups, and favorable international environment. The Korean people are known to be highly motivated to work and possess a high need achievement needs. And as a reflection of their Confucian values, Koreans have a great desire for education. Design factors are those elements that are used as instruments for Korea's economic development programs. These include export-oriented economic policies, big businesses, public enterprises, labor management, and aggressive management styles.

Many of the factors that contributed to Korea's economic success have changed in recent years. The civilian-dominated government now keeps big businesses at arm's length. Today's businesses can no longer depend on government for financial support and monopolistic protection from competition. Workers no longer toil under arduous working conditions with low pay. The Confucian virtues of loyalty and filial piety have been replaced by the materialistic pursuit of individual happiness and success. The Korean export strategy based on cost leadership has been challenged by newly developing countries in Asia. Technology transfer from other advanced nations has become increasingly difficult as they fear the boomerang effect. Korea's trading partners now demand the opening of its market to their products, while they are less generous on granting Korea access to their markets.

These changing business environments present formidable challenges for Korean firms. In the absence of governmental protection, Korean firms need to modify their managerial practices to become more competitive in the domestic and international markets. As protection is removed worldwide under the multilateral trade agreements of the new GATT (General Agreement on Tariffs and Trade), well-managed multinational firms can enter the Korean market and dominate its previously sheltered agricultural and service industries. In the global market too, only those Korean firms that can compete on product quality and price with other developing and advanced nations will survive. Are Korean firms prepared to meet these challenges? This book is written with this question in mind.

References

Amsden, A.H. (1989): *Asia's Next Giant: South Korea and Late Industrialization*. New York: Oxford University Press.

Bank of Korea (1987): *Financial Statement Analysis*. Seoul: Bank of Korea.

Business Korea (1993): "Chaebols Under Fire," 10(12):18-20.

Caiden, G.E. and Kim, B.W. (1991): *A Dragon Progress: Development Administration in Korea*. West Hartford: Kumarian Press.

Chang, C.S. and Chang, N.J. (1994): *The Korean Managerial System: Cultural, Political, Economic Foundations*. Westport, CT: Quorum.

Chang, S. (1993): "Korea Reunification: What Price Unity?" *Business Korea*, 10(10):26-29.

Chun, S.K. (1994): "Samsung Group: CEO Lee Pursues Endless Management Reforms,"*Business Korea*, 12(2):30-31.

Chung, K.H. (1977): *Motivational Theories and Practices*. Columbus, OH: Grid Publishing.

Chung, K.H. and Lee, H.C. (1989): *Korean Managerial Dynamics*. New York: Praeger.

Darlin, D. (1994): "A Korean Deal Emerges,"*Forbes*, (September 12): 178-180.

Economic Planning Board (1987): *Social Indicators in Korea*. Seoul: Economic Planning Board, the Republic of Korea.

Fiedler, F.E. (1967): *The Theory of Leadership Effectiveness*. New York: McGraw-Hill.

Hamilton, G.G. and Orru, M. (1989): "Organizational Structure of East Asian Companies," in K.H. Chung and L.H. Lee (eds.), *Korean Managerial Dynamics*. New York: Praeger, pp. 39-50.

Hong, W.T. (1991): "Export-Oriented Growth and Equity in Korea," The National Bureau of Economic Research Second Annual Conference on Economics, Taipei, 19-21 June.

Institute for South-North Korea Studies (1993): *True Story of Kim Jong Il*. Seoul: Institute for South-North Korea Studies.

Jones, L.P. (1976): *Public Enterprise and Economic Development: The Korean Case*. Seoul: Korea Development Institute Press.

Jones, L.P. and SaKong, Il. (1980): *Government, Business, and Entrepreneur Ship*. Cambridge, MA: Harvard University Press.

Jung, K.H. (1989): "Business-Government Relations in Korea," in K.H. Chung and H.C. Lee (eds.), *Korean Managerial Dynamics*. New York: Praeger, pp. 11-26.

Jung, K.H. (1994): "Changing Business-Government Relations," A Yonsei University Working Paper.

Kang, B.K. (1989): "Economic Development Strategy and Income Distribution in Korea," Korea Development Institute Research Material, Seoul: KDI.

Kang, S.Y. (1994): "Hyundai's Planned Steel Mill: To Repeat POSCO's Legend?" *Business Korea*, 12(2):21-22.

Kahl, J.A. (1959): "Some Social Concomitants of Industrialization and Urbanization," *Human Organization*, 18(Summer):53-74.

Kahl, J.A. (1965): "Some Measurement of Achievement Orientation," *American Journal of Sociology*, 70:199-211.

Kim, B.P. (1992): *Two Koreas in Development*. New Brunswick, NJ: Transaction Publishers.

Kim, K.D. (1984): *Man and Society in Korea's Economic Growth: Sociological Studies*. Seoul: Seoul National University Press.

Kim, K.D. (1993): *Korean Value Systems and Social Consciousness*. Seoul: Bakyoungsa.

Kim, L.S. (1980): "Stages of Development of Industrial Technology in A Developing Country: A Model," *Research Policy*, 9:254- 277.

Kim, M.S. (1986): "Study on Public Expenditures on Education," *Korea Development Review*, 8(4):110-133.

Kim, T.K. (1982): *Korean Value Systems*. Seoul: Munwhasa.

Klernan, T. (1992): "The Northern Option," *Korea Business World*, 8(4):18-21.

Lee, B.J. (1994): "North Korea: Behind Closed Door," *Business Korea*, 12(3):21-23.

Lee, H.C. (1994): "Preparation for North-South Economic Cooperation by Four Korean Chaebols," *Korea Times-Washington Edition*, August 1:6-7.

Lee, K.U. and Lee, J.H. (1990): *Business Group and Concentration of Economic Power*. Seoul: Korea Economic Development Institute.

McClelland, D.C. (1961): *The Achieving Society*. Princeton, NJ: Von Nostrand Reinhold.

McClelland, D.C. (1962): "Business Drive and National Achievement," *Harvard Business Review*, 66:99-112.

Moon, P.Y. (1991): "The Saemaul (New Community) Movement 1971," in S.J. Cho and Y.H. Kim (eds.), *Economic Development in the Republic of Korea*. Honolulu: East-West Center, pp. 371-404.

Moskowitz, K. (1989): "Ownership and Management of Korean Firm," in K.H. Chung and H.C. Lee (eds.), *Korean Managerial Dynamics*. New York: Praeger, pp. 51-64.

Nash, M. (1954): "Social Prerequisites to Economic Growth in Latin America and Southeast Asia," *Economic Development and Cultural Change*, 12(3):225-242.

Park, S.W. and Green, G.P. (1994): "Agrarian Transformation and Colonialism: An Historical Comparative Study of Korea and the Philippines," *Yeungnam University Working Paper Series*. Daegu, Korea: Yeungnam University.

Republic of Korea (1993): *New Five-Year Economic Plan: 1993-97.* Seoul: Government Printing Office, Republic of Korea.

SaKong, Il. (1993): *Korea in the World Economy*. Washington, DC: Institute for International Economics.

Shin, Y.K. (1985): *Industrial Organization Theory*. Seoul: Seoul National University Press.

Sohn, J.A. (1993a): "President Kim's Reform Policy: Bloodless Revolution," *Business Korea*, 10(10):19-22.

Sohn, J.A. (1993b): "Samsung Group: Embracing Breathtaking Changes," *Business Korea*, 11(2):15-19.

Sohn, J.A. (1994): "Samsung's Grand Ambitions," *Business Korea*, 11(12):23-25.

Song, B.N. (1990): *The Rise of the Korean Economy*. New York: Oxford University Press.

Spengler, J.J. (1961): "Theory, Ideology, Non-Economic Values, and Politico-Economic Development," in R. Braibaniti and J.J. Spengler (eds.), *Tradition, Values, and Socio-Economic Development*. Durham, NC: Duke University Press, pp. 1-56.

The Economist (1996): "What Price an Hour's Work," 341(7990):77.

Tu, W.M. (1984): *Confucian Ethics Today: The Singapore Challenge*. Singapore: Federal Publications.

Weber, M. (1930): *The protestant Ethic and the Spirit of Capitalism*. London: Allen an Unwin.

Weber, M. (1951): *The Religion of China: Confucianism and Taoism*. New York: The Free Press.

Yoo, Y.O. (1994): "A Symbolistic Study of the Possibility of De-Kimilsungization of Juche Ideology--With a Focus on the Prospects for North Korea's Adopting the Chinese Model," *East Asian Review*, 6(1):37-60.

Chapter 2
Business and Government Relations

2.1 Introduction

The symbiotic relationship between business and government in Korea was formed in the early 1960s when the military-dominated authoritarian government established economic development as its primary goal. The relationship could be characterized as a vertical one where the government took firm control of business through the allocation of financial resources and entry permits for new business. This vertical relationship was reinforced by Korea's Confucian culture, in which government officials were highly respected. The Korean industrial system, which tied the government and business sectors together, has been called "Korea, Inc.,"because it was managed as if it were a company (Jones and SaKong, 1980). Within Korea, Inc., the nation's President acted as the CEO (Chief Executive Officer), ministers in the economically-oriented ministries as chiefs of staff, and heads of private and public firms as COOs (Chief Operating Officers).

In the 1990s, however, there are some signs that the traditional Korea, Inc. has outlived its usefulness. The state-led economic planning was effective during the early stage of economic development as a means of providing the needed capital and developing the basic infrastructure. As the economy has grown and become more open to the world economy, tight control of the economy by bureaucrats has become less effective and efficient. In addition, the political reform process, which started in 1987 and culminated in the installation of the civilian-dominated government in 1993, has changed the traditional vertical relationship among the political elite, government bureaucrats, and the private business. Now the government has become just one of many stakeholders that business has to deal with in a more pluralistic and democratic society.

This chapter focuses on the relationship between business and government in the process of developing the Korean economy. To this end, it discusses the essence of Korean government's economic and industrial planning, the government role in capital formation and resource allocation, development of big business groups, and changing patterns of business-government relations. As the economy has expanded, however, the role of government in business has changed, and so has the relationship between business and government.

2.2 Economic Development Plans

Prior to the 1950s, the Korean economy was primarily an agrarian economy. Developmental efforts other than what the Japanese occupation had contributed to the economy between 1910 and 1936 were non-existent. Korea's formal developmental efforts started after the Korean War. The Korean economy has developed through roughly five distinctive phases: reconstruction (1953-1961), economic take-off (1962-1971), heavy and chemical industry drive (1972-1981), structural adjustment (1982-1986), democratic reform (1987-1992), and globalization (1993-1997) (Choi and Lee, 1990; OECD, 1994).

2.2.1 Reconstruction Phase (1953-1961)

With the end of World War II, Korea gained independence from Japanese rule. After the war, the U.S. military government ruled South Korea until the Korean government under President Syngman Rhee was installed in 1948. Soon after this installment, but before any economic plan was contemplated, the Korean War broke out and lasted three years. After the Korean War, President Rhee's government focused its energy on the survival and rehabilitation of the war-torn economy. Feeding the hungry population and sustaining the then current level of consumption for the population were the major concerns of President Rhee. The U.S. educated President Rhee believed in a free-market economic system and consequently played a passive role in economic development.

President Rhee's government, however, laid an important groundwork for future economic development by initiating the development of import-substitution industries for domestic consumption, investing in education for human resource development and carrying out a land reform policy for more equitable income distribution (Mason et al., 1980; Jones and SaKong, 1980). Although the economy grew slowly, the level of education rose substantially during this period, providing an impetus for future development. President Rhee was ousted by a student revolt in April 1960. Mr. Chang Myon was elected as President, but his regime was toppled by a military coup led by General Park Chung Hee in May, 1961.

2.2.2 Economic Take-off Phase (1962-1971)

The newly established military-dominated government under General Park placed economic development at the top of its political agenda and started to mobilize the nation's resources to this end. In order to mobilize the nation's internal and external resources, several important institutional reform measures were introduced.

First, the Economic Planning Board (EPB) was created in 1961 to draw up economic plans and to provide economic policy coordination. The head of EPB served as Deputy Prime Minister to signify the importance of economic policy coordination among ministries. Second, commercial banks were nationalized so that the government could control the allocation of financial resources. Additionally, the roles of existing state-owned special banks (Bank of Korea and Korea Development Bank) were expanded or new banks (Industrial Bank of Korea and Korea Export-Import Bank) were created to support the government's economic plans. Third, the Korea Trade Promotion Corporation (KOTRA) was funded in 1964 to promote exports and to carry out market research abroad. The government also authorized the Korean Traders Association (KTA) to collect one percent of the value of imports to be used as an export promotion fund. Finally, the national Taxation Administration Office was established in 1965 to collect taxes that were needed to support the nation's economic plans.

The government led the nation's economy by means of economic and industrial planning. The terms "economic planning" and "industrial planning" are often used interchangeably, but a distinction can be made. Economic planning is seen as the government's overall plans for resource mobilization, resource allocation, and economic growth targets; industrial planning connotes the selective support of certain industries by the government. In the context of the Korean economy, industrial planning can be seen as an instrument for economic development.

The nation's first serious economic development plan (1962-1966) was launched in 1962; a series of five-year plans followed thereafter. During this take-off period, the government focused on the development of an economy built on a combination of import-substitution and export-oriented businesses by building up basic industries (e.g., cement, fertilizer, and petroleum), labor-intensive light manufacturing industries (e.g., textile, footwear, plywood, and wigs) and infrastructure (e.g., communications, electricity, and transportation). Because Korea lacked natural resources and had a limited domestic market, it pursued an export-oriented growth strategy to pay for raw materials, technology, and intermediate industrial goods needed for its industrialization programs. Exporters were provided with loans at preferential interest rates and foreign currencies at favorable exchange rates. In addition, manufacturers were exempted from import duties on raw materials and intermediate goods imported for exports.

As a result, exports grew at an average rate of 38.8 percent annually during this period (International Monetary Fund [IMF], *International Financial Statistics*, 1991). Initially, exports were limited to low-skilled, labor-intensive manufacturing products, but by 1971 they were diversified into relatively more sophisticated, capital-intensive products such as consumer electronics, steel plates, and ships. This export growth paved the way for high economic growth and accelerated Korea's industrialization process. Export growth brought in foreign currencies and opened markets for future economic expansion.

2.2.3 Heavy Industry Phase (1972-1981)

Once basic industries and infrastructure were in place, the government placed emphasized the development of heavy and chemical industries (HCI) (Choi and Lee, 1990; Song, 1990; SaKong, 1993). In 1973, the government announced the Heavy and Chemical Industry Declaration, meant to strengthen the automobile, steel, nonferrous metal, shipbuilding, industrial machinery, electronic, and petrochemical industries. In promoting HCI programs, the government selectively channeled a large portion of the nation's financial resources into well-established businesses in the targeted industries. Such financial allocations were called "policy loans." Almost 60 percent of the total bank loans from 1975 to 1977 and close to 95 percent of policy loans in 1978 were devoted to heavy and chemical industries (SaKong, 1993, p. 57).

The heavy industry promotion drive caused a major structural change in the economy and at the same time created a sectoral imbalance. On the positive side, HCI's share in the manufacturing sector increased from 34.9 percent in 1972 to 51.2 percent in 1982 (Economic Planning Board, [EPB] 1980, 1986, *Major Statistics of the Korean Economy*). Also, the share of HCI in the total manufactured good exports increased from 25.3 percent in 1972 to 52.8 percent in 1982 (Korea Foreign Trade Association, *Yearbook*, various issues). HCI programs also propelled Korea into a nation of world-class big business groups that are the envy of other newly industrializing countries.

On the negative side, however, the preferential treatment given to HCI created sectoral imbalances between heavy and light industries and between big businesses and small-medium industries. As the nation's financial resources were devoted to heavy and chemical industries, other industries were financially strapped. Another issue was the problem of inefficiency. As resources were allocated preferentially in the absence of competition, overcapacity and inefficiency resulted. Examples include Korea Heavy Industries, Hankook Heavy Machinery, and Okpo Shipyard that were later taken over by other companies. Eventually, the HCI as a whole had to be restructured because many companies went bankrupt.

2.2.4 Structural Adjustment Phase (1982-1986)

In the late 1970s and early 1980s, the Korea economy was experiencing high inflation (as high as 25.6 percent in 1980), low economic growth (minus 4.8 percent in 1980), and heavy foreign debt (the highest level of $46.7 billion in 1985) (Bank of Korea, *Economic Statistical Yearbook*, various years; Economic Planning Board, *Major Statistics in the Korean Economy*, various years). Excessive investment in heavy and chemical industries in the 1970s, the worldwide recession that followed the second oil crisis in 1979, and the political instability following President Park's assassination in 1979 contributed to economic difficulties in the early 1980s. Additionally, the newly developing countries in Asia (e.g., China, Indonesia, Malaysia, and Thailand) were challenging Korea's export drive in the low-end of the labor-intensive products, contributing to the negative growth in Korea's exports (minus 8.0 percent in 1982).

In order to deal with these problems, the Chun Doo Hwan government undertook several structural adjustment measures: price stabilization, financial sector liberalization, balanced growth, and import liberalization (Choi and Lee, 1990; Song, 1990; Suh, 1992). First, the growth of money supply was reduced to a target level of 15 percent annually during the fifth five-year planning period (1982-86), compared to an annual growth rate of 24.7 percent during the fourth planning period (1977-81). Second, commercial banks were privatized between 1981 and 1983, and policy loans favoring heavy industries were eliminated. Third, the Fair Trade Act was enacted in 1981 to promote market competition and to prevent the concentration of economic power in the hands of large businesses; the growth of small and medium-sized firms was promoted in the 1980s. Fourth, to reduce trade deficit, intensive efforts were made to promote exports and at the same time to liberalize restrictions on imports.

As a result of these measures, the inflation rate was kept under five percent annually; the trade balance began to show a surplus during the fifth economic planning period. A trade surplus of $4.2 billion was recorded in 1986. However, the concentration of economic power in the hands of *chaebols* accelerated during this period. Public suspicion of conspiracy between government and *chaebols* as well as major corruptions in the political elite caused social unrest, eventually bringing down Chun's regime.

2.2.5 Democratic Reform Phase (1987-92)

As the Korean populace gained economic security, resulting from economic growth, they began to demand political freedom and an equitable distribution of income. A series of student demonstrations against the military-dominated authoritarian government finally resulted in a political democratization in 1987. Followed by the political reform, the newly elected Roh Tae Woo government introduced a variety of economic liberalization measures including free labor movement, privatization of public enterprises, import liberalization, and reduction of various financial subsidies.

The newly acquired political freedom, economic liberalization, the 1988 Seoul Olympic Games, and the "three lows" (low oil prices, low exchange rates, and low interest rates) all helped to invigorate the Korean economy during the sixth planning period (1987-1992). The economy (GNP) grew at an annual rate of 9.9 percent during the period, and the highest level of trade surplus in Korea's history ($8.8 billion) was recorded in 1988. However, the liberalization of the labor movement caused labor costs to rise at an annual rate of 12.75 percent, and consumer prices went up by 7 percent annually. The heated economy, coupled with exorbitant price increases in real estate, stimulated conspicuous consumption, causing a widespread disharmony between the haves and have-nots.

2.2.6 Globalization Phase (1993-1997)

The state-guided industrial planning in Korea accelerated the economic growth for three decades. By the end of the sixth planning period in 1992, Korea achieved its industrialization goal:the development of the industrial sector and an export-oriented economy. The Korean industrial development strategy was based on an unbalanced growth between different sectors of the economy. The challenge now for the civilian dominated government under President Kim Young Sam and for the future administration is to sustain economic growth and at the same time to achieve an equitable distribution of income.

Another challenge is the globalization of the Korean economy by increasing free trade, liberalizing the financial market, and adopting economic regulations consistent with international standards. Restrictions on outward as wells as inward foreign direct investment need to be eased;

financial markets should be opened to foreign investors; and expenditures on research and development need to be increased to at least by four percent of GNP (OECD, 1994). If all goes well, Korea's GNP per capita is expected to rise to approximately $20,000 by year 2005.

The role of government in guiding the nation's economy is likely to be minimized because the economy has become too big and complex to be managed by the "visible hand" of the government's technocrats. The "invisible hand" of the market has to replace the visible hand of the government in managing the nation's business affairs. Whether or not the government will leave the task of managing the nation's business affairs to the invisible hand of the market remains to be seen. This point will be further examined in a later section.

2.2.7 Change in Industrial Structure

The core of Korea's economic planning during the past three decades was the promotion of economic growth through exports. From the outset, economic planners were keenly aware of the need for exporting manufactured goods to pay for imports of foods, raw materials, and intermediate industrial goods. In the absence of natural resources and a sizeable domestic market, Korea had to depend on overseas' resource supplies and markets for its products. In the early 1960s, primary goods such as silk, tungsten, and fishery products were exported. As industrialization progressed, light-manufactured goods such as textiles, footwear, synthetic products, and plywood replaced primary goods. By the early 1980s, labor-intensive light-manufactured goods were replaced by capital-intensive products, including steel products, ships, petroleum products, and tires. In the second-half of the 1980s, the export of manufactured goods gave way to the export of technology-intensive industrial products such as automobiles, computers, consumer electronics, and semi-conductors.

The change in Korea's export structure is reflected in the change of its industrial structure. As exports moved from primary goods to light manufacturing goods, and then to capital and technology-intensive products, the proportion of the primary sector (especially agriculture) in the nation's gross national product (GNP) had declined from 41.0 percent in 1965 to under 7.0 percent in 1995. In comparison, the manufacturing sector increased from under 19.3 percent to 27.5 during the same period. The service sector increased from 39.7 percent to 65.5 for the same period (Exhibit 2.1).

Korea's industrial structure is unique in two respects. First, the proportion of the manufacturing sector in Korea's GDP is substantially higher than that of other advanced nations in Western Europe and North

America, where the manufacturing sector accounts for about 20 percent of their GDP (Song, 1990, p. 108). Korea expanded its manufacturing sector to pursue an export-oriented growth strategy and pay for raw materials, intermediate goods, and food. Only Japan (30 percent) and Germany (32 percent) share a similar industrial structure. Second, the industrial structures in other developing nations normally moved from "early industries" such as foods and textiles to "middle industries" such as wood products, rubber products, and chemicals, and then to "late industries" such as heavy machinery, metal, and petro-chemical products (Chenery and Taylor, 1968). Korea, however, moved from the early industries directly to late industries, a result of the government's HCI drive in the 1970s (Song, 1990).

In order to achieve a balance in its industrial structure, Korea needs to put more resources into the development of medium-sized firms, which are more likely to be in "middle industries." Furthermore, "late industries" are primarily the users of "middle-level" technologies. As such, while "late industries" provide Korea with a strong industrial base, they do not give Korea a competitive edge in a technological sense. As Korea wants to become an advanced economy, it needs to invest more in "high-tech industries," including electronics, telecommunications, bio-engineering, and superconductivity. This point will be further elaborated on in Chapter 5.

Exhibit 2.1: Growth National Product by Industry (in %)

		Sector	
Year	Primary	Secondary	Tertiary
1965	41.0	19.3	39.7
1975	27.8	20.8	45.4
1985	13.2	32.4	54.4
1995	7.0	27.5	65.5

Notes: The primary sector includes agricultural, fishery, and forestry. The secondary sector includes manufacturing and mining. The tertiary sector includes services and other infrastructure industries. The 1995 figures are estimations.

Source: Bank of Korea (various years): *Korea Statistical Yearbook*. Seoul: National Statistical Office, Republic of Korea.

2.3 Capital Formation and Resource Allocation

As noted earlier, the Korean economy during its developmental stages was guided by the government's economic planners. The government was heavily involved not only in planning but also in implementing its economic plans by enlisting the private sector. The government induced the private sector to carry out its economic plans by means of financial and administrative support. As a start, the government played a decisive role in the formulation of capital in the hands of a few selected businesses (*chaebols*). There were at least three ways that the government helped *chaebols* to accumulate their wealth: the sale of government properties, credit market distortion through "policy loans," and the manipulation of foreign exchange rates (Jung, 1989).

In the event that the private sector was not able to respond adequately to the government's developmental needs, the government became directly involved in investing and even managing the industrial enterprises. The share of public sector investment in the nation's total investment averaged about 35 percent between 1963 and 1971; it leveled off at around 30 percent by the mid-1980s (SaKong, 1993; Lee, 1990). The private sector was responsible for 65 percent of total investment between 1963 and 1979; and its share gradually increased to around 70 percent by the mid-1980s. The heavy reliance on public enterprises was inevitable during the early stages of economic development due to the lack of capital formation in the private sector. As the economy matured, however, the necessity for government's direct involvement in the nation's business affairs decreased. In the following sections, we will see how the government helped the private sector in its capital formation process.

2.3.1 Sales of Government Properties

The first sale of government properties to civilians involved the disposal of "enemy properties" that were left behind by the Japanese in the aftermath of World War II. The terms of sale were based on estimated values of these properties, which were paid off over a ten year period (Chung, 1986). In order to attract potential buyers, these properties were often undervalued. Moreover, the buyer was required to put down only a ten percent downpayment, with the rest to be paid in the subsequent years. It was apparent that, during the inflationary period in the 1950s and 1960s, installment payments became windfall profits for the purchaser. At least 13 *chaebols* took advantage of these sales.

The second occasion was the sale of government-owned properties in the 1960s. Again, high inflation and the terms of sale were such that purchasers were able to accumulate significant wealth. For example, Hanjin Group bought the government-owned Korean Airlines in 1969 and paid for it over the next ten years. At least 20 *chaebols* acquired more than one public enterprise during this period, and most of them were profitable transactions for the buyers (Chung, 1986).

In some cases, however, there were no eager buyers for government properties. In order to make them more attractive, the government had to increase inducement packages. For example, Hankook Machinery was initially purchased by Shinjin Group in 1969, but the acquired firm was never profitable and had to be repossessed by a government-controlled bank. The company was again acquired by the Daewoo Group in 1975 at the request of the government, and it eventually became profitable under Daewoo management. Such deals were most common in the restructuring phase in the 1970s.

2.3.2 Credit Market Distortion

The government heavily relied on financial policy tools to induce businesses to follow its lead in economic development. In the early 1960s, commercial banks were nationalized by limiting shareholders' voting rights. Along with government-owned banks, the nation's banking systems channelled financial resources into certain industries selected for growth, and credit markets were distorted in favor of those big businesses favored by government.

Bank loans made for such purpose were called "policy loans," which amounted closer to 50 percent of the total available loans in the 1970s. The majority of these loans initially went to support export-oriented activities and then to promote heavy and chemical industries (SaKong, 1981). *Chaebols* which were favored by the government, were the beneficiaries of such policy loans. As the nation's financial resources were channelled into a few selected firms, the rest of the economy encountered a chronic state of credit shortage, forcing other firms to rely on curb markets (Kim, 1994). Policy loans helped *chaebols* to become even larger and caused a structural imbalance between large and small companies.

These policy loans in most cases came with preferential interest rates when compared with ordinary bank loans. For example, the interest rates for policy loans were 5.8 percent for the period of 1961-70, compared with 20.2 percent and 51.6 percent for ordinary bank and curb market loans respectively (Chung, 1986). When inflation rates, which averaged 14.2 percent in the 1960s, are taken into account, the real interest rates (ordinary bank loan rates minus inflation rates) were relatively low. Real interest rates for policy loans were, however, negative.

This credit distortion between 1960 and 1980 led *chaebols* to become overly dependent on borrowed funds. The equity-to-assets ratio for Korean firms, at its lowest point in 1980, was 17.3 percent, compared to 30.1 and 46.4 percent for Japanese and U.S. firms respectively in 1980 (Kim, 1990). This ratio is even worse when it is calculated on the market-based value of assets rather than on the book-value-based assessment. The ratio for Korean firms was 11.0 percent, compared to 45.4 and 49.4 percent for Japanese and U.S. firms, using the same assessment criterion.

Although the equity-to-assets ratio was extremely low, *chaebols* perceived the risk of bankruptcy to be low because there was an implicit understanding that the government would bail them out in case of financial troubles. Since *chaebol* companies expanded their businesses in response to the government's economic plans, they expected the government's protection. Because of this understanding, *chaebols* invested heavily into risky projects that they otherwise would not have undertaken. Under this arrangement, the burden of risky investments was shared by all sectors of the economy, while the gains from such investments went to *chaebols*. Chung (1986) estimated that the top 50 *chaebols* gained more than 50 percent of their wealth from this credit market distortion.

2.3.3 Manipulation of Foreign Exchange Rates

The foreign exchange market was also distorted to favor exporters. In the 1950s and early 1960s, the official exchange rates remained low, less than 50 percent of the real value of foreign currencies (Hong, 1976). Overvalued Korean currency made imports inexpensive but hindered exports. It was estimated that excess profits generated from overvalued domestic currency amounted to more than 88 percent of the amount of money that importers actually paid. After the military government took power in 1961, official exchange rates were adjusted to the market value to stimulate exports. However, the official exchange rates still remained low due to high inflation, benefiting importers.

Although the distorted exchange rates discouraged exports, exporters nevertheless benefitted by linking imports to exports. Foreign currencies were made available at favorable exchange rates to exporters who imported capital goods and raw materials to produce exportable goods. Also, other forms of incentives such as taxes, tariffs, and subsidies were used to promote exports. Thus, exporters had ample opportunities to gain windfall profits from the exchange market distortion.

The government experimented with various exchange rate systems to achieve a balance between keeping inflation down and promoting exports. Until 1965, complicated multiple exchange rate systems were used to favor targeted imports and exports at the same time. In 1965, a floating, unified exchange rate policy was introduced to maintain the stability of exchange rates. In 1974, the Korean *won* was pegged to the U.S. dollar. Since 1980, the exchange rate was determined by the movements of the exchange rates of major trading partners. This new system maintains exchange rates more realistically and is still in force.

Chung (1986) estimated that the total contribution of government to the accumulation of wealth to *chaebols* by the above three measures (sales of government properties, credit distortion, and control of foreign currencies) amounted to 80 percent of the equity of the top 50 *chaebols* in 1980. In addition, other forms of incentives (tax incentives, direct subsidies, tariff protection, and labor movement restrictions) benefitted *chaebols* greatly. Regardless of the accuracy of these estimates, the measures described here clearly show how critical the role of government was in the development of Korean *chaebols* and how critical the *chaebols* have been in the development of the government's industrialization programs. In the following section, we will review the process by which *chaebols* were enticed, nurtured, protected, and controlled by government.

2.4 Emergence of Korean *Chaebols*

Until 1876, when the first modern treaty (known as the Treaty of Kanghwa) was signed with Japan, Korea had an agrarian economy. With the opening-up of the country to Japan and the West, Korea began to develop an industrial economy with the introduction of electricity, communication facilities, and railroads (Song, 1990). During the Japanese occupation (1910-45), Korea's industrial sector expanded under Japanese ownership and management. A number of Korean entrepreneurs, such as Park Hung Sik (Whasin Department Stores), Kim Song Su (Kyungsung Textile), Paek Yun Soo (Taechang Trading), Park Sung Jik (Kongiksa), Son Bong Jo (Yungshisa), Choi Kee Chang (Kaesong Electric), Son Chang Soon (Samkong Knitwear), Park Tae Hong (Saechang) to name a few emerged during the Japanese colonial period (Chang and Chang, 1994; Juhn, 1994). These entrepreneurs were relatively undercapitalized and lacked the skills to match Japanese competition. They merely survived in the hostile climate of colonial rule.

The end of World War II did not produce a change in the business climate in Korea. The tragic division of the country after World War II and the subsequent Korean War in the early 1950s further retarded economic development in Korea. However, several entrepreneurs, noticeably Chung Ju Yung (Hyundai), Lee Byung Chul (Samsung), Koo In Hoe (Lucky), Kim Sung Kwon (Ssangyong), Park In Chun (Kumho), and Kim Chul Ho (Kia) had emerged as leaders of *chaebols* during the post-World War II period and eventually became the present-day *chaebols*. Another group of entrepreneurs, noticeably Kim Woo Choong (Daewoo), Choi Jong Hyun (Sunkyong), and Cho Choong Hoon (Hanjin) emerged as *chaebol* leaders after the Korean War. In this section, we will review the process by which these entrepreneurs emerged as present-day *chaebols*.

2.4.1 Emergence of *Chaebols*

Generally speaking, the mid-1950s could be construed as the period for the emergence of Korean *chaebols*. Due to the devastating destruction of economic assets during the Korean War, businesses had to reconstruct their production capacities. During this reconstruction period, import substitution and construction projects such as textiles, sugar refineries, cement, and fertilizers were started by private businesses with government assistance and foreign aid. As a result, the Korean economy expanded at an annual rate of 4.7 percent between 1954 and 1960 (Cho, 1994). The manufacturing sector grew at an annual rate of 12.2 percent during the same period, resulting in a change of the sector's contribution to the nation's GNP from 14.0 percent in 1954 to 20.5 percent in 1960.

Although the government aided the reconstruction effort of private businessmen, its involvement in business occurred within the context of a free market economy. Some writers argued that entrepreneurs accumulated their wealth during this period by extracting favorable concessions from the government in the form of low interest loans, import rights, favorable exchange rates, and low cost acquisition of government properties (Jones and SaKong, 1980; Shin, 1984). It is generally believed that entrepreneurial activities were aided by government during this period, but such an aid should not be considered as a reflection of formal economic planning. This assertion is based on the following observations.

First, President Syngman Rhee was a firm believer of a free market economy. Second, the U.S. military administration influenced the Korean economic policy during the early years of the first Republic. Third, the Korean government at that time lacked suitable institutions and know-how to lead the economy. Finally, the Korean people might have reacted adversely to any attempt at control in response to the painful memory of the controlled economy during the Japanese colonial period. For these reasons, until the early 1960s, the strong interventionist characteristics of Korean government had not emerged.

During this short period of a relatively free-wheeling capitalistic economic environment, a few entrepreneurial firms, notably Samsung, Lucky, Ssangyong, Sambo, Tongyang, and Taehan had already emerged as *chaebols*. The rapid pace of their capital accumulation made them easy targets for criticism during the transitional period between the civil revolution in 1960 and the military coup of 1962. After the downfall of the Rhee regime in April 1960, the Chang Myun government embarked on a policy of cleaning up "illegal and unfair profiteering" by *chaebols*. In August 1960, 24 companies were fined for tax evasion and unfair profits, but they refused to comply with the government demands (Park, 1982). This matter had not been resolved by May 1961, when General Park Chung Hee took over the Chang government.

2.4.2 Government Control of *Chaebols*

The military government resumed the task of cleaning up the so-called corrupt businessmen. Soon after the military coup in 1961, the heads of ten prominent *chaebols* were arrested and ordered to return profits that were judged to be gained unfairly. Shocked by this event, six out of ten executives declared that they would voluntarily give up their private property to the government. Upon gaining control of *chaebols*, the military government soon relaxed its strong antibusiness attitude and reduced its moves to seize private property. *Chaebols* paid only about $16 million in fines and were allowed to keep most of their assets (Jones and SaKong, 1980, p. 272). In return, *chaebols* were asked to take part in the government's effort to industrialize the nation.

These events did much to shape the image of *chaebols* among the general populace and to define subsequent business-government relations in Korea. Big business entrepreneurs had to publicly confess that they had evaded taxes and profited unfairly and illegally. The image of *chaebols* was badly tarnished, and this unfavorable image has lingered into the present time. The superior position of government relative to business was firmly established during the course of settling these events. It was clear to everyone that the government is in the driver's seat.

Another event further solidified the government's control over *chaebols*. In the early 1960s, privately-held commercial banks were put under the control of government by limiting private shareholders' voting rights. In addition, the government established a number of state-owned banks and expanded existing state-owned banks. Unlike Japanese big businesses, which controlled commercial banks in their group, Korean businesses had to rely on government-controlled banks for business expansion and working capital. This arrangement resulted in business having a greater dependency on government. As businesses voluntarily or involuntarily took on big and risky ventures, their dependency on government for cheap loans inevitably increased.

In this political climate, business firms that were friendly with the government received ample support in pursuing their business ventures, and those who failed to maintain such a relationship were deprived of support. As a result, there were changes in the ranking of Korean *chaebols* during this period of rapid growth. Exhibit 2.2 shows the top ten *chaebols* in 1965, 1975, 1985 and 1995. As noted, the ranking changed greatly between 1965 and 1975, but very little between 1975 and 1985. The change in business leadership indicated that the military government actively identified loyal and effective entrepreneurs and channeled funds to them (Chung, 1985).

Exhibit 2.2: Top Ten Business Groups in Korea

1965	1975	1985	1995
Samsung	Samsung	Lucky-Goldstar (LG)	Hyundai
Lucky	Lucky	Hyndai	Samsung
Ssangyong	Hyundai	Samsung	LG
Panbon	Hanjin	Sunkyong	Daewoo
Sambo	Hyosung	Daewoo	Sunkyong
Samyangsa	Ssangyong	Ssangyong	Ssangyong
Tongyang	Daewoo	Hanjin	Kia
Taehan	Doosan	KoreaExplosives	Hanjin
Kaeppong	Dong-A	Daelim	Hanwha
Hwashin	ShinDong-A	Hyosung	Lotte

2.4.3 Concentration of Economic Power

As noted earlier, the government policy for developing heavy and chemical industries (HCI) in the 1970s accelerated the concentration of economic power in the hands of a few selected *chaebols*. In order to promote these industries, President Park cajoled a small group of trusted and well-established entrepreneurs to invest heavily in massive industrial projects (e.g., automobile, shipbuilding, oil refineries, and chemical plants) and provided them with various financial incentives and administrative support. When industrial projects were too big and risky for the private sector, the government became directly involved. The creation of Pohang Steel (POSCO) is a case in point.

Once the HCI plan was drawn up, the administrative machinery went into work. Through its control of the banking systems, the government devoted almost 60 percent of the nation's total bank loans to the HCI projects in the second-half of the 1970s (Lee, 1991; SaKong, 1993). *Chaebols* that were selected for these projects received even greater benefits--low interest loans, tax benefits, favorable exchange rates, and exclusive business licenses.

Furthermore, they had direct access to the President, his trusted assistants, and cabinet ministries for personal consultation (Clifford, 1994, pp. 115-123). The direct involvement of President Park, the administrative support of governmental bureaucrats, and the tight credit control in favor of HCI projects made big business groups even bigger.

The effect of the HCI programs on the concentration of economic power was staggering. The top 10 *chaebols* accounted for 23.4 percent of the GDP in 1987, and the top 46 *chaebols* 43.0 percent (SaKong, 1993, p. 247). Their sales relative to Korea's GNP grew from 15 percent in 1974 to 50 percent in 1980 and about 70 percent in 1984. In 1984, the 3 largest *chaebols* accounted for 36 percent of GNP. The size of these business groups became large enough to be listed in the *Fortune Global 500*. By 1984, 9 Korean big businesses were on the list, 11 in 1987, and 12 in 1996. The difference in size, even among the large *chaebols*, was significant. The fourth largest *chaebols*, Daewoo, was only about one-half the size of Samsung in terms of sales.

2.4.4 Restructuring of *Chaebols*

The rapid growth of *chaebols* in the 1970s and 1980s caught the eye of political elite. As early as 1974, President Park expressed concern over concentration of economic power. On May 29th of that year, President Park directed the economic ministries and the Bank of Korea to take the following actions:

(1) to induce *chaebols* to list their stocks on the open capital market;
(2) to closely supervise tax payments received from and bank credits extended to *chaebols*;
(3) to restrict overly leveraged firms from entering into new businesses.

This was the first concrete evidence that the government was concerned about excessive concentration of economic power in the hands of *chaebols*.

The Park government's efforts to restructure *chaebols,* however, did not produce any measurable impact. The drive to promote the HCI overshadowed the need to restructure *chaebols*. In fact, as noted earlier, concentration of economic power accelerated in the 1970s. Furthermore, the government was really not in a position of restructuring *chaebols* because of its dependency on *chaebols* to carry out its HCI projects and to compensate for any political shortcomings for being a military dictatorship. HCI projects needed economies of scale, and any restructuring efforts might have squelched the energy of *chaebols,* which were the workhorses in the government's economic drive.

The aggressive investment in HCI projects, the unchecked growth of big businesses, the political uncertainty in the aftermath of President Park's assassination, and the unfavorable international business environment all contributed to the downturn of the Korean economy in the late 1970s and early 1980s. Critics argued that HCI projects were too costly and inefficient for the Korean economy to sustain (Kim, 1985; Yoo, 1989). During the period of the HCI drive, business investments were made not on the basis of economic merits but on political mandates, resulting in economic inefficiencies.

With the increased liquidity of funds, big businesses expanded into new businesses both related and unrelated to their core competencies, commonly known as "octopus-style diversification." The number of firms owned by the top 30 *chaebols* increased from 304 in 1974 to 608 in 1980 (Lee, K.T., 1991, p. 480). Such an unchecked growth of *chaebols* into unrelated businesses, especially by means of acquiring unprofitable firms, further contributed to economic inefficiencies (Kim, 1985). Furthermore, the two oil crises in the mid and late 1970s led to a global economic downturn, which in turn reduced the demands for Korean exports. These unfavorable forces led to a triple malaise in the economy--high inflation, slow or even negative economic growth, and an unfavorable balance of payment in the early 1980s.

President Chun Doo Whan, who took over the government in 1979, made some serious attempts to improve the financial situation of big businesses. The actions taken by President Chun in 1980 included:

(1) forced divestment of subsidiaries owned by the top twenty *chaebols*;
(2) compulsory sale of real estate not used for business purposes;
(3) abolishment of trade associations that might hinder competition;
(4) close supervision of and restrictions on bank credits extended to excessively leveraged firms;
(5) stricter enforcement of external auditing on big businesses.

The centerpiece of these actions was the forced sale of real estate owned by *chaebols*. The proceeds of these sales were used to improve the capital structure of highly leveraged firms.

This reform effort was vigorously pursued in the first two years but was relaxed later. Scandals involving President Chun's family members, however, made it difficult for the president to push forward with his reforms (Clifford, 1994, pp. 194-203). While the Chun's government pushed hard for reforms, his relatives were allegedly peddling influence for their own personal gains, weakening the government's moral posture. During the first 2 years of Chun's presidency, about $50 billion (257 billion Korean wons) worth of real estate owned by *chaebols* were sold, but more than 8 times the amount of real estate sold was subsequently acquired by the same *chaebols*.

In the same fashion, 140 firms belonging to the top 20 *chaebols* were either divested or merged with other group companies, but 99 new firms were established by the same groups (Jung, 1989).

Nevertheless, the Chun government made continuous efforts to check the growth of *chaebols*. The system of credit supervision for large *chaebols* was reintroduced in 1984, freezing the total amount of bank credits available to the top five *chaebols* and setting ceilings for the top 30. In selected cases, bank credit was completely withdrawn from unprofitable companies, which led to the demise of Kukje (a *chaebol* group) in 1985. In 1986, the antitrust regulations and fair trade laws were amended to prevent the "octopus-style diversification" by *chaebols*. Under this law, *chaebols* were prevented from investing in their group firms by means of limiting cross-equity holding (inter-locking ownership) to not more than 40 percent of the firm's net asset value. With this measure, the ratio of their cross-equity holding to net asset value declined from 43.6 percent in 1987 to 32.1 percent in 1990 (SaKong, 1993, p. 63).

2.4.5 Assertion of *Chaebols*

The government's effort to control the growth of *chaebols* succeeded somewhat in the 1980s, but by the late 1980s *chaebols* had accumulated sufficient economic resources at their disposal and had became less dependent on government subsidies for survival. A number of factors attributed to their fortune.

First, the government's dependency on *chaebols* for its economic ends firmly had established *chaebols* as a formidable force. As long as *chaebols* met the government's performance expectations, they were left free to expand their operations in new fields, causing them to become even larger. The Korean economy relied so much on *chaebols* that it was difficult for the government to curtail their activities without adversely affecting its performance.

Second, by the early 1980s the world economy had recovered from a prolonged recession caused by the two oil crises in the 1970s. Blessed with the falling dollar value (Korean wons were pegged to the U.S. dollars), low oil prices, and relatively low interest rates during that time, the Korean economy was able to create an export boom. Exports had quadrupled during the 1980s, growing from $17.2 billion in 1880 to $71.8 billion in 1990, resulting in the highest trade surplus of $8.8 billion in 1988. Armed with proceeds from exports, *chaebols* depended less on government. Riding the tide of political and economic liberalization movements in the late 1980s, *chaebols* raised relatively inexpensive capital through foreign capital markets by means of issuing bonds and swap arrangements (Clifford, 1994, pp. 243-251).

Finally, the fact that government bureaucrats changed hands but *chaebols*' leaders remained unchanged enhanced the power of *chaebols*. The political elites who harried *chaebols* in the 1960s had all disappeared from influential government positions by the early 1980s. Likewise, those bureaucrats who attempted to control *chaebols* during the Fifth Republic were gone by the late 1980s with the fall of President Chun from power. President Roh Tae Woo, who took over the Sixth Republic, declared political reform processes, including the liberalization of *chaebols* from government control. Saddled with charges of corruption and brutal human rights violations of the previous government, the Roh government was not in a position to deal with *chaebols* forcefully. President Roh, nevertheless, demanded *chaebols* to focus on a few selected business lines by divesting other businesses to reduce economic power concentration, but his demands were largely ignored.

2.5 Emerging Business-Government Relations

The concentration of economic power in the hands of a few *chaebols* has been a concern for Presidents Park, Chun, and Roh, but not much has been accomplished in reforming this situation due to their dependency on *chaebols* for their political and economic ends. The situation, however, has changed in recent years as a result of changing political, economic, and international environments. The civilian government of President Kim Young Sam, which began in 1993, has taken a different approach to business-government relations. Unlike previous military-dominated governments, the civilian government has maintained an arm's length relationship with *chaebols*. President Kim underscored this point in 1993 by declaring his intention of not accepting any financial contributions from business during his tenure as president. Additionally, a new election law was passed by the National Assembly in early 1994 to strictly limit the amount of political contributions made to any candidate. This severance of financial ties will undoubtedly minimize the symbiotic relationship between government and *chaebols*.

A number of reform measures, begun by President Roh, picked up the speed under the new civilian government. Significant changes that have taken place in recent years include the liberalization of labor movement, financial industry reform, and the end of industrial policy. These changes altered the business-government relationship from one of traditional symbiotic ties to one of dealing at arm's length. That does not mean that *chaebol* will be left free to pursue their economic ends. As long as *chaebols* influence the economic well-being of the nation, their activities will be monitored by the government.

2.5.1 Liberated Labor-Management Relations

In the 1960s and 1970s the government suppressed the labor movement to control labor costs. In 1971, the Special Act on National Security required prior government approval of any labor negotiations. This Act was lifted in 1981 to restore the rights of labor in collective bargaining. However, new restrictions were imposed. In order to weaken the power of labor unions, the government banned industry-wide labor unions and restructured them around individual companies called "enterprise unions." Enterprise unions were managed by labor-management council, composed of managers and labor representatives. The idea was to promote the common interests of labor and management.

The problem, however, was that labor representatives were appointed by management and acted more for the benefits of management than for labor. Even when genuine disputes occurred, labor-management councils could not function as bargaining units due to their lack of experience in collective bargaining. In most labor disputes, government officials would be called in to settle the differences, and settlements tended to favor management because such settlements served the government's industrial policy (Kim, 1988). During this period, labor-management relations were replaced by labor-government relations.

The political reform in 1987 removed government intervention in labor-management practices and restored the rights of workers in the labor movement (Lee, 1988). The newly amended Trade Union Act of 1988 protects such unfair labor practices by employers as discrimination against workers who attempt to join or organize a union, rejection of a collective bargaining agreement, and interfering with workers in the formation and operation of a union. Union shops are now legal provided that more than two-thirds of employees are union members. Workers are also free to establish industry-based national unions.

Labor-management relations in Korea have entered a new era in which employers and employees themselves have to deal with their problems face-to-face without government intervention. The government, unlike its past repressive response to any labor initiative, is now taking a hands-off policy, insisting that labor disputes be handled by employers and employees themselves. This has been a new experience for labor and management because in the past three decades they never had opportunities to negotiate wages and grievances through a well-established bargaining process. This lack of experience in negotiation caused a wave of labor disputes in the latter part of the 1980s. More on labor relations will be discussed in Chapter 8.

2.5.2 Financial Industry Reforms

Another far-reaching government measure was the liberalization of the financial market. The financial sector had probably been the most heavily regulated industry in the Korean economy and at the same time was the most backward industry. In the early 1960s, the government took control of banking systems to mobilize the nation's financial resources to support its industrialization efforts. All phases of financial operations, from entry and monetary supply, to interest rate determinations were heavily regulated by the Ministry of Finance. The Kim Administration introduced a major financial industry restructuring plan in 1993. This plan included interest rate deregulation, phasing out policy loans, elimination of credit control system, reduction of government control on foreign exchanges, and financial market liberalization (Kim, 1993).

Under the new plan, commercial banks gained freedom in their selection of top management, setting interest rates and shareholder dividends, and establishing branch offices (*Business Korea*, 1994a, pp. 36-37). No longer are the top management of commercial banks descended from the Ministry of Finance or the Bank of Korea. As commercial banks are made free to set interest rates on deposits and loans, the gaps between official and real market rates are narrowed. Also, under the reform plan, commercial banks gradually phase out policy loan requirements. Currently, commercial banks are required to set aside 40 percent of their loan funds for small businesses (*Business Korea*, 1994a). Such policy loans are, however, likely to be replaced with other forms of governmental assistance programs administered by government-owned special banks.

The reform also calls for the opening up of Korea's financial markets to the world. Korea's trading partners have demanded that the Korean government open its financial markets wider and eliminate discriminatory practices against foreign financial institutions. Because Korea aspires to be a free-trader and becomes a member of the WTO and OECD, it has no choice but to accommodate the foreign partners' demands. Thirty-seven foreign banks are currently operating in Korea. Riding on the wave of financial market reforms, the foreign exchange market has been deregulated. Foreign exchange service fees are liberated; foreign currency transfers are less restrictive (*Business Korea*, 1995a, pp. 44-45).

These financial reforms will have a far-reaching impact on the relationship between Korean businesses and government and on global industrial competitiveness. These reforms will undoubtedly reduce the dependency of businesses on government. No longer can businesses depend on preferential policy loans from the government. On the other hand, businesses are free to search low cost capital overseas. Companies such as Kia Motors and Hansol Paper recently issued floating-rate notes in foreign capital markets (*Business Korea*, 1995b, pp.: 21-23), and Pohang Steel has registered in the New York Stock Exchange for its equity financing. For the financial institutions, deregulation will bring tough competition from abroad.

2.5.3 End of Industrial Policy

The Kim's administration is committed to the gradual ending of industrial policies which choose and support winners and protect domestic industries. In the absence of capital, technology, raw materials, and managerial skills, the previous administrations played a crucial role in capital formation, resource mobilization, resource allocation, technology development, and managerial intervention. However, as the economy has grown, it has become increasingly difficulty for the government to plan centrally and guide the nation's economic affairs. Government intervention in the past often resulted in market distortions and inefficiencies in the economy.

Another change is to end the protection of domestic industries. Domestic industries had been protected from foreign competition because it was thought that they were too young to compete with foreign industrial giants. Now that the nation has become a leading foreign trader, this argument is not longer valid. Furthermore, the newly established multilateral trade agreement demands that Korean domestic industries be opened to foreign competition. This opening will undoubtedly change the business-government relations from one of traditional administrative decree to one of the rule-based regulation. Foreign competitors usually demand internationally accepted rules and regulations. Despite the government's announced policy of liberalizing the economy, however, it is still heavily involved in entry and exit decisions. For example, the government initially blocked Samsung from entering the automobile industry (*Business Korea*, 1994b, pp. 21-23). The government blocked Samsung's entry into the automobile industry for the reason of excessive competition, but it finally gave in to Samsung's wish.

Although the government is now attempting to deregulate the whole economy, it will take time for bureaucrats to take their hands off the areas they have been involved in for such a long time. Because the symbiotic relationship has benefitted both business and government for such a long time, it will not be eliminated overnight. Furthermore, in a Confucian culture, people tend to trust bureaucrats more than they do businessmen and they like to see government exercise some form of control over business. As a result, some form of influence will be maintained. But government's role will not be as a direct interventionist but as an overseer. In any event, the traditional mode of business-government relations, commonly known as Korea, Inc., is forever gone in the new era.

2.5.4 Today's *Chaebol* Issues

The government may not directly intervene business affairs of big businesses, but it will continuously monitor their activities. As noted earlier, the government perceives *chaebols* to be its own creation and thus believes it has the responsibility to monitor them. Because *chaebols* have accumulated wealth with the aid of government, the government, as well as the public, perceive *chaebols* to be public entities. Furthermore, *chaebols* are far from being popular among the populace. A recent study reveals that *chaebols* have a serious image problem among the general population (Jung, 1991; Janelli, 1993, pp. 81-88). Negative images associated with *chaebols* include excessive real estate speculation, excessive concentration of economic power, diversification of business lines, inadequate concern for environment, poor labor-management relations, and lack of separation of ownership and management. As long as people see *chaebols* to be unpopular public entities, they will demand that the government control *chaebols*.

In response to these demands, the government will exert its influence on some issues considered to be important to the public and to the performance of the economy. The *chaebol* issue today is focused on three interrelated areas: legitimacy, equity, and efficiency (SaKong, 1993). The legitimacy issue stems from the fact that *chaebols* have in large part accumulated their wealth through preferential treatment by the government. *Chaebols* had unfair advantage over other small and medium-sized firms in getting bank credits, foreign exchanges, and tax benefits. In the minds of many Koreans, *chaebols* grew at the expense of non-*chaebol* firms and taxpayers. Furthermore, *chaebols* pose formidable entry barriers to other firms, lowering the level of competition in the overall economy.

The legitimacy issue has become relatively less important in recent years mainly because the government has curtailed its preferential treatments of *chaebols*. The Korean people generally accept the fact that capital formation in the hands of a few *chaebols* was essential for the nation's economic development, and that *chaebols* contributed to their economic well-being. And yet, people are still uneasy about the concentration of economic power in the hands of a few *chaebols*. They fear that *chaebols* will extend their power beyond the sphere of business into other sectors of the society, including politics.

The equity (fairness) issue is closely related to the legitimacy issue. The Korean economy expanded under the policy of "growth first, distribution later." People understood the necessity of such a policy in the early years of economic development. However, it has become an issue when a large share of the nation's wealth continues to remain in the hands of a few *chaebols*. As long as the nation's wealth remains in the hands of a few *chaebols*, *chaebols* will be criticized for being unfair. How can this problem be solved? In the U.S., the separation of ownership and management occurred gradually through the sale of common stock to the public, diluting ownership structure. In Japan, the breakup of *zaibatsus* (financial cliques) by the Occupied Forces Supreme Command at the end of Word War II changed the ownership structure. In Korea, the change of ownership structure, in the absence of forceful governmental intervention, will only come gradually.

There are several forces that will bring about the dilution of ownership structure and the eventual separation of ownership and management. First, as inheritance and gift taxes are administered more strictly, the intergenerational transfer of wealth will be more difficult and costly. Second, the growth of *chaebols* will require equity financing, diluting the ownership concentration. This will become more evident as the government curtails preferential treatments for *chaebols*. Third, the government is likely to limit the cross-holding of stocks among member companies in the same business group. Inter-locking stock ownership has been used as a means of exercising ownership control with limited equity. Finally, *chaebols* are forced to rely on professional managers to manage their firms in an increasingly competitive business world. Chapter 3 deals with this ownership issue.

Efficiency is closely related to the diversification strategy of *chaebols*. *Chaebols* have pursued an aggressive diversification strategy by over-extending themselves into various related and unrelated businesses. Studies suggest that firms with unrelated diversification tend to perform less effectively than firms with related-diversification (Rumelt, 1974; Bettis and Hall, 1982; Varadarajan and Ramanujam, 1987; Lubatkin and Rogers, 1989). In an era of global competition, mediocre companies cannot survive for long. Korean *chaebols*, unless their resources are focused on a few selected product lines, will not be competitive in the global market. Global competition will gradually force Korean companies to be more selective in their product lines (see Chapter 4).

In order to increase efficiency, *chaebols* are being asked by the government to reduce the number of affiliated companies. By eliminating unprofitable product lines, *chaebols* can become more competitive. However, the government's attempts to control *chaebols* have been largely unsuccessful due to the failure of government to follow through. In the past, politicians' financial dependency on *chaebols* interfered with their resolve. The situation is markedly different from the past; the civilian government is more forceful in dealing with *chaebols*. As a result, *chaebols* have taken voluntary actions in streamlining their unprofitable affiliates (*Business Korea*, 1993: pp. 18-20).

2.5.5 Models of Business-Government Relations

The changing patterns of business-government relations in Korea can be seen through a framework for analyzing the various roles that a government can take in managing a nation's economy. The government can play the role of subsidizer and/or regulator. Depending on how these two roles are adopted, four patterns of business-government relations can emerge: laissez-faire, mercantilism, paternalism, and constitutionalism (Cho, 1992). A government, which provides nominal subsidies to and imposes minimal regulatory guidelines on business, is regarded as a *laissez-faire* government. The Syngman Rhee government (1948-1960) could be classified as a *laissez-faire* government as it promoted a free-market economy. A government, which provides ample subsidies to and imposes minimal regulatory measures, is regarded as a *mercantilistic* government. Korea's economic take-off phase (1962-1971) could be regarded as a mercantilistic age. During this phase, the government fully supported businesses without imposing heavy regulatory constraints.

In the 1970s, businesses were not only provided with ample subsidies but also encumbered with heavy regulatory measures. As the size of businesses increased, so did the government's attempt to control them. Such a relationship between business and government can be characterized as *paternalistic*. The growth of businesses also meant a lessening need for governmental subsidies. The combined forces of less dependency on subsidies and increasing need for regulatory controls produced an age of *constitutionalism* in the 1980s. During this age, the primary role of government is to become a rule-setter.

What lies ahead for the business-government relations in the 1990s? It appears that the age of constitutionalism is likely to continue during this period, because the government and the general public perceive big businesses to be public entities that need to be controlled. From a purely economic standpoint, government intervention can only lead to another round of market distortions and economic inefficiencies. In the absence of governmental intervention, free-market competition will force businesses to be competitive. However, as people fear an unchecked growth of businesses, they will demand that government exert some control on big businesses.

2.6 Summary

The Korean economy has been characterized as a state-led economy. In this state-led economy, the government has played three distinctive roles: formulating economic plans, formatting and allocating capital formation, and building world-class big businesses. The government developed a series of five-year economic development plans and carried them out through the efforts of the private sector. From the outset, the government recognized the importance of the private sector in its developmental efforts. Because the lack of capital formation and technology, the government took the initiative in accumulating capital in the hands of a few selected entrepreneurs and guided their activities. This symbiotic working relationship succeeded handsomely, in bringing about the nation's economic growth and the development of world-class big businesses.

There are some signs that the symbiotic relationship between business and government has outlived its usefulness. The state-led economic model was effective in providing the needed capital for businesses and building the nation's economic infrastructure. As the economy grew and became increasingly complex, however, the tight control of business activities by government technocrats became less effective. Government intervention distorted the market economy, causing economic inefficiency. Furthermore, the private sector accumulated the needed capital, technology, and managerial skills to do better jobs in managing its business affairs.

Traditionally, the relationship between business and government has been vertical: government led business. The vertical relationship that developed during the past three decades is changing. The political reform that started in 1987 and the establishment of the civilian government have changed the traditional vertical relationship among the power elites in Korea: politicians, bureaucrats, and businessmen. Now the political and governmental bureaucrats have to deal with business leaders on a horizontal level. Furthermore, the tenure of politicians and bureaucrats is limited, but that of business executives is unlimited. This change will undoubtedly enhance the position of business in its relation to government.

The emerging pattern of business-government relations does not mean that business will be free of government's influence. As long as government perceives *chaebols* to be its own creation and the general populace trusts government more so than business, the influence of government on business is likely to continue. The role of government in the nation's business affairs, however, is likely to change from that of an active supporter to that of a regulator. It is hoped that the new business-government relations are not adversary in nature. Business and government need to continuously cooperate to cope with increasing global industrial competition and with the disparity that exist between big businesses and other segments of the society.

References

Bank of Korea (various years): *Economic Statistics Yearbook.* Seoul: Bank of Korea.

Bettis, R.A. and Hall, W.K. (1982): "Diversification Strategy, Accounting Determined Risk, and Accounting Determined Return," *Academy of Management Journal*, 25(2):785-799.

Business Korea (1993): "Chaebol Under Fire," 10(12):18-20.

Business Korea (1994a): "Free at Last?" 11(9):36-37.

Business Korea (1994b): "Samsung Clinches Victory Over Existing Auto Makers," 12(6):21-23.

Business Korea (1995a): "Financial Sector Liberalization," 12(12):44-45.

Business Korea (1995b): "Foreign Exchange Restrictions Liberalized," 12(8):21-23.

Chang, C.S. and Chang, N.J. (1994): *The Korean Management System.* Westport, CT: Quorum Books.

Chenery, H.B. and Taylor, L. (1968): "Development Patterns Among Countries and Over Time," *Review of Economics and Statistics,* 10(4):391-416.

Cho, D.S. (1992): "From Subsidizer to Regulator--The Changing Role of Korean Government," *Long Range Planning*, 25(6):48-55.

Cho, D.S. (1994): *Study of Korean Chaebols*. Seoul: Daily Economic News.

Cho, L.J. and Kim, Y.H. (1994): *Korea's Political Economy: An Institutional Perspective.* Boulder,CO: Westview Press.

Choi, K. and Lee, Y.S. (1990): "The Role of the Korean Government in Industrialization," in C.H. Lee and I. Yamazawa (eds.), *The Economic Development of Japan and Korea*. New York: Praeger, pp. 53-72.

Chung, Y.I. (1985): "Chaebol Entrepreneurs in the Early Stage of Korean Economic Development," *Journal of Modern Korean Studies*, 2:15-29.

Chung, Y.I. (1986): "Capital Accumulation of Chaebol in Korea During the Early Stages Economic Development." Paper presented at the Korean Economic Conference, Seoul.

Clifford, M.S. (1994): *Troubled Tiger: Businessmen, Bureaucrats, and Generals in South Korea*. New York:M.E. Sharpe.

Corbo, V. and Suh, S.M. (1992): *Structural Adjustment in a Newly Industrialized Country*. Baltimore: Johns Hopkins University Press.

Economic Planning Board (EPB)(various years): *Major Statistics of the Korean Economy* Seoul: Korean Government Printing Office.

Hong, W.T. (1976): *Factor Supply and Factor Intensity of Trade in Korea*. Seoul: KDI Press.

International Monetary Fund (IMF)(various years): *International Financial Statistics.* Washington, DC: International Monetary Fund.

Janelli, R.L. (1993): *Making Capitalism: The Social and Cultural Construction of a South Korean Conglomerate*. Stanford, CA: Stanford University Press.

Jones, L.P. and SaKong, Il. (1980): *Government, Business, and Entrepreneurship in Economic Development: The Korean Case*. Cambridge, MA: Harvard University Press.

Juhn, S.I. (1994): *Korean Entrepreneurship in Historical Perspectives*. Seoul: Seoul National University Press.

Jung, K.H. (1989): "Business and Government Relations in Korea," in K.H. Chung and H.C. Lee (eds.), *Korean Managerial Dynamics*. New York: Praeger, pp. 11-26.

Jung, K.H. (1991): *Diversification and Industrial Competitiveness*. Seoul: Korea Economic Research Institute.

Kim, E.H. (1990): "Financing Korean Corporations: Evidence and Theory," in J.K. Kwon (ed.), *Korean Economic Development*. New York: Greenwood Press, pp. 185-206.

Kim, H.J. (1988): "Industrial Relations in Korea: Issues and Perspectives," *Journal of East and West Studies*, 17(2): 1-16.

Kim, H.W. (1985): *The Korean Economy: Past Performance, Current Reforms, and Future Prospects*. Seoul: Korea Development Institute.

Kim, J.M. (1993): "Financial Industry Restructuring: Cornerstone for Economy's Growth and Stability," *Business Korea,* 10 (11):32-35.

Kim, P.J. (1994): "Financial Institutions," in L.J. Cho and Y.H. Kim (eds.), *Korea's Political Economy: An Institutional Perspective*. Boulder, CO: Westview Press, pp. 273-320.

Korea Foreign Trade Association (various years): *Yearbook*. Seoul: Korea Foreign Trade Association.

Lee, C.P. (1990): "The Role of Trade in Korea's Economic Development," in C.H. Lee and I. Yamazawa (eds.), *The Economic Development of Japan and Korea*. New York: Praeger, pp. 19-32.

Lee, J.T. (1988): "Labor Politics and Industrial Relations in Korea," *Journal of East and West Studies*, 17(2):17-30.

Lee, K.T. (1991): "Policy Measures to Reduce Industrial Concentration," in L.J. Cho and Y.H. Kim (eds.), *Economic Development in the Republic of Korea*. Honolulu: East-West Center, pp.431-472.

Lee, S.C. (1991): "The Heavy and Chemical Industries Promotion Plan (1973-79)," in L.J. Cho and Y.H. Kim (eds.), *Economic Development in the Republic of Korea: A Policy Perspective*. Honolulu: University of Hawaii Press, pp. 431-472.

Lubatkin, M. and Rogers, R. (1989): "Diversification, System Risk, and Shareholder Return: A Capital Market Extension of Rumelt's Study," *Academy of Management Journal*, 32(2):454- 465.

Mason, E.S., Kim, M.J., Perkins, D.H., Kim, K.S., and Cole, D.C. (1980): *Economic and Social Modernization of the Republic of Korea*. Cambridge, MA: Harvard University Press.

McMillan, C.J. (1996): *The Japanese Industrial System*. Third Revised Edition. Berlin, New York: Walter de Gruyter.

OECD (1994): *OECD Economic Surveys: Korea*. Paris: Organization for Economic Cooperation and Development.

Park, B.Y. (1982): *Chaebols and Politics*. Seoul:Hankook Yanseo.

Rumelt, R. (1974): *Strategy, Structure and Economic Performance*. Cambridge: Harvard University Press.

SaKong, Il. (1981): "Development Strategy and Finance in Korea," *Economic Development and Finance in Korea*. Seoul: Korea Investment and Finance Co.

SaKong, Il. (1993): *Korea in the World Economy*. Washington, DC: Institute for International Economics.

Shin, Y.K. (1984): *Characteristics of Korean Business*. Seoul: Seoul National University Press.

Song, B.N. (1990): *The Rise of the Korean Economy*. Hong Kong: Oxford University Press.

Suh, S.M. (1992): "The Economy in Historical Perspective," in V. Corbo and S.M. Suh (eds.), *Structural Adjustment in A Newly Industrialized Country*. Baltimore: John Hopkins University Press, pp. 6-34.

Varadarajan, P. and Ramanujam, V. (1987): "Diversification and Performance: A Re-examination Using a New Two-dimensional Conceptualization of Diversity in Firms," *Academy of Management Journal*, 30(2):380-393.

Yoo, J.H. (1989): *The Government in Korean Economic Growth*. Seoul: Korea Development Institute.

Chapter 3
Characteristics of Korean Firms

3.1 Introduction

There are many large public and private enterprises in Korea. As noted in Chapter 1, public enterprises laid the foundation on which private firms could build Korea's economy. The government used the public sector primarily to build the infrastructure of the economy. Korea Electric Power, Korea Telecommunications, Korea Highway Corporation, Korea Development Bank, and Pohang Steel are examples. While the public sector played an important role in building the infrastructure of the economy, the private sector provided the primary engine for Korea's economic growth.

Most large business firms are privately owned and managed by the founders and their families, commonly known as *chaebol* (Cho, 1995; Hattori, 1989; Steers et al., 1989; Yoo and Lee, 1987). The top 30 Korean *chaebols* practically dominate all industrial sectors: airlines, automobile, consumer electronics, construction, shipbuilding, steel-making, retailing, insurance, and others. As *chaebols* are becoming increasingly powerful, so are concerns for their legitimacy and economic efficiency. As it stands now, *chaebol* families (founders and their families), with ownership of about ten percent of the total outstanding shares, have absolute control over their business groups. Minority shareholders with more than 50 percent ownership (57.3 percent in 1995) collectively have no influence on corporate governance (*Korea Daily Economic News*, June 16, 1995). An argument can be made that economic inefficiency is caused by excessive diversification and the lack of separating management from ownership. The former leads to fragmentation of managerial attention and resources, and the latter limits the pool of well-trained managerial talents.

This chapter examines the characteristics of Korea *chaebols* and discusses issues related to the ownership and governance structure of Korean firms. It is speculated here that as the Korean economy expands, *chaebols* will need additional financing through capital markets, causing a gradual dilution of ownership control by *chaebol* families. This in turn will lead to gradual separation of ownership and management. As ownership structure changes, so will corporate governance structure. This chapter will debates the pros cons of different forms of corporate governance structures.

3.2 Characteristics of Korean *Chaebols*

Korean *chaebols* are unique in a sense that they are created by the government. The military-dominated government in the three decades since 1961 actively created and/or supported private business in order to carry out its industrialization programs. Policy instruments included low-interest loans, favorable foreign exchange rates, preferential tax treatments, and licenses for new businesses. Those firms that stayed on favorable terms with the government participated in the industrialization programs and were major beneficiaries of such government support. Subsequently, they emerged as powerful *chaebols*.

Korean *chaebols* are in some ways similar to Japanese *keiretsus* (business groups) and American-style conglomerates. They all are large and highly diversified companies. They, however, differ greatly in their ownership and governance structure. While Korean *chaebols* are mostly owned and managed by *chaebol* families, Japanese *keiretsus* are largely owned by other member companies and managed by professional managers. In the U.S., most conglomerates are mostly owned by individual and institutional investors and are managed by professional managers.

Korean *chaebols* are characterized by family ownership control, interlocking ownership, heavy debt-financing, and aggressive diversification. *Chaebol* families own far less than 50 percent of *chaebol*-related companies, but they have absolute control over their business groups. Interlocking ownership and debt-financing allow them to control *chaebol*-related companies with very little equity of their own. They are also highly diversified, creating a enormous power base for *chaebol* families. These points are further elaborated in the following sections.

3.2.1 *Chaebol* Family Ownership

There are 30 large business groups that are classified as *chaebols* and subjected to the special rules of the Fair Trade Act (OECD, 1994). Most of these business groups are owned and managed by founders and their families (in short, *chaebol* families). These *chaebols* are reluctant to go public for the fear of losing control. For example, in 1995, only 172 out of 623 companies (27 percent) in the 30 business groups were listed in the stock exchange. The Kia Group was the first business group that broke out the traditional ownership pattern by publicly trading more than one-half of its affiliated companies' stocks.

Chaebol's ownership can be classified into three categories: *chaebol* families, member companies within the same business group, and minority shareholders (individual and institutional investors). Until 1992, about half of the total paid-in capital of these top 30 groups were held by *chaebol* families and member companies within the group. Since then, the ownership share of these companies by *chaebol* families and member companies declined, on the average, to lower than 50 percent. In 1995, *chaebol* families owned on the average 10.5 percent of the total outstanding stock; member companies owned 32.4 percent through cross-shareholdings, making the internal ownership 43 percent. Minority shareholders owned the remaining 57 percent (Exhibit 3.1). If cross-shareholdings were barred, the ratio between inside and outside ownership would have been 15 percent versus 85 percent.

The pattern of ownership structure in Korean *chaebols* can be classified into three types (Hattori, 1989). Exhibit 3.2 depicts the ownership structure of Korean *chaebols*. Type I refers to direct ownership, in which the *chaebol* family directly owns the companies. Hanjin Group is a prime example. Type II is a nucleus company structure, where the *chaebol* family designates a nucleus company, which in turn owns its group-affiliated companies. Daewoo Group represents Type II; Daewoo Foundation serves as its nucleus company. Type III signifies an interlocking ownership structure (cross-shareholding), in which the *chaebol* family owns a nuclear company and/or an intermediary such as a cultural foundation, which in turn has interlocking ownership with member companies. Samsung Group is an example of Type III.

There has been a trend for Korean *chaebols* to move from Type I toward Type III as they grow. For example, Hanjin Group uses Korean Air as its lead company in controlling its affiliated companies. When companies are relatively small, the *chaebol* family owns and controls them directly. As these companies grow, taking on external capital, the ability of *chaebol* companies to control them declines. In order to maintain ownership control, the *chaebol* family tends to set up a lead or nucleus company to control the group's affiliated companies. As long as the *chaebol* family has ownership control of the lead company, which in turn has control over its subsidiaries, the family can control the subsidiaries without owning them directly.

Exhibit 3.1: Ownership of Korean Business Groups by Insiders (in %)

Business Group	Founder	Relatives	Member Companies	Total
Hyundai	3.7	12.1	44.6	60.4
Samsung	1.5	1.3	46.3	49.3
LG	0.1	5.6	33.0	39.7
Daewoo	3.9	2.8	34.6	41.4
Sunkyong	10.9	6.5	33.5	51.2
Ssangyong	2.9	1.3	28.9	33.1
Hanjin	7.5	12.6	18.2	40.3
Kia	17.1	0.4	4.2	21.9
Hanwha	3.6	1.8	31.2	36.7
Lotte	0.8	2.5	18.8	22.3
Kumho	0.6	1.8	37.7	40.3
Doosan	2.8	11.2	37.0	51.6
Daelim	0.3	8.6	28.3	37.6
Dong-A	10.7	9.0	20.0	40.1
Hanla	23.2	7.4	27.3	57.8
Dongkook	4.2	11.3	31.2	46.6
Hyosung	12.1	1.5	29.3	43.6
Hanbo	57.1	31.1	0.0	88.3
Dongyang	1.5	4.8	38.2	46.1
Hanil	8.3	7.4	26.9	43.1
Kolong	1.8	9.3	35.5	47.6
Kohap	3.4	2.4	40.7	46.7
Jinro	11.3	3.8	31.7	47.2
Haitai	3.8	1.1	28.7	34.0
Sammi	6.5	7.1	17.2	30.9
Dongboo	11.2	3.9	24.9	40.4
Woosung	7.4	14.9	37.6	62.6
Kukdong	1.6	4.4	16.3	25.0
Byucksan	2.9	11.9	26.3	41.3
Miwon	12.1	6.1	30.9	49.8
Average	4.9	5.6	32.8	43.3

Source: Adapted from *Korean Economic News*, July 1, 1995.

Exhibit 3.2: Ownership Patterns of Korean *Chaebols*

Type I Direct Ownership Structure

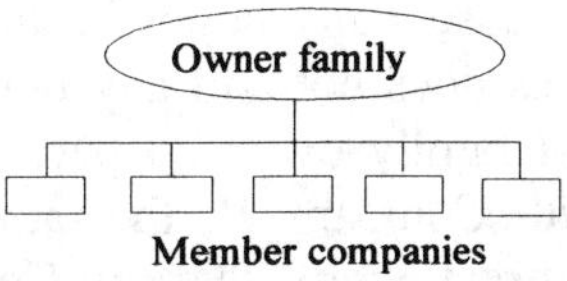

Type II Holding Company Structure

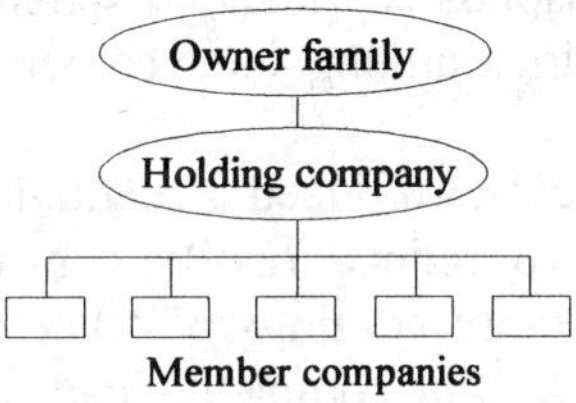

Type III Mutual Ownership Structure

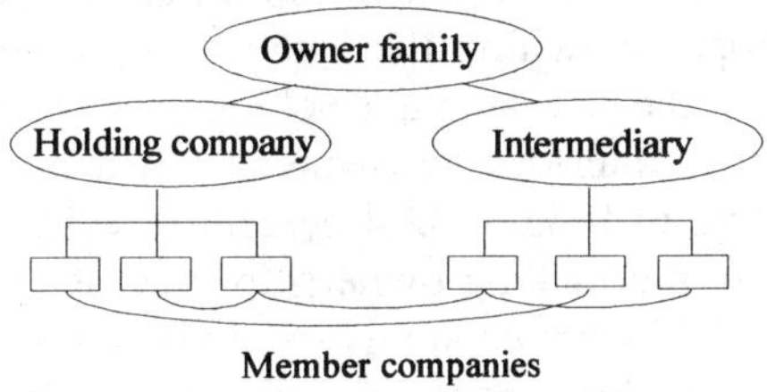

Source: Adapted from Hattori, T. (1989): "Japanese Zaibatsu and Korea Chaebol," in K.H. Chung and H.C. Lee (eds.), *Korean Managerial Dynamics*. New York: Praeger.

3.2.2 Interlocking Ownership

Publicly-held companies within a *chaebol* group are traded as independent companies. Although these companies are listed as independent companies, they are linked by means of interlocking ownership (or cross-shareholding). Interlocking ownership gives *chaebol* families the ability to control affiliated companies with a limited equity of their own. By holding each other's shares, the percentage of ownership by a *chaebol* family in relation to a firm's outstanding capital will increase. As shown in Exhibit 3.1, *chaebol* families on the average own only about 10 percent of the total outstanding capital, but the interlocking ownership of 33 percent gives them an effective ownership control share of 43 percent. Even though minority shareholders collectively own more than 50 percent of a company's outstanding capital, they do not have ownership control because their shares are largely fragmented and their rights to challenge management has not been protected.

Interlocking ownership share is essentially bogus because the swapping of stock between members companies does not add any new capital except on paper. For example, if a *chaebol* family owns 20 percent of Company A, which has cross-shareholding with Company B, the family can control the two companies even if it has no direct equity share in Company B. If cross-shareholding is barred, or a consolidated financial statement is forced on a business group, cross-shareholdings among its member companies will be canceled out.

In 1994, the Korean government introduced a regulation to control cross-shareholding schemes in order to reduce family control of big business groups. Under this regulation, equity holdings of other member companies cannot exceed 25 percent, and *chaebol* companies had to achieve this limit within three years. Since a member firm with more than 25 percent ownership of other member companies within the same business group needs to reduce its ownership share, the overall interlocking ownership in a firm's capital structure will decline. Interlocking ownership had been already declining from about 40 percent in 1983 to 32.4 percent in 1995.

Along with the decline in interlocking ownership, the ownership share by founder families is declining. As the economy expands, the need for capital expenditure increases. In a rapidly expanding economy, the need for capital expansion outpaces a firm's ability to generate the needed capital internally. To keep up with capital expansion, the firm has to raise the needed capital either though equity or debt financing. Owner-managers who are concerned with ownership control will prefer debt-financing over equity financing. But there is a limit as to how far a firm can rely on debt-financing, as we will see later. Consequently, the dependency on equity-financing will increase, diluting the ownership share of *chaebol* families. Family ownership share has declined from 17.2 percent in 1983 to 10.5 percent in 1995.

Although family ownership has decreased over the years, Korean *chaebols* are not likely lose ownership control soon. Berle and Means (1932) suggested that when ownership was concentrated in a relatively small number of shareholders, a majority shareholder with 20 percent equity ownership could effectively control a firm. When equity ownership is widely distributed, a majority shareholder with 10 percent equity ownership could control the firm (Larner, 1966). In some cases, as little as 5 percent ownership was sufficient for corporate control (Herman, 1981). Presently, Korean *chaebols* have more than 40 percent of effective ownership control.

3.2.3 Debt-based Capital Structure

The capital structure of Korean big businesses reveals that the ratio of equity-to-total assets is relatively lower in comparison with firms in other industrial countries. Between 1977 and 1988, the ratio for large Korean companies was 21.4, compared to 29.4, and 46.9 percent for their counterparts in Japan and U.S. on the book-value basis. On the basis of market value, the ratios are 16.3, 44.2, and 45.3 percents respectively (Kim, 1990). In 1995, the ratio on a book-value-basis was 19.9 percent for Korean companies (*Korean Economic News*, July 1, 1995).

There are several reasons for the high financial leverage enjoyed by Korean firms (Kim, 1990). First, during the past decades, the government used policy loans as a means of promoting targeted industries in the Korean economy. Interest rates for these loans were substantially lower than the market and inflation rates, creating opportunities for eligible firms to make substantial windfall profits.

Second, during the same decades, the government bailed out many insolvent businesses. These bailouts were to protect workers from being unemployed, to avoid the adverse effect of big business failures on the whole economy, and to protect the financial reputation of Korean firms overseas. These bailouts, as they removed fear of bankruptcy, encouraged firms to increase their dependency on government-backed loans. The larger the size of loans, the lesser the chance for defaulting. Unfortunately, the burdens associated with bailouts and resulting economic inefficiencies were borne by the taxpayers.

Finally, higher dependency on debt financing makes it possible for *chaebol* families to control their firms with a relatively small equity of their own. Note that the equity-to-total capital for large Korean companies is about 20 percent; only about 15 percent of their equity is contributed by *chaebol* families. This means *chaebol* families contribute only about 3 percent of their wealth to the total capitalization of their business groups and yet exercise absolute control over their business groups by means of interlocking ownership and debt-financing.

As noted in Chapter 1, the civilian government under President Kim limited the use of policy loans for *chaebols*. The issue of fairness and the concern of excessive concentration of economic power in the hands of *chaebols* led to the curtailment of governmental supports for *chaebols*. Furthermore, the government has introduced a new law to control the practice of mutual loans guaranteed among member companies within a business group (*Hankook Ilbo*, May 11, 1996, p. 9). As a result, the *chaebols*' ability to raise capital through debt-financing has been curtailed. Any future capital expansion by *chaebols* must come from the equity market.

The Korean economy is an investment-driven economy; its international competitiveness has been gained by producing globally-standardized products such as automobiles and consumer electronics and by using large scale economies (Porter, 1990, pp. 685-690). To be more competitive in the global market, Korean companies should not only increase their economies of scale but also become more innovative. Increasing economies of scale and innovation both require additional investment. Since Korean firms are already over leveraged, they have to meet the increased capital needs through equity-financing. The question is whether or not Korean firms will depend on equity-financing to the point where they may lose ownership control. If Korean firms are preoccupied with the maintenance of ownership control, they are likely to remain as small and inconsequential companies.

3.2.4 Unrelated Diversification

When a firm enters a new business area which is not tied to its current product or market, it is called diversification. There are a variety of reasons for diversification. When a firm's current product line matures or even declines, the firm may have to search for new business opportunities. Alternatively, when the firm is very successful in an industry and has substantial surplus resources, the firm may also need new businesses to invest. Or, the firm may diversify simply to expand its business domain and increase its economic power.

Alfred Chandler (1962) found that firms in the U.S. historically tended to grow and diversify in a distinctive pattern. In the introductory stage, firms specialize in single product lines. In the next, successful companies emerged as dominant forces in their chosen industries. In the third stage, successful companies increased the number of product lines related to their core businesses and expanded geographically. This is commonly referred to as *related diversification*. In the last stage, firms diversified into businesses unrelated to their core technological competencies (*unrelated diversification*). Understandably, firms that were diversified into related businesses by capitalizing on the existing technology tended to perform better than those which diversified into unrelated fields (Rumelt, 1974; Peters and Waterman, 1982; Prahalad and Hamel, 1990).

The unrelated diversification mode is most prevalent among Korean business groups (Jung, 1991). There are several reasons for such diversification. First, Korea has been a newly expanding economy, presenting *chaebols* with new business opportunities. Second, the Korean market is relatively small. A successful company reaches a saturated market with a relatively small scale of operation and soon needs to find new business opportunities. Third, *chaebols* pursued their growth strategies through diversification in order to gain status as big businesses, because government favored big businesses as an instrument for the nation's economic development. Since the government supported and protected big businesses from domestic as well as foreign competition, Korean *chaebols* increased their size by means of diversification with little risk to themselves. Finally, failed firms were often rescued by government and assigned to successful business groups (Lee, 1991).

Cho (1989) revealed that diversification generally had a positive effect on corporate growth and profitability to a certain point, but beyond that point it had a negative effect. This study seemed to support the research findings by Rumelt (1974) that rated the effect of related diversification on corporate performance more favorably than that of unrelated diversification. Successful firms tend to diversify into businesses that can build, draw strength from, and expand technological strength around their core businesses. Yoshihara (1981) too found in Japan that as a firm adds new businesses, its size increases. However, as the firm attempts to add more new businesses aggressively, it tends to add new businesses with marginal profitability and with low growth potential.

A Korean *chaebol* as a business group is large, but its subsidiaries are relatively small in size. Many *chaebol* companies are into capital-intensive industries (e.g., automobile, consumer electronics, oil refineries, and chemicals). These require "minimum efficient economies of scale" to become competitive in the international market (Chandler, 1986). And yet, their scales are relatively smaller than those of Japanese and American firms (Lee, 1991). For example, the sizes of American and Japanese automobile companies are on the average more than 13 times larger than those of Korean counterparts. In the case of consumer electronics, it is about 10 times. This observation implies that Korean *chaebols* need to focus their resources in a few selected fields to gain efficient economies of scale by consolidating far-flung operations.

3.3 Corporate Governance in Korea

Large Korean firms are primarily owned, managed, and controlled by *chaebols* families. If they are 100 percent financed by founders and their families, there is no need to debate corporate governance issues. Owner-managers can manage these firms as they wish. The problem, however, is that since more than 50 percent of their outstanding shares are owned by outside minority investors, there is a strong need for monitoring their performance.

In addition, there are other constituents who have contributed to the success of Korean *chaebols*. Government-controlled banks carried the burden of providing "policy loans" to *chaebols*. Labor toiled worked hard at low pay under the policy of "growth first, distribution later." The general public carried the tax burdens of providing subsidies to *chaebols* and bailing out failed companies.

As multiple stakeholders contributed to the growth of *chaebol* firms, they should have some influence on the governance of these firms. As it stands now, the *chaebol* families have absolute control of their firms; there is no effective corporate governance mechanism that protects the interests of multiple stakeholders other than *chaebol* families. The government is supposed to protect the interests of minority stakeholders. However, the military-dominated government in the past decades was pro-*chaebol* at the expense of other stakeholders. The newly-constituted civilian government has been slow in dealing with the governance issue for the fear of destabilizing the economy. As a result, owner-managers exercise firm control over their companies though they have less than ten percent ownership. In the following sections, we will first examine the current status of corporate governance in Korea.

3.3.1 Internal Control Mechanisms

There are basically two types of control mechanisms: internal and external (Walsh and Seward, 1990). These control systems are designed to bring the interests of managers and other stakeholders into congruence. Internal controls include boards of directors, labor unions, and minority shareholders. External controls are market forces, mergers and acquisitions, and government regulations.

Internal Executive Boards. Required by law, the board of directors in a publicly held company is charged with the responsibility of safeguarding corporate assets for corporate stakeholders. More specifically, the board of directors is responsible for selecting top management teams, evaluating their performance, deciding executive compensation, and reviewing major investment decisions. Since the board is responsible for monitoring the performance of management, it should be independent of the managerial influence. Having board members from outside of the organization is often suggested as a way to maintain such independence (Pearce and Zahra, 1991).

In Korean companies, there are no outside directors on the board. All board members are inside executive directors who are appointed by the chairman and who perform day-to-day managerial functions as president, executive vice president, managing director (Daily and Schwenk, 1996). As a result, the board does not function as an independent decision making body, monitoring the performance of top management. Board meetings are where the chairman communicates his wishes to the members. At present, presidents of a *chaebol*'s affiliated companies are appointed by the chairman, and the chairman's position is kept within the *chaebol* family.

Currently, there are outside directors on the board of state-owned enterprises. However, since all major decisions are made by government bureaucrats in various ministries, the role of the board of directors is largely ceremonial. Given this experience, one can not expect that the board of directors in both publicly-held and state-owned companies will function effectively even if they have outside directors.

The future challenge for large Korean firms is to find a way to govern themselves internally in order to meet the needs of various stakeholders. Failure to do so will continuously create conflicts between various stakeholders--*chaebol* families, minority shareholders, labor, government, and the general public. *Chaebols* have been criticized for exploiting workers, exploiting minority shareholders, profiting from real estate speculations, buying special favors from government, and so forth.

Workers and Labor Union. In the absence of adequate internal governance systems, workers and labor unions often emerge as internal control mechanisms by challenging management. Until recently, workers did not even have the rights to organize, negotiate, and take collective actions, let alone express their views on social and political issues. Labor-management councils existed in large corporations, but they largely served as advisory groups rather than as decision-making bodies. Workers demanded participation in managerial decisions related to their work, wages, and fringe benefits. Only recently have they gained the right to exercise their basic rights.

Workers and unions do not have a systematic way of monitoring the performance of management, but they nevertheless influence top management's decisions through their collective activities. Their concerns are mainly focused on improving wages and working conditions. Occasionally, however, they express their views on social and political issues affecting their welfare in the workplace to have an influence on managerial decisions. And if their demands are not met, they take their grievances to the streets for public support.

Although workers have emerged as a "watch dog" or pressure group monitoring the performance of top management, one cannot expect them to serve as an effective corporate control mechanism in achieving a balance between *chaebol* owners and the interests of major stakeholders. First, their primary goal is to protect their own interests. These interests are often in conflict with the interests of other stakeholders such as shareholders, consumers, and taxpayers. Secondly, even if we assume that they are fair-minded in pursuing the interests of all stakeholders, they may not have the needed expertise and experience of monitoring managerial performance.

Minority Shareholders. Minority shareholders own about 57 percent of the total outstanding stock of publicly-traded *chaebol* companies. As noted earlier, if cross-shareholdings are removed, they own as much as 85 percent of these companies. And yet they do not have much influence on the management of their firms. As noted earlier, there are two basic reasons for their plight. First, they are too fragmented to emerge as a force with which management has to deal. Secondly, there has not been an effective legal framework to protect the interests of minority shareholders.

Because there is no effective control mechanism protecting minority shareholders, *chaebol* families can transfer resources between member companies benefitting themselves at the expense of other shareholders. For example, assume that a *chaebol* family owns only 10 percent of Company A, a highly successful business unit, and 100 percent of Company B, an unsuccessful business unit. Under the current practice, the *chaebol* family can transfer Company A's resources to rescue Company B through interlocking ownership. Since the *chaebol* family wholly owns Company B, the family gains at the expense of minority shareholders of Company B.

In 1996, the government introduced a bill to protect the interests of minority shareholders. In the past, a group of minority shareholders with at least five percent of collective ownership shares was able to bring a suit against management. The new law lowers the required ownership share to three percent, and in some case a minority shareholder with just one share will be allowed to file suit against the management. Even with this provision, minority shareholders are not well protected. Their rights need to be strengthened to encourage the participation of the general public in the nation's capital market.

3.3.2 External Control Mechanisms

There are several control mechanisms that originate externally: government, financial institutions, and capital markets. When internally-based mechanisms of corporate governance do not function effectively, externally-based control mechanisms tend to emerge as alternatives.

Government Controls. Perhaps, the most powerful external control comes from the political elite and the governmental bureaucracy. Since they have in the past provided financial and administrative supports for businesses, they had the power to monitor the performance of large corporations. Government has made several attempts to curtail the power of *chaebols*. For example, the Fair Trade Act (1986) was enacted to prohibit cross-shareholding among member companies within a business group. This law was amended in 1992 and 1994, requiring *chaebols* to dispose any cross-shareholdings involving more than 25 percent of ownership by a member company. This law is designed to control the misuse of cross-listings as a means of inflating the ownership share of *chaebol* families.

Recently, a series of laws was introduced to curtail the power of *chaebols*. For example, the practice of guaranteeing loans for other companies within a business group will be gradually phased out eventually being eliminated by 2001. Minority shareholders will be given the right to sue management at a minimal cost to themselves. Interorganizational transactions among member companies will be required to be publicized. Fair and open trades are likely to be emphasized in coming years, although the government often times backpedaling its commitment.

Although the government has been playing an important role in corporate governance in Korea, its effectiveness has not been felt. During the years of military-dominated administrations, political contributions and bribes often compromised the effectiveness of governmental efforts to monitor *chaebols*. The indictment of two former presidents for taking bribes in addition to other charges attested to this problem. In the 1990s, as the government has curtailed financial and administrative supports for business, its leverage on *chaebols* has declined. Additionally, the government started to deregulate the business sector, reducing its direct intervention on corporate governance.

Financial Institutions. Financial institutions such as banks, pension funds, and insurance companies can serve as external control agents. After all, large Korean firms heavily depend on financial institutions for their capital requirements. Financial institutions are major stakeholders for *chaebols*: banks are their fund providers and other financial institutions are their shareholders. As bank loans (especially unproductive ones) mounted, some government officials at one point even suggested a debt-equity swap by which a certain portion of bank loans would turn into equity. If that happened, banks would have become the largest shareholder. This idea was never taken seriously because it violates the basic tenets of private property rights.

In Japan and Germany, banks play a major role in corporate governance. In fact, they are the largest shareholders of large Japanese and German companies. In Korea, however, banks have not been a major force in corporate governance. During the years of military-dominated administrations, commercial banks were nationalized under the control of the government to be used as the administrative agents of developmental funds. As a result, banks failed to develop their capacity to own other companies and monitor their performance.

The role of other financial institutions (pension funds, mutual funds, and insurance companies) in corporate governance also has been minimal, but it is likely to increase. At the moment, institutional shareholders do not have much power in monitoring Korean companies. However, as family ownership of large corporations is diluted, the share of institutional ownership will increase. As their share increases, it would be natural for them to monitor the performance of the firms they have invested. In addition, financial institutions should play the role of agent for small investors. This trend is already evident in advanced countries such as the U.S. and Germany. In the U.S., as will be shown later, institutional shareholders exert enormous power in monitoring the performance of large U.S.corporations.

Market-based Controls. There are basically two types of market-based controls: consumers and stock market. In a free-market economy, consumers and capital markets have enormous power over corporations. In the past, a limited number of *chaebols* were protected from foreign competition and were able to cooperate with each other to minimize competition (Choi, 1995).

However, in the new age of open markets, consumers will have a wide range of products at varying prices. Domestic producers who are not able to compete on quality and price will be at risk. The challenge for them will be to make continuous investments in improving product quality and production efficiency and in providing their companies with an infusion of highly trained managerial talents.

Other market-based control mechanisms are mergers and acquisitions. In the U.S., the capital market plays an important role in monitoring and disciplining U.S. corporations. Underperforming companies become a target for acquisition by other companies or corporate raiders. Because underperformance is reflected in a firm's stock value, other management teams are likely to offer themselves to the shareholders as alternatives to the incumbent management.

At present, the Korean government requires a report on the buyer's intention when the acquisition of a firm's stock involves more than ten percent. This requirement discourages the possibility of a hostile takeover, reducing the role of the stock market in corporate governance. This requirement is to be lifted in 1997, making mergers and acquisitions possible. However, mergers and acquisitions will not become commonplace in Korea because such measures are likely to be pursued by *chaebols* and perceived as an attempt to increase their economic power. On the other hand, *chaebol* families whose ownership share is nominal will be challenged by minority shareholders for corporate control. For example, recently *chaebols* companies such as Hanwha, Deahan Pulp, Shinhan, and Hanmi Bank have become the takeover targets.

As we can see here, there is no effective corporate governance mechanism that can balance the interests of various stakeholders in Korean *chaebols*. By default, *chaebol* families control large Korean businesses as if they owned them outright. The ownership and governance structure of Korean *chaebols* raise two questions: legitimacy and efficiency. Is it fair for a *chaebol* family to control a business group with less than three percent equity ownership of its total assets? Can a business group survive in an age of unlimited global competition without focusing its resources on a few selected businesses especially without the involvement of talented professional managers? These questions call for the development of effective governance mechanisms.

3.4 Comparative Governance Structures

The corporate governance system in Korea is at the crossroads. If the ownership of *chaebol* companies is retained in the hands of a few *chaebol* families, Korean firms are likely to remain small and less competitive, because their ability to raise the needed capital and managerial talents from external sources will be limited. An example can be found in the British economy. In a large number of British companies, except for British Petroleum, Imperial Chemical, and a few others, owner-families retain ownership control and occupy top management. They manage these companies with the assistance of professional salaried managers. As a result, British companies remain relatively small compared with those of other industrial nations.

If Korean *chaebols* want to compete in the global marketplace, they may have to raise the needed capital though external capital markets, diluting ownership control of *chaebol* families. If that happens, who is going to control them? In the U.S., the dilution of family ownership led to the emergence of professional manager. This eventually led to the separation of management and corporate control from ownership. In Japan, professional managers replaced founder families and gained corporate control. Will Korean firms follow the U.S. or Japanese mode of corporate governance? Or, will they follow the British pattern in sustaining family ownership control? Before we speculate on the corporate governance structure in Korea for the future, let us first look at the governance structures of other industrialized countries.

3.4.1 U.S. Corporate Governance

In the U.S., corporate governance structure has evolved through four phases: family, financial, managerial, and then much later, investor controls (Exhibit 3.3). In the late 18th century, most firms were small, privately owned, financed, and managed by owners and their families. Because the economies of scale were small, owner-managers were directly involved in all phases of managerial decisions, including financing, production, sales, and services. Chandler (1980) called it *family capitalism.* By the mid-19th century, the U.S. economy expanded due to the expansion of railroad and communication systems after the Civil War. Such expansion required capital beyond what owner-managers could generate internally. In order to meet this capital expansion need, they borrowed money from banks, insurance companies, and other financial institutions. Industrial firms that heavily relied on bank loans were under the control of bankers. Chandler called it *financial capitalism.*

Exhibit 3.3: Development of Capitalism and Ownership structure

	Family Capitalism	Financial Capitalism	Managerial Capitalism	Investor Capitalism
Source of Capital	Family and retained earnings	Retained earnings and debt-financing	Retained earnings, debt-financing and equity financing	Retained earnings, debt-financing and equity financing
Ownership Structure	Founder and family	Founder, family, and financial institution	Individual shareholders	Individual and institutional shareholders
Corporate Governance	Founder and family	Founder, family, and financial institution	Professional managers	Institutional investors

Source: Adapted from Lim, U.K. (1989): *Corporate Ownership Structure and Development of Capital Market.* Seoul: Korea Credit Analysis Corporation, p.12.

The increasing power of financial institutions, however, created fear among corporate managers of being taken over by bankers. Speculative transactions of stocks, use of inside information for personal gains, monopoly of financial transactions, and corporate control by banks further contributed to this fear. To curtail the influence of banks on industrial firms, the government enacted a series of banking laws such as the National Banking Act of 1864 and the Banking Act of 1933. In order to overcome the limitations associated with internal and debt financing, businesses started to raise capital through stock markets, diluting ownership control. As owner families were losing ownership control, professional managers emerged to replace them, ushering in an era of *managerial capitalism.*

Agency Problems. The reliance on equity financing and professional managers greatly contributed to the growth of U.S. firms. As corporate size and complexity increased, an increasing number of professional managers were hired to run large corporations. As the power of professional managers increased, however, the relationship between shareholders (principals) and managers (agents) became strained. Because principals and agents differ in their personal goals, conflicts can occur when agents with little or no ownership make managerial decisions (Berle and Means, 1932; Jensen and Meckling, 1976; Fama and Jensen, 1983; Williamson, 1988). Professional managers (agents) may pursue courses of action that benefit them (e.g., personal monetary gain, power enhancement, and perquisites) at times at the expense of owners' goals (e.g., capital appreciation, high profits, and dividend increases). Conflicts that exist between principals and agents are called *agency problems.*

Various governance mechanisms have been established to deal with agency problems: outcome-based compensation, managerial stock ownership, and boards of directors (Walsh and Seward, 1990). Outcome-based compensation encourages managers to achieve organizational goals because their rewards are tied to their performance. Management stock ownership encourages managers to align their interests with those of other shareholders. As managers increase their ownership share, they share the interests of shareholders. Ultimately, the board of directors is established to protect the interests of shareholders. Since individual shareholders cannot monitor managerial actions on a regular basis, they send their representatives to the board.

Board of Directors. In theory, shareholders control their firms through a governance system called *board of directors.* In this governance structure, the roles of ownership, governance, and management are differentiated. Shareholders exercise their ownership rights by electing the board of directors who represent them at board meetings and vote on issues such as mergers and acquisitions at annual shareholder meetings. The board of directors elects top management, evaluates management performance, approves executive compensation, and decides on issues that call for stockholder approval. Management then performs day-to-day managerial functions.

The boards of directors can be an effective corporate governance mechanism if its members can be independent in selecting, evaluating, and rewarding top management. Board members, however, cannot be independent for several reasons. First, their selection is largely influenced by top management. Because ownership of publicly-held companies is widely dispersed, no single shareholder can influence the election of directors. Under these circumstances, top management presents a slate of candidates for election largely by proxy. Management's candidates are rarely defeated (Bacon and Brown, 1977; Jacobs, 1991).

Second, chief executive officers (CEOs) often serve as chairs on corporate boards. A related problem is the duality of membership on boards while serving in top management. It has been observed that about 80 percent of the CEOs in U.S. corporations also serve as chairs on their boards of directors (Dayton and Keener, 1987; Lorsch and MacIver, 1989; Rechner and Dayton, 1991). If CEOs serve on boards, especially as chairs, it will be difficult for board members to be independent in evaluating top management's performance (Dayton and Keener, 1987).

Finally, boards of directors are often consisted of insiders, who are less likely to be objective in evaluating top management's performance. Because they are either employees or family members, they are more likely to align their interests with top management than with outside shareholders. Outside members with no affiliation with the firm are often recommended to be on the board in order to serve the interests of minority shareholders (Fama and Jensen, 1983; Byrd and Hickman, 1992).

It has been suggested that a proper mix of inside and outside directors makes an effective board. Insiders will bring expertise, while outsiders bring independence. To ensure the board's independence, there should be a sufficient number of independent outsiders. At the same time, too many independent outsiders can hinder the board's effectiveness due to their lack of expertise in the firm's operations. Historically, insider directors outnumbered outsiders in U.S. corporations, justifying the criticism that inside directors rubber stamp top management's decisions (Herman, 1981; Pearce and Zahra, 1991). In recent years, however, board members who will take active roles in meeting their legal responsibilities have been selected from both inside and outside(Pozen, 1994).

Investor Capitalism. Traditionally, shareholders who are unhappy with corporate performance would rather divest their shareholdings than challenge management. However, beginning in the mid-1980s, institutional investors (e.g., bank trust departments, pension funds, mutual funds, and insurance companies) started to organize themselves to exert influence on corporate management. For example, the Council of Institutional Investors (organized in 1985), Institutional Shareholder Services (established in 1985), and United Shareholders Association (1986) are organized to challenge management on issues related to corporate governance, corporate performance, and executive governance.

The power of institutional investors increases as their equity shareholdings increase. The percentage of equity shareholdings by institutional investors in U.S. corporations went from less than 20 percent in 1965 to about 50 percent in 1990. For example, in 1990, institutional investors held 52 percent of General Electric, 59 percent of Johnson and Johnson, and 83 percent of Intel. The amount of shares held by institutional shareholdings have increased but concentrated in the hands of a few institutional investors. Most large companies have a large number of institutional investors, but the 20 largest investors account for more than a third (34.1 percent) of the total outstanding shares (Lowenstein, 1991). As a result, many companies find that a majority of their stocks are under the control of a few powerful institutional investors.

Institutional investors are barred from direct involvement in management by the Security Exchange rules, but they nevertheless influence corporate governance in a number of ways. First, they nominate and vote for board members who are likely to represent their interests at board meetings. Second, they participate in takeover activities when the companies in which they have invested perform poorly. They also challenge management by means of proxy contests during hostile takeover bids. Finally, they pursue resolutions to change corporate governance structures, which are called *shareholder proposals*. Examples include rescinding anti-takeover measures such as poison pills and golden parachutes that make unfriendly takeovers costly (Useem, 1993). Corporate managers respond to these challenges because failure to do so can mean loosing their jobs.

Institutional activism is said to reduce agency problems that occur between shareholders and managers because managers become more responsive in meeting shareholders' demands for high profits, increased stock prices, and performance-based compensation for executives (Pozen, 1994). Shareholder value has increased in the 1990s partially due to management's relentless efforts to improve profits and stock prices. But critics argue that this increase in shareholder values came at the expense of workers who lost their jobs in corporate downsizing, restructuring, as well as in outsourcing processes and long-term investments that are needed to sustain corporate survivability (Jacobs, 1991). As a result of the increasing power of institutional owners, the U.S. corporate governance has moved away from a *manager-controlled* to a *investor-controlled system* (Useem, 1996).

In summary, corporate controls in the U.S. are exercised through internal and external control mechanisms. The centerpiece of the internal control system is the board of directors, which oversees the performance of top management to protect the shareholders' interests. This control mechanism often fails when the board is composed of inside directors who rubber stamp top management's decisions. To ensure the board's independence, independent outside directors are appointed as a means of insuring that boards will be more objective in judging the performance of top management. A proper mix of inside and outside directors usually produces an effective board and contributes to the firm's economic well-being. When internal control systems fail, external control systems such as takeover threats and institutional investors become active in governing Corporate America.

3.4.2 Japanese Corporate Governance

Corporate ownership and governance structures in Japan differ considerably from those in the U.S. Unlike U.S. large corporations mostly owned by individual shareholders, large Japanese corporations are mostly owned by financial and nonfinancial institutions and controlled by managers with little ownership (Yoshimori, 1995). Prior to World War II, large Japanese business groups such as Mitsui, Mitsubishi, and Sumitomo were owned by Mitsui, Iwasaki, and Sumitomo *zaibatsu* families respectively (Hattori, 1989). After the World War II, the Allied Forces Supreme Command led the dissolution of *zaibatsu* groups. In response, *zaibatsu* families voluntarily submitted dissolution proposals to the Supreme Command and gradually relinquished their ownership interest and removed themselves from managerial positions.

When the occupied forces left Japan in 1951, the companies in the old *zaibatsu* companies regrouped themselves as *keiretsu* groups. However, the postwar *keiretsu* companies were different from prewar *zaibatsu* groups (Okumura, 1976). First, unlike the *zaibatsu* companies owned by founder families, *keiretsu* companies are largely owned by other companies in the same business group. Second, companies in each business group are listed as separate companies on the stock exchange, but they coordinate their activities through interlocking ownership. Finally, corporate control is exercised by means of horizontal and vertical institutional ownership.

Institutional Ownership Control. A peculiar aspect of Japanese corporate governance is control through institutional ownership. Almost three-quarters of the total outstanding corporate equity of all listed Japanese companies is held by other companies--mostly financial and nonfinancial companies, compared to about one-third in the U.S. (Prowse, 1992). As noted earlier, there is a difference in institutional ownership between Japan and the U.S. In Japan, the majority institutional owners are other companies in the same business group. In contrast, the majority of institutional owners in the United States are mutual funds and pension funds, which buy and sell stocks for individual investors. That means the ultimate ownership of institutional shareholdings lies in institutions in Japan and individual investors in the U.S. This difference has a profound effect on how corporations are governed in Japan and the U.S.

Institutional ownership in Japan comes in basically two forms. The first is interlocking ownership among major firms (member companies) within a business group. Interlocking ownership of each other's company is usually under ten percent. The second is institutional ownership of subsidiaries by *keiretsu* companies. These subsidiaries may own stocks of their parent companies, but their shares are relatively small. Interlocking ownership among member companies within a *keiretsu* group has led to horizontal internal firm control; ownership of subsidiaries has led to vertical interfirm control (Okumura, 1982). The relationship among member companies is relatively informal in nature; no one member exercises dominant control over others. In contrast, the relationship between a *keiretsu* company and its subsidiaries is hierarchical; subsidiaries subordinate their operations according to the plans of their parent companies.

Horizontal Interfirm Control. Horizontal interfirm control is exercised through the meetings of presidents of member companies and interlocking directorship. For example, the presidents of Mitsubishi member companies meet on Fridays in a group called the *Kinyokai* Club to discuss matters related to the group as a whole. Similarly, the presidents of Mitsui member companies meet on Tuesdays, and the presidents of Sumitomo meet on Wednesdays. Additionally, many of the executives of member companies within a group hold directorships in other member companies. Some of them hold multiple directorships. Ten to twenty percent of these executives hold directorships in other member companies or multiple directorships (JFTC, 1992; Ueda, 1994).

Although no one member company dominates the entire group, *keiretsu* banks and insurance companies have stronger voices in the governance of other member companies because their shares of interlocking ownership are usually higher than those of other member companies and they also are the chief sources of debt financing for their member firms. Higher percentages of interlocking ownership allow them to have proportionally higher percentages of interlocking directorships. Financial institutions also influence the corporate governance of indebted firms by means of debt service covenants. Creditors can force debtors to accept managerial intervention and dissolution.

Vertical Interfirm Control. The relationship between *keiretsu* companies and their subsidiaries is vertical. *Keiretsu* member companies dictate the corporate governance and management of their subsidiaries and affiliated companies by prescribing a set of regulations for managing them such as the basic management doctrine, rules of transactions, appointment of key personnel, and others. They also monitor the performance of their subsidiaries and affiliated companies. If the performance of a subsidiary does not meet the parent company's expectations, the parent company provides the needed managerial, financial, and/or technical assistance. Frequently, the parent company's personnel are dispatched to the affected subsidiary.

Member companies of a *keiretsu* group have numerous subsidiaries and affiliated companies. For example, Mitsubishi Heavy Industries has more than 40 subsidiaries and another 300 affiliated companies (Okumura, 1982). Each of these subsidiaries and affiliated companies has subsidiaries and affiliated companies. There are also subcontractors working for the Mitsubishi subsidiaries and affiliated companies. All these subsidiaries and affiliated companies are related to Mitsubishi Heavy Industries by performing upstream and/or downstream activities.

Vertical interfirm control is usually exercised in times of financial crises. During normal courses of business, individual companies are usually left alone. Firms monitor themselves through internal control mechanisms. They have their own boards of directors to monitor their performance. These boards are mostly composed of internal executive directors who have managerial responsibilities (Tricker, 1994, pp. 19-22). Even when executives from other companies are on the board, they are considered insiders because they are from member companies within the same business group.

Inside Executive Directors. A typical Japanese Board is composed of Chairman, President, Vice-Presidents, Senior managing directors, managing directors, directors, and statutory auditors. They are all executive directors with little stock ownership promoted from the company's managerial ranks. Non-executive directors from outside rarely exist in Japanese corporations. The closest to such appointments would be directors from affiliated companies. What all this means is that Japanese corporations are controlled and management by professional managers with little ownership interests, characterizing a purely manager-controlled corporate governance system.

Because there is no representation of individual shareholders on the board, professional managers are given opportunities to engage in opportunistic behaviors (higher pay, perks, and empire building) for themselves. Rather than searching for ways to enhance shareholders' wealth, they will be more interested in increasing the size of their firms in ways that can lead to higher pay, perks, power, and survival. Japanese managers place a high premium on corporate growth, in contrast to American managers who emphasize profit maximization (Chung and Lee, 1989, pp. 163-180). Lower pressure for profit maximization allows Japanese firms to undertake investment projects that American counterparts would avoid. This stimulates Japanese firms to expand.

Do Japanese managers recklessly pursue opportunistic behavior? To some extent, they do. Japanese managers are more concerned with corporate growth than with profitability (Chung and Lee, 1989). The ROI for Japanese manufacturing firms for the decade of 1984-1993 averaged five percent annually, compared with seven percent for U.S. manufacturing firms. They pay themselves and their employees generous salaries, bonuses, and other fringe benefits. They rarely lay-off their employees. However, the interfirm control through interlocking ownership prevents them from pursuing unrealistic opportunistic behavior. In fact, it is much easier to engage in such opportunistic behavior in U.S. corporations because CEOs in U.S. firms deal with a single board to get their pay raises or perks. In contrast, Japanese CEOs must deal with an intricate web of interfirm control mechanisms to achieve the same goals.

3.4.3 European Governance Structure

The European Union is not a single country. As such, there is no single form of corporate governance structure. The corporate governance structure is divided along ideological lines: owners versus other stakeholders (mostly workers and private versus public ownership [Alkhafaji, 1989]). One extreme is the British corporate governance structure that stresses the importance of private ownership of business and the right of owners in corporate governance. Most British companies are owned by a large number of shareholders, which are comprised both of private investors and institutions such as insurance companies, investment companies, and pension funds. Shareholders have the right to elect their representatives on the board of directors to protect their rights. However, in Britain, the existing board nominates the slate of candidates, who are rarely defeated. As the existing board usually is composed of majority owners (founding families), the British system essentially resembles the owner-controlled governance structure.

On the other extreme is the French system that stresses the importance of public ownership and the role of government in corporate governance. The national government is heavily involved in the nation's economic affairs. Public enterprises have monopolies in railroad, electricity, and tobacco industries, and compete with private enterprises in air transportation, automobile, banking, and oil refineries. State government also participates and exercises supervision in joint ventures with the private sector. Even in private enterprises, the government sets rules related to the workweek, overtime compensation, and paid vacations. Because of the public nature of French enterprises, corporate boards are largely composed of outside directors monitoring French enterprises.

The Germanic system, falling between these two extremes, recognizes the importance of duality in corporate governance (Charkham, 1994). There are public enterprises in Germany, but the private sector dominates the German economy. Private enterprises are owned by individual shareholders and financial institutions. In general, both private and public corporations are independent of the government in their governance. However, the co-determination Act of 1976 gives workers the right to participate in corporate governance. German corporate boards are divided into *Vorstand* (management) and *Aufsichtsrat* (supervisory). The *Vorstand* runs the company and is responsible for the firm's performance. The *Aufsichtsrat* appoints the *Vorstand* members and supervises their activities. By the co-determination Act, half of the *Aufsichtsrat* comes from workers and the other half from shareholders.

3.5 Options for Korean *Chaebols*

The corporate governance structure in Korea is in the process of changing. Faced with the globalization of the world economy, Korean firms do not have much choice but to expand. To do so will require massive investments to enhance their capacities to develop new products, improve product quality, and achieve economic efficiency. As their ability to raise such investments is internally limited, they need to rely on external capital markets, diluting ownership control of *chaebol* families. If the current trend of ownership dilution continues, it will probably take 10 to 15 years before the *chaebol* families will have only one or two percent of the total outstanding capital among large business groups. How fast the dilution of ownership will actually occur depends on several factors such as the *chaebol* families' desire to maintain ownership control and the laws governing cross-shareholdings, mutual loan guarantees, minority shareholder rights, and inheritance taxes. Undoubtedly, *chaebol* families will attempt to maintain ownership control by all means. Whether the government has the will to enforce the laws and facilitate the dilution process is another matter.

Ownership control by *chaebol* families so far has been protected by means of cross-shareholding and suppressing minority shareholders in corporate governance. Korean *chaebols* are not likely to give up their controlling interest; they will fight to maintain ownership control by means of restricting public offerings of their ownership shares, strengthening cross-shareholding systems, providing managerial education and training of their offspring, and/or buying political influences by means of political contributions and bribes. The only way in which the corporate governance system is changed is through two forces: gradual dilution of ownership control and changing laws governing ownership structure.

The government over the years has attempted to curb the power of *chaebols*, but their efforts have been largely unsuccessful. As pointed out in

Chapter 2, *chaebol* families outlived policy makers who were behind reform movements. The political will to reform the *chaebol* structure became unglued when those reform-minded policy makers left office. Furthermore, the dependency of politicians on *chaebols* for their political funds in the past also weakened the political will to reform. Even the civilian government under President Kim Young Sam seems to find it difficult to restructure *chaebols* for the fear of disrupting their normal economic activities.

The current government nevertheless continues to press for a major reform in corporate governance in Korea by changing commercial laws to curtail the power of *chaebol* families (POSRI, 1995; *Hankook Ilbo*, May 7, 1996, p. 14). The new laws limit the amount of cross-shareholdings, curtail mutual loan guarantees among affiliated companies, give minority shareholders the right to take collective action against the *chaebol*-controlled management, and demand the publication of consolidated financial statements of *chaebol* companies.

These laws will not directly force *chaebols* to reduce their ownership control but will force them to make a choice between *chaebol* ownership control or gradual dilution of ownership control. Since *chaebol* families no longer can maintain controlling ownership share by means of cross-shareholdings and external debts through mutual loan guarantees, any growth of their firms must come from either internally generated earnings or by selling ownership shares to external shareholders. The choice they have now is to either remain as small companies by protecting ownership control or to expand their operations by diluting it. If a *chaebol* family decides to remain small, it will lose a competitive edge that comes from the economies of scale. On the other hand, if it decides to expand, the dilution of ownership control becomes inevitable and the separation of ownership and management will follow.

Gradual dilution of ownership control is likely to occur as Korea pursues globalization. One overriding weakness of Korean firms in global competition is the lack of economies of scale. To be competitive in the international market, a firm must maintain a minimum efficiency scale. For example, in the case of the automobile industry, the minimum efficiency scale (MES) for manufacturing is estimated to be around 300,000 units per year. If marketing and R&D costs are added, the MES is likely to be more than one million units. Korean business groups as a whole are large in size, but individual firms within a business group are relatively small. If Korean firms want to compete effectively in the global market, they need to increase the level of investment in product innovation, product quality, and manufacturing efficiency by focusing their resources in a few selected industries.

The need for additional capital is likely to force Korean *chaebols* to rely on external capital markets, diluting their ownership control shares. In the first half or the 1990s, the Korean economy grew at an annual rate of about eight percent, and its inflation rate was about six percent. If a company wants to keep abreast of the national economy, its annual sales should grow at a rate of 14 percent. If we assume that the sales-to-asset ratio remains at the same level, the required assets should also grow at an annual rate of 14 percent. Assuming also that the equity-to-asset ratio remains at the same level, the company should increase its capital by 14 percent per annum. This means that the firm's capital should double every six years. It is apparent that even a very rich *chaebol* family will find it difficult to keep up with such capital requirements without loosing ownership control.

Even if the government is not actively involved in the transformation process, if *chaebol* firms want to grow and remain competitive, they do not have much choice but to raise the needed capital through equity sharing with minority shareholders and in the process must accept the dilution of ownership control. A combination of internal and external forces will gradually lead to the separation of ownership and control. We will probably witness such events in large publicly-listed companies in the next decade or so. On the other hand, if *chaebol* families want to hold on to their ownership control and refuse to expand, they can do so at the expense of losing business opportunities.

In the meantime, the existing governance systems must be revised to deal with the issues of fairness and economic efficiency. There should be some control mechanisms to monitor managerial decisions of owner-managers who have absolute control over the whole business group. Government efforts to ban cross-shareholding and mutual loan guarantees should be strengthened, regulations on takeovers should be lifted; minority shareholders should be given the right to challenge management. In addition, the role of the board of directors should be strengthened to monitor the performance of owner managers; that means, the board should have some outside directors who can be independent in judging managerial performance.

At the same time, utmost care must be taken in order to not disturb managerial stability in the short run. Corporate governance is a sensitive issue which touches upon corporate control over financial and human resources. A proper balance should be maintained between economic efficiency and equity in devising corporate governance systems. It should be kept in mind that the current entrepreneurial capitalism in Korea has created a dynamic economy. Any premature intervention on corporate governance by the government could result in serious repercussions. The new corporate governance system should evolve over time through trial and error. Only in the next decade will witness the emergence of a workable corporate governance system that is capable of sustaining the Korean capitalistic system.

3.6 Summary

Korean *chaebols* are the creation of interventionist economic policies that have been in force since 1962 when President Park Chung Hee initiated an aggressive industrialization effort. In the absence of private capital formation, the government actively created and/or supported private businesses to carry out its industrialization programs by means of providing low-interest loans, favorable foreign exchange rates, tax incentives, subsidies, and administrative supports. Those firms that maintained favorable terms with government policy-makers were the beneficiaries of these governmental programs. As long as they used these resources to support the government's economic goals, they were continuously supported and eventually emerged as powerful *chaebols*.

The combined sales of the top four *chaebols* (Hyundai, Samsung, LG, and Daewoo) represent a colossal 84 percent of Korea's GDP, and their exports account for almost 60 percents of Korea's total exports. Their share of manufacturing value-added also amounts to more than 30 percent of Korea's GDP. *Chaebols* are highly diversified, ranging from airlines, automobiles, consumer electronics, shipbuilding, construction, retailing, transportation, and others. Few industries are untouched by *chaebols*.

The concentration of economic power in the hands of a few *chaebols* has become a major issue in Korea, reflecting concerns over fairness and efficiency. As it stands now, *chaebol* families with about ten percent of ownership share have almost absolute control over whole *chaebol* business groups. As their businesses expand, their controlling ownership share will be further diluted. And yet, they have not yet devised adequate corporate governance systems to accommodate changing ownership patterns.

The ownership control by *chaebol* families creates agency problems for minority shareholders (small and institutional investors) who own more than 50 percent of the total outstanding capitalization of the top 30 *chaebols*. Such governance systems also limit the firm's capacity to raise external capital for business expansion and to attract managerial talents outside their families. If a *chaebol* firm wants to grow, it has to raise external capital and bring in external managerial talents. In the process it must gradually accept the dilution of ownership control.

As a *chaebol* company gradually loses ownership control, the separation of ownership and management will eventually follow. A new governance system consisting a board of directors must be developed. Board members are selected to represent the interests of various stakeholders of a company including majority and minority shareholders and probably employees. This board will select its CEO and a top management team to manage the company at maximum efficiency. Their performance will be judged by the board internally and the market externally.

References

Alkhafaji, A.F. (1989): *A Stakeholder Approach to Corporate Governance*. New York: Quorum Books.

Anderson, C.R. and Paine, F.T. (1978): "PIMS: A Reexamination," *Academy of Management Review*, 3(3):602-612.

Bacon, J. and Brown, J.K. (1977): *The Board of Directors: Perspectives and Practices in Nine Countries*. New York: The Conference Board.

Berle, A.A. and Means, G.C. (1932): *The Modern Corporation and Private Property*. New York: McMillan.

Byrd, J.W. and Hickman, K.A. (1992): "Do Outside Directors Monitor Managers?" *Journal of Financial Economics*, 32:195-221.

Chandler, A.D. (1962): *Strategy and Structure*. Cambridge, MA: MIP Press.

Chandler, A.D. (1980): "The United States: Seedbed of Managerial Capitalism," in A.D. Chandler and H. Daems (eds.), *Managerial Hierarchies*. Cambridge, MA: Harvard University Press, pp. 9-40.

Chandler, A.Jr. (1986): "The Evolution of Modern Global Competition," in M.E. Porter (ed.), *Competition in Global Industries*. Boston: Harvard Business School Press, pp. 405-448.

Charkham, J.P. (1994): *Keeping Good Company: A Study of Corporate Governance in Five Countries*. New York: Oxford Press.

Cho, D.S. (1989): "Diversification Strategy of Korean Firms, " in K.H. Chung and H.C. Lee (eds.), *Korean Managerial Dynamics*. New York: Praeger, pp. 99-112.

Cho, D.S. (1995): *Study of Korean Chaebol*. Seoul: Daily Economic Newspapers.

Choi, J.P. (1995): "Industrial Structure and Market Competition," in POSRI, *Large Enterprises in Korea: Who Own and Control?*. Seoul: POSCO Research Institute, pp. 116-139.

Chung, K.H. and Lee, H.C.(eds.)(1989): *Korean Managerial Dynamics*. New York: Praeger.

Chung, K.S. (1994): *Governance Structure and Firm Competitiveness*. Seoul: Korea Institute of Finance.

Daily, C.M. and Schwenk, C. (1996): "Chief Executive Officers, Top Management Teams, and Boards of Directors: Congruent or Countervailing Forces?" *Journal of Management*, 22(2):185- 208.

Dayton, D.R. and Keener, I.K. (1987): "Composition and CEO Duality in Board of Directors: An International Perspective," *Journal of International Business Studies*, 18(4):33-42.

Fama, E.F. (1980): "Agency Problems and the Theory of the Firm," *Journal of Political Economy*, 88:288-307.

Fama, E.F. and Jensen, M.C. (1983): "Separation of Ownership and Control," *Journal of Law and Economics*, 26:301-325.

Hattori, T. (1989): "Japanese Zaibatsu and Korean Chaebols," in K.H. Chung and H.C. Lee (eds.), *Korean Managerial Dynamics*. New York: Praeger, pp. 79-95.

Herman, E.S. (1981): *Corporate Control & Corporate Power*. Cambridge: Cambridge University Press.

Jacobs, M.T. (1991): *Short-Term America*. Boston: Harvard Business School Press.

JFTC (1992): *Six Largest Business Groups in Japan*. Tokyo: Japanese Fair Trade Commission.

Jensen, M.C. and Meckling, W.H. (1976): "Theory of the Firm: Managerial Behavior, Agency Costs and Ownership Structure," *Journal of Financial Economics*, 3:305-360.

Jung, K.H. (1991): *Diversification and International Competitiveness of Korean Business*. Seoul: Korea Economic Research Institute.

Gerlack, M.L. (1992): "The Japanese Corporate Network: A Blockmodel Analysis," *Administrative Science Quarterly*, 37:105-139.

KERI (1993): *Financial Liberalization and Bank-Firm Relations*. Seoul: Korea Economic Research Institute.

Kim, E.H. (1990): "Financing Korean Corporations: Evidence and Theory," in J.K. Kwon (ed.), *Korean Economic Development*. New York: Greenwood Press, pp. 341-358.

Larner, R. (1966): "Ownership and Control in the 200 Largest Nonfinancial Corporations: 1929-1963," *American Economic Review*, 56(4):777-787.

Lee, S.H. (1991): *Separation of Ownership and Management: Managerial Modernization and Economic Democratization*. Seoul: Social Science Research Institute, Seoul National University.

Lim, U.K. (1989): *Corporate Ownership Structure and Development of Capital Markets*, Seoul: Korea Credit Analysis Corp.

Lim, U.K. (1989): *Ownership Structure of Listed Companies and Managerial Control Issues*. Seoul: Council of Listed Companies.

Lorsch, J.W. and MacIver, M. (1989): *Pawns or Potentates: The Reality of America's Corporate Boards*. Boston: Harvard Business School Press.

Lowenstein, L. (1991): *Sense and Nonsense in Corporate Finance*. Reading, MA: Addison-Wesley.

Nishiyama, T. (1982): "The Structure of Managerial Control: Who Owns and Controls Japanese Businesses?" *Japanese Economic Studies*, Fall:37-77.

OECD (1994): *OECD Economic Surveys: Korea*. Paris: Organization for Economic Development and Cooperation.

Okumura, H. (1976): *Six Largest Business Groups in Japan*. Tokyo: Diamond Publishing.

Okumura, H. (1982): "Interfirm Relations in an Enterprise Group: The Case of Mitsubishi," *Japanese Economic Studies*, Summer:53-82.

Pearce, J.A. and Zahra, S.A. (1991): "The Relative Power of CEOs and Boards of Directors: Associations with Corporate Performance," *Strategic Management Journal*, 12:135-153.

Peters, T.J. and Waterman, R.H. (1982): *In Search of Excellence*. New York: Harper and Row.

Porter, M.E. (1990): *The Competitive Advantages of Nations*. New York: The Free Press.

POSRI (1995): *Large Businesses in Korea: Who Own and Control*. Seoul: POSCO Research Institute.

Pozen, R.C. (1994): "Institutional Investors: The Reluctant Activists," *Harvard Business Review*, 72(1):140-149.

Prahalad, C.K. and Hamel, G. (1990): "The Core Competence of the Corporation," *Harvard Business Review*, 68(May-June):79- 91.

Prowse, S.D. (1992): "The Structure of Corporate Ownership in Japan," *Journal of Finance*, 47(3):1121-1140.

Rechner, P.L. and Dayton, D.R. (1991): "CEO Duality and Organizational Performance," *Strategic Management Journal*, 12:155-160.

Rhodes, S.A. (1973): "The Effect of Diversification and Industry Profit Performance in 241 Manufacturing Industries: 1963," *The Review of Economics and Statistics*, (May):146-155.

Rumelt, R. (1974): *Strategy, Structure, and Economic Performance*. Boston: Harvard Business School.

Steers, R.M., Shin, Y.K., and Ungson, G.R. (1989): *The Chaebol*. New York: Harper and Row.

Tricker, R.I. (1994): "Japanese Company Boards and Their Directors," in R.I. Tricker (ed.), *International Corporate Governance*. New York: Prentice Hall, pp. 19-22.

Ueda, Y. (1994): "Intercorporate Networks in Japan: A Study of Interlocking Directorates in Modern Large Corporations," in R.I. Tricker (ed.), *International Corporate Governance*. New York: Prentice Hall, pp. 49-61.

Useem, M. (1993): *Executive Defense: Shareholder Power and External Reorganization*. Cambridge, MA: Harvard University Press.

Useem, M. (1996): *Investor Capitalism: How Money Managers Are Changing the Face of Corporate America*. New York: Basic Books.

Walsh, J.P. and Seward, J.K. (1990): "On the Efficiency of Internal and External Corporate Control Mechanisms," *Academy of Management Review*, 15(3):421-458.

Wernerfelt, B. (1986): "The Relationship between Market Share and Profitability," *Journal of Business Strategy*, (Spring):67-74.

Williamson, O.E. (1988): "Corporate Finance and Corporate Governance," *Journal of Finance*, 43:567-591.

Whitley, R.D. (1991): "The Social Construction of Business Systems in East Asia," *Organizational Studies,* 12(1):1-28.

Yoo, S.J. and S.M. Lee. (1987): "Managerial Style and Practice of Korean Chaebols," *California Management Review,* (Summer):95-110.

Yoshihara, H. (1981): *Diversification Strategies of Japanese Firms*. Tokyo: Japan Economic Newspaper.

Yoshimori, M. (1995): "Whose Company is It? The Concept of the Corporation in Japan and the West," *Long Range Planning*, 28(4):33-44.

Chapter 4
Globalization of Korean Firms

4.1 Introduction

Globalization means different things to different people. To some, it may mean increasing imports and exports, while to others it may mean becoming multinational companies (MNCs) or opening one's domestic market to MNCs. If it is defined in terms of imports and exports, Korea is already there. By the mid-1990s, Korea has become the world's tenth largest trading nation; its two-way trade amounted to $260 billion. Globalization is, however, more than importing and exporting merchandise. A nation's trade volume can increase by means of mercantilism--importing raw materials, exporting finished goods, and protecting one's domestic market. Globalization in this chapter is defined in the context of global free trade and economic activities. That means trading nations open their domestic markets to foreign competitors, allow foreign direct investment (FDI) by MNCs, and engage in the global market as exporters, importers, and foreign direct investors.

If globalization is defined as opening domestic market to foreign competition and inward as well as outward FDI, Korea is far behind. Until recently, Korean firms had been protected from foreign competition in their domestic market. They were export-oriented but their manufacturing activities were primarily domestically-oriented. Inward and outward FDI was relatively scarce. Korean firms became globally recognizable business groups (*chaebols*) primarily owing to the financial backing and domestic market protection of the government, low-cost but highly disciplined labor, and entrepreneurial talents. But they were not globalized in the context of global free trade and open competition. Their growth primarily came from increasing economies of scale and a high degree of diversification in their domestic markets rather than from venturing into foreign markets as MNCs.

The business environments that were conducive to the growth of Korean firms by means of diversification have changed drastically in the 1990s. There are internal and external forces that have changed ways in which Korean firms conduct their businesses. Internally, Korea is no longer a low wage country; the political reform in the late 1980s lifted the lid on wage increases. Furthermore, cost advantages that stem from economies of scale are copied by other newly developing countries. Korean consumers also have changed; they now demand high quality as well as variety of goods and services, regardless of their origin. Externally, as Korea became a powerful trading nation, its partners demanded its domestic market to be opened to their products. As Korean wages rise, it lost cost advantages to countries such as China, Indonesia, and India. In response to these pressures, Korean firms began to increase their manufacturing operations overseas, thereby ushering in an age of globalization.

This chapter deals with challenges that lie ahead for Korean firms to compete in their domestic and international markets in a more open global economy. It is argued here that the high degree of diversification pursued by Korean firms is a serious hindrance in achieving the competitiveness required in the new global business environment. Korean firms need to focus their energies and resources on developing competitive advantages. To do so would require the triple task of restructuring their diversified portfolio, relocating their manufacturing operations overseas, and developing a new core competence based on technology and managerial know-how.

4.2 Growth Through Diversification

It was pointed out in Chapter 3 that Korean firms in the 1960s were developed as import-substitution industries such as cement, fertilizer, and oil refining. An outward-looking export drive, started in the early 1970s, developed light manufacturing industries such as apparel and shoes. After the fall of South Vietnam and a partial pullout of U.S. troops from Korea in the mid-1970s, the Korean government initiated the development of heavy and chemical industries such as machinery, petrochemicals, steel, and shipbuilding. This was followed by the development of consumer electronics and automobiles as growth industries. During these developmental periods, business groups that were favored by the government were given opportunities to expand into various related and unrelated industries. Even small business groups emulated large ones and attempted to diversify even when their scales were relatively small. In this section, we will analyze the diversification patterns of Korean business groups and explain why they have pursued such a diversification strategy. Afterward, it will describe how the changing business environments necessitated the restructuring of Korean firms toward globalization.

4.2.1 Patterns of Diversification

The selection of a business domain is a critical part of corporate strategy, and it is determined by two elements: product and market. According to Ansoff (1965), there are four possible domains of product and market for business growth. First, a firm may pursue growth in the existing product/market domain. When a firm's market position is strong in that industry, it would be wise for the firm to remain in it. This strategy should be the least risky because the firm has developed a core competence in that domain. Second, a firm may introduce the existing product into a new market segment or geographical area. Exporting to a new country is an example of such a new market development. Third, a firm may introduce a new product to the existing market. Given the rapid technological change, it is essential for any firm to keep abreast of new technological developments in a chosen industry. Finally, a firm may venture into a new business domain, which is not tied to its existing product or market.

Depending on how product-market mixes are configured, a firm's business domain strategy can be classified into five categories: single business, dominant business, vertical integration, related diversification, and unrelated diversification (Aaker, 1995; Rumelt, 1974). When a firm remains in an existing product-market domain, it is called a single business. When a firm expands its market share through product innovation and market development, it is called a dominant business. When a firm enters a new business, which is not tied to its current product or market, it is called diversification. Diversification can be further classified into three types: vertical, related, and unrelated. Vertical diversification occurs when a firm integrates business activities along its value chains such as suppliers (backward) and retailers (forward). Related diversification refers to a situation where a new business area entered by a firm shares its existing managerial know-how, technology, and resources. When a new product-market domain is not related to the existing business, it is called an unrelated diversification.

Although the rationale for business domain classification is relatively easy to understand conceptually, actual measurement of business domain strategy is often complicated due to the difficulty of defining the degree of relatedness between different business units. To overcome this difficulty, Rumelt (1974) devised a framework for classifying business domain strategy. If one business unit accounts for more than 95 percent of the total sales of a company or business group, it is called a single business. If one business unit accounts for more than 70 percent but less than 95 percent of the firm's sales, its is called a dominant business. If the total sales of vertically integrated business units account for more than 70 percent of the group's sales, it is called a vertical type. If the sales of related business units account for more than 70 percent of the group's sales, it is called a related type. The rest is called an unrelated type, in which no single business unit primarily accounts for the group's sales.

Using this framework, 108 large Korean business groups were studied to determine their diversification strategies in 1984 and 1989 respectively (Jung, 1991). Because the samples were selected at different time periods, they were not the same but comparable. Between 1984 and 1989 business groups moved toward a higher degree of diversification. In 1989, 71 percent of the large Korea business groups were in three types of diversification (vertical, related, and unrelated), up from 58 percent in 1984. Only 7 percent were classified as single businesses and 22 percent were dominant businesses in 1989, compared to 11 percent single and 31 percent dominant businesses in 1984.

When the diversification pattern of Korean business groups is compared with that of American and Japanese companies, the former shows a higher degree of diversification than the latter, especially in unrelated diversification. Comparative data of American and Japanese companies are relatively old but useful because their history is much longer and also their sizes are much larger than Korean companies. Japanese corporations were more specialized in 1973 than were Korean business groups in 1989. American companies were highly diversified in 1969, but related diversification was most prevalent. Korean business groups, although they were smaller than American companies, have chosen an unrelated diversification strategy more often than have the latter.

4.2.2 Unrelated Diversification

There are several reasons for unrelated diversification. The first is when the existing industry has reached a maturity or declining stage of the product life cycle. At that point, the firm needs to search for new growth opportunities. The second is when a firm is very successful in an industry and has substantial resources. It may then have to find new business opportunities for its surplus resources. The third is the motivation of owner-managers to diversify their risk. Lastly, a firm may pursue diversification strategy just to expand its economic power. These reasons explain why diversification strategy, especially an unrelated one, is most frequently pursued by firms operating in small, protected, and underdeveloped markets.

More specifically, the following points seem to be germane to the Korean case. First, the Korean economy has been rapidly expanding, providing new business opportunities for existing firms. Newly developing economy means that there are underdeveloped supporting industries such as suppliers of raw materials and retailers. Since the Korean economy lacked such supporting industries, Korean firms had to develop such industries themselves rather than wait for others to develop them. For example, Hyundai might have entered the highway construction and shipbuilding industries to promote its automobile industry. Highways and cargo ships are complemental to the automobile industry.

Second, the government industrial policy often provided business groups with an incentive to diversify. Protected from foreign competition and often financially supported by the government, they were encouraged to go into various unrelated businesses with little risk to themselves. Especially, in the 1970s, the government provided strong incentives for business groups to venture into new heavy and chemical industries. Given the large minimum efficient scale required in these industries, the government had to restrict the new entrants, creating an artificial oligopoly, to protect the selected few.

Third, the Korean market during the early stage of economic development was relatively small. As a result, a successful company reached a market saturation with a relatively small scale of operations. At this point, the company had a choice between expanding its manufacturing operations overseas as a means of gaining foreign markets or venturing into a new product-market domain at home. Rather than entering foreign markets as manufacturers, Korean business groups pursued an export strategy and at the same time pursued diversification at home.

Fourth, the high degree of diversification coincided with the motives of owner-managers. When ownership and management are separated, such as in the U.S., stock investors would not pay a premium for a highly diversified company because they can easily diversify their risk by investing in several bluechip stocks in different industries of their choice. Owner-managers, however, may find it beneficial to have a diversified business portfolio to minimize their risk. Additionally, owner-managers draw benefits from managing a large diversified business group because it gives them bargaining power in business transactions, political power in the national economy, and social status.

Finally, Korean firms initially built their competitiveness through borrowed technology, economies of scale, low labor cost, and domestic market protection. Competitive advantages that they have built tended to be location-specific that could not be easily transferred to foreign countries. Because their products were undifferentiated and their managers lacked local expertise of foreign markets, Korean firms did not have much choice but to diversify their businesses domestically.

In short, there were many reasons why Korean business groups pursued a high degree of diversification: market protection, underdeveloped markets, high transaction costs, and risk reduction. Many of these reasons are now gone or disappearing. Consequently, it can be argued that the high degree of diversification may have outlived its usefulness in the new open economy. The new open economy demands that Korean firms have to be globalized.

4.3 Pressure for Globalization

Korean companies are now faced with completely different business environments than they were used to in the previous decades. These changes can be described in three aspects. First, Korean firms are now exposed to foreign competition without market protection. Market-opening measures have occurred voluntarily as well as involuntarily. Second, the locational advantages (low-cost and high-quality labor, low financial costs, and government subsidies) that Korean firms used to enjoy as a production base have deteriorated. Attractive locations have appeared in China, Southeast Asia and Eastern Europe. Finally, Korean customer have changed. With increased income, they now demand high quality goods and services. All these changes occurred in a relatively short period of time, putting pressure on Korean firms to change. Let us elaborate each of these aspects.

4.3.1 Opening of Domestic market

Market-opening measures are taken by the Korean government in response to various external and internal pressures. Externally, Uruguay Round (UR), World Trade Organization (WTO), Asia-Pacific Economic Cooperation (APEC), Organization of Economic Cooperation and Development (OECD), and U.S.A. have had significant impacts on the Korean economy. The successful conclusion of UR, which resulted in the creation of WTO, means that Korean businesses have to be open to foreign competition. In terms of the manufacturing industry, the impact of the UR is relatively small. Because tariffs have been lowered gradually in the last decade, the average tariff rate for manufactured products had reached approximately eight percent by 1995. The service industry is a different story. Korea made market opening concessions in 78 out of the 155 service industry segments in response to the world trade agreements. Significantly affected services industries include telecommunications, distribution, and finance. In addition, stricter enforcement of intellectual property rights is expected. Although the new trade agreements are generally good for Korean exporters, the opening of domestic market means more competition from foreign MNCs.

APEC is expected to bring added pressure for opening the Korean market to foreign competition starting in 1997. The target year to complete free trade and investment in the APEC is 2010 for industrialized economies and 2020 for less industrialized ones. As one of the leading industrialized economies in Asia, Korea has to demonstrate leadership in pushing for the success of APEC by opening its domestic market for its neighbors.

Korea's new membership in OECD in 1996 creates an added pressure for globalization of its industries. As a condition for joining OECD, Korea has to take certain market opening measures, especially in the financial market and other service industries. More significantly, Korea has to align its trade and investment policies with those of industrialized nations. The immediate impact of OECD will be removing trade restriction against certain Japanese imports, which are in direct competition with Korean products, such as automobile, television, and VCRs. This will be a serious challenge for Korean business groups in their domestic and global markets.

Bilaterally, the U.S. has put constant pressure on Korea to liberalize its trade and investment regulation, separate from other multilateral negotiations such as WTO. For example, the U.S. government has brought pressure on the Korean government to create favorable conditions for importing foreign cars into Korea. Although the tariff rate for imported cars was already low at eight percent, there were some restrictions in financing and advertising. Also the consumption tax favored small-engine cars where Korean products were more competitive. Starting in 1996, all these restrictions were gradually removed in response to pressure coming from the U.S. government. The U.S. government identified the telecommunication industry as the next target for import liberalization. Since the American market is relatively more important for Korean exporters than the Korean market is for U.S. exports to Korea, bilateral pressures have worked more favorablely for the U.S.

The second change that has forced Korean firms to restructure is the deteriorating locational advantage as a production base. Since the democratization process started in 1987, Korean workers have gained economic and political power, resulting in double-digit wage increases annually between 1988 and 1995. Korean wages are now the second highest in Asia just behind Japan. High wages together with high rental costs led Korea into becoming a country with high costs of doing business. Korea's overall global industrial competitiveness sunk to 24th and 25th in 1994 and 1996 respectively. That means Korea is no longer an attractive manufacturing location for multinationals and even for Korean companies.

Additionally, Korea is viewed by many foreign and even domestic companies as a country with excessive government regulation (Sherman, 1996; Holmes and Kirkpatrick, 1996). This is evident when Korea is compared with advanced nations such as the U.S.A., U.K., and Japan and other Asian NICs (newly industrialized countries), such as Hong Kong, Singapore, and Taiwan. Korea is also lagging behind other NICs in infrastructure such as transportation and communications. In other words, other Asian NICs have more attractive locational advantages than Korea. At the same time, China, Indonesia, Vietnam, and others Southeast Asian countries provide MNCs with lost-cost labor. As a result, Korea is seen as one of the least attractive destinations for FDI, ranking ninth among the ten largest economies in Asia in terms of total inward foreign investment, followed only by the Philippines.

As Korea becomes a high-cost location for doing business, some Korean firms are now moving out of the country in search of low labor and other production costs. Footwear, textile, and other light manufacturing industries have now relocated to China and Southeast Asia. Heavy industries, requiring large scale facilities, still remain in the country but are under pressure to relocate labor-intensive processes overseas. For example, automobile companies have keep their production facilities in the country until recently, but are investing heavily overseas due to high costs and saturated domestic market.

The third environmental shift is a change in consumer tastes and preferences. Two factors contributed to the change in consumer tastes and preferences. The first is the market-opening measures taken by the government in recent years. As the domestic market opens to foreign competition, Korean consumers have more choices and find foreign products to be better in product quality and design and competitive in price. As a result, a variety of foreign-made goods such as automobiles, cigarettes, electrical appliances, consumer electronics, cosmetics, and sporting goods are making major inroad into Korean markets. Even day-to-day necessities such as chopsticks, utensils, fruits, and food stuffs are now imported.

The second is the rising level of incomes and savings. GNP per capita reached the level of $10,000 in 1995. Korean consumers have more cash available for consumption now than ever before because sizeable consumer credits were not available to them in the past. For example, the credit available for housing is very limited, so one had to save at least 60 to 70 percent of the housing cost to make a purchase. People saved a higher percentage of their earnings in the past because there were not many opportunities to spend due to various austerity measures taken by the government. For example, foreign travel for pleasure was limited until the early 1990s. Heavy taxation of foreign products discouraged demand for them in the past. As these restrictions have been removed, the demand for foreign-made goods has increased rapidly.

If this trend continues, there will be a major shake-up in Korean industries. As the economy is exposed to international competition, companies that have been protected from foreign competition until now are finding themselves vulnerable. In a protected market where entry is restricted and there is little competition, both strong and weak competitors could coexist and survive. But, in a competitive market, strong competitors take a bigger share of the market. Constantly, weaker ones are either forced out of market or have to find a niche. Korean big businesses (*chaebols*) that gain industrial competitiveness through globalization are likely to survive and even prosper. But, those with poor business portfolios and a poor market position, lacking global exposure, will find themselves relegated to playing minor roles.

Globalization is defended on a theoretical ground. Studies suggest that globalization has positive impacts on a firm's growth and profitability for several reasons (Rugman, 1979; Dubin, 1980; Caves, 1982; Kim et al., 1989). First, globalization gives a multinational company an opportunity to establish an oligopolistic or monopolistic position in the global market (Rugman, 1979). Second, a firm's proprietary skills can be fully utilized through globalization (Dubin, 1980). Third, there is a positive relationship between international operations and product differentiation and such a relationship creates entry barriers for potential competitors (Caves, 1982). Fourth, international market diversification provides a firm with stability (Rugman, 1979; Caves 1982). Finally, global players gain technological and managerial skills by competing with the best global players in the world.

4.3.2 Foreign Direct Investment

Faced with the competitive domestic market and deteriorating locational advantages, Korean companies began to move their manufacturing operations overseas in recent years (Halsey, 1996). Although Korean firms are latecomers in investing overseas, the pace of FDI has accelerated in recent years. Outward FDI by Korean firms has increased from $1.6 billion in 1990 to $5.0 billion in 1996 (*Hankook Ilbo*, January 24, 1997, p. 8). The cumulative value of Korean outward FDI between 1990 and 1996 is $19.6 billion (Exhibit 4.1). The size of individual investment projects increased in recent years. For example, the amount of outward FDI almost doubled between 1994 and 1995, but the total number of projects decreased from 1,946 to 1,557 during the same period, suggesting that large business groups such as Daewoo, Hyundai, Kia, and Samsung, began to move into foreign markets in recent years. This point will be further elaborated later.

Exhibit 4.1: Outward Foreign Direct Investment

Year	Investment (in million $)	Projects (no.)
1990	1,610	515
1991	1,510	527
1992	1,206	631
1993	1,875	1,049
1994	3,580	1,946
1995	4,913	1,557
1996	5,049	1,565

Source: Bank of Korea (various years): *Biannual Survey of FDI Trend*. Seoul: Bank of Korea.

Destinations for Korea's outward FDI also changed drastically in recent years. By the end of 1990, North America was the biggest recipient of Korean FDI. But in the first half of the 1990s, Asian countries have become the target for Korea FDI. By the end of 1995, the U.S. and China were the major recipients of Korea's FDI (Exhibit 4.2). Out of the ten largest FDI by Korean firms, six were Asian countries and four were western countries. It is noteworthy that China has emerged as the number one recipient of Korean FDI in terms of the number of projects, a result of the formal diplomatic relationship between the two countries in 1992.

Exhibit 4.2: Ten Largest Countries for Korea's Foreign Direct Investment: Cumulative Value as of December 1995

Country	Investment (in million $)	Projects (no.)
U.S.A.	3,879	719
China	2,809	2,239
Indonesia	945	262
Japan	451	171
Canada	445	47
Germany	288	67
Malaysia	277	132
Great Britain	244	52
Hong Kong	241	226
Philippines	215	338

Source: Bank of Korea (1996): *Biannual Survey of FDI Trend*. Seoul: Bank of Korea.

There are basically three types of outward FDI: export platform, host market, and strategic moves. Most FDI by Korea firms in developing countries in the early stage were the export platform type--bringing raw materials from home, processing them at a host country, and re-exporting them to other countries. This type of FDI was usually found in labor intensive and light manufacturing activities such as textiles, footwear, plywood, and others, requiring relatively small amount of investment. For example, the majority of 1,290 Korean FDI projects went to China to take advantage of inexpensive Chinese labor in the early 1990s, and the average size of these projects was less than $1 million.

In recent years, as host countries gained economic strength, their markets have become important to Korean overseas investors. Korean firms responded to this importance by increasing the size of their FDI and the number of contracts with local people and businesses. For example, by the mid-1990s, the average size of Korean FDI projects in China was larger and these projects were targeted at the Chinese domestic market. Such projects tend to have significant impact on the host country economy in terms of technology transfer. But they also have some adverse effects such as foreign ownership and dependency on MNCs. Although the export platform type of FDI is still important in low-labor cost countries in Southeast Asia, the tendency now is to take host country markets seriously.

Finally, Korean FDI in advanced countries tends to be more strategically oriented. They are there not only to take advantage of large consumer markets but also to have access to advanced technology available in these countries. Two industries are most important to Korean firms in this regard: consumer electronics and automobiles. Since the mid-1990s, electronics companies such as Samsung and LG (Lucky-Goldstar) have been spearheading FDI in the U.S. and European markets. In recent years, the Korean automotive industry has also become an important player in the global market. Although Korean automakers are not yet a major player in the U.S. and West European markets, they actively participate in those markets to have access to advanced technology, to acquire advanced marketing skills, and to learn to compete with the best automakers in the world.

4.3.3 Cultural Globalization

As Korean firms venture into foreign countries, they are faced with problems of managing cultural differences. According to the world competitiveness reports by the Switzerland-based International Management Development (IMD), Korea ranked the last (41st) in cultural openness in 1994 (Kang, 1994). It is not surprising to see such a poor cultural ranking because the traditional Korean culture (Confucianism) tends to be anti-outsiders and xenophobic. Confucianism stresses the importance of harmony, peace, and respect among kinships at the expense of maintaining harmonious relationships with outsiders (Kim and Kim, 1989). In other words, Confucian ethics are limited to one's family and circle of friends, and immediate work groups, but do not applied to outsiders. To many Koreans, sharing common school background, family clan, and hometown are often more important in getting jobs and being promoted than having professional expertise.

Given this cultural background, Koreans are not well trained to deal with outsiders including foreign nationals. Initial reports are mixed. On one hand, Korean managers were praised for showing personal interests in workers by visiting their employees in hospitals at a Korean-owned plant in the U.S. On the other hand, they were criticized for being harsh in dealing with workers at Korean-owned firms in China and Pakistan (*Wall Street Journal*, July 23, 1996, p. A19). There were some incidents where foreign workers in Korea were mistreated by their employers and coworkers (Kim, 1994). Even now, there are reports that foreign workers are generally poorly paid and often physically abused.

By way of meeting the global challenge, President Kim Young Sam in 1994 declared the globalization movement in Korea. This movement implies that Korea will join the global community as a free trader and that Korea businesses will be abided by the business codes of conduct generally adopted by MNCs. To achieve this end, Koreans are encouraged to learn foreign languages and to travel abroad to experience foreign cultures. At the same time, Korean firms are urged to develop industrial competitiveness to survive in the open global market. In response, a great number of foreign language instructors are hired by Korean schools at various levels and an increasing number of Koreans travel abroad. Korean firms also have increased overseas educational opportunities for their employees; big business groups send a large number of their managers for short as well as long-term educational and managerial training sessions in the U.S., Europe, and Asian countries.

Undoubtedly all these globalization efforts will help to globalize Korean firms and their managers. Korean managers will not only learn more about the managerial practices of their trading partners, but also learn more about the cultural differences of people they are dealing with. But a lingering question is how well Korean managers are prepared to deal effectively with foreign nationals with cultural differences. Korean managers are likely to find that adopting new corporate strategy, organizational structure, and technology is much easier than dealing with people from different cultures. The Confucian culture of honoring inner circles of people at the expense of excluding outsiders needs to be modified before any behavioral change of dealing with foreign nationals is attempted. This point will be further elaborated in Chapter 6.

4.4 Globalization Trend in Industry

As noted early, electronics and automobile industries lead the globalization of Korean firms. Other industries such as memory chips, petrochemicals, heavy machinery, and telecommunications may follow the footsteps of electronics and automobiles. But for the time being, Korean firms seem to be betting on these two industries. In the following section, we will examine these two industries as examples of Korea's FDI.

4.4.1 Electronic Industry

Electronics companies such as Samsung, LG, and Daewoo are in the forefront of the globalization push among Korean companies. Their strategic moves in recent years include a series of acquisitions in advanced countries to upgrade their technology and establishing integrated production bases in several countries to enhance their cost competitiveness. There are several elements that characterize Korean FDI. First, Korean electronics firms attempt to achieve technological parity with Japanese, American, and European companies through acquisitions in advanced countries. Samsung's acquisition of AST Research and LG's acquisition of Zenith Corporation are prime examples. Second, they have developed regional strategies in FDI. FDI is made in developing countries to take advantage of low cost labor and in advanced countries to position themselves as major players in the increasingly complex and competitive electronics industry. Finally, they have established multiple strategic alliances with major MNCs in the industry in order to have access to overseas markets as well as technology.

Samsung Electronics illustrates the globalization of Korean electronics companies. The company has made FDI aggressively in recent years, and its global expansion has involved three distinctive strategies. The first is to enhance the technological capacity by acquiring high-tech companies in advanced countries. Samsung's recent acquisitions include 100 percent of IGT Corp, a specialist in telecommunications, 20 percent stake of Array, 100 percent of Harris Microwave Semiconductors, and 40 percent of AST Research in the U.S. Others include 51 percent of Lux (CAD/CAM software) and 50 percent of Union Optical (microelectronics) in Japan.

The second is to set up production facilities in developing countries such as China, Malaysia, and Mexico to maintain cost leadership. These overseas facilities are used not only to meet local demands but also to export to other countries. For example, Samsung products made in these countries can be exported to Korea and the U.S. Additionally, it has an integrated production site in the U.K. to be used as an export platform into other European countries.

Finally, Samsung has divided the world market into five regions: China, Japan, Southeast Asia, Europe and the Americas. For example, Samsung's Southeast Asia headquarters in Singapore is responsible for 15 countries in that region. It has 12 plants in 5 countries: 4 in Malaysia, 3 in Indonesia, 3 in Thailand, 1 in Vietnam, and 1 in India. In addition, there are 15 sales subsidiaries and 31 branch offices in that region. In 1996, Samsung in Southeast Asia employed 16,000 local nationals and 140 Korean expatriates.

Samsung uses its global configuration and coordination as a strategic weapon (Porter, 1986). In order to achieve economies of scale in production, it makes essential parts, such as picture tubes and tuners, in one location and supplies them to assembly operations dispersed in different countries. Local assembly operations are important because most ASEAN countries levy higher tariffs on imported finished goods than on imported parts. Currently, Malaysia is the base for parts manufacturing due to its cost advantages. But as the cost structure and tax situation change, so does the manufacturing configuration. Overall, cost competition makes it essential for Samsung to standardize its products. But Samsung is likely to pursue some degree of localization to meet some peculiar needs of its host markets. An example is to adopt karaoke machines to accommodate some peculiarities in leisure culture in the region.

4.4.2 Automotive Industry

Traditionally, the Asian automotive industry has been dominated by Japanese companies: mainly, Toyota, Nissan, Honda, and Mitsubishi. Recently, however, American and European automotive companies are making major inroads into the Asian market. Ford and GM have expanded car production in Asia, especially in China and Thailand. Volkswagen is already the leading carmaker in China, and other European companies have also expanded their marketing efforts in Asia.

Until recently, Korean automotive companies have stayed home, except for Hyundai's assembly plant in Quebec, Canada, which was discontinued due to high costs and poor sales in North America. There are three reasons why Korean companies have stayed home until recently. First, the technology licensing agreements with foreign partners prevented them from exporting to certain overseas markets. Hyundai was the exception because it had complete freedom in exporting its products even though it had a strategic alliance with Mitsubishi. Daewoo and Kia had to accept some territorial restrictions in return for technological licensing with foreign partners. Recently, however, as these two companies were able to design and manufacture their own cars without relying on foreign partners, they have gained freedom in exporting and assembling in foreign countries.

Korean automakers gained autonomy in exporting and overseas manufacturing but were suddenly faced with steep competition in their domestic and international markets. The government's liberal import policy will mean increased competition in their domestic market, especially in the luxury car market where profit margins are higher. In addition, production costs are rising due to increasing labor costs and R&D expenditures. As these costs increase, so the required economies of scale. Currently, Korean automakers have a production capacity of two million cars annually. This capacity is planned to be increased to six million units by the year 2000 (Sohn, 1996a). If Samsung enters the auto industry, the capacity will be further expanded. This expansion plan is in part necessitated by the huge new product development costs.

The domestic market in Korea is only around 1.8 millions cars a year. That means, the rest of the 6 million units has to be sold overseas. Increasing competition and high domestic labor costs make it necessary that Korean automakers move overseas. FDI by Korean automakers is already a reality. Kia has been assembling cars in the Philippines and Taiwan and recently has begun assembling cars in Vietnam. Indonesia and Malaysia are the next target countries. Hyundai has been assembling 25,000 cars annually in Thailand, the Philippines, and Indonesia under licensing agreements. Daewoo Motors, the weakest among the three in the domestic market, has been very aggressive in expanding overseas. The company has invested in ten countries in Southeast Asia, Eastern Europe, and Central Asia during the first part of 1990s to either manufacture or assemble cars and also open R&D centers in three European countries.

4.5 Strategic Options for Korean Firms

The rising production cost at home, import liberalization, the changing demands of Korean consumers, and the WTO have created pressures for Korean businesses to become global companies. Korean firms are meeting these pressures by relocating production bases overseas, acquiring advanced technologies, and increasing economies of scale. Such responses are, however, not enough to overcome the basic structural weaknesses of Korean firms; that is a lack of strong global presence. In industries that produce and sell globally standardized products such as appliances, automobiles, consumer electronics, tires, and telecommunications, companies with strong global presence tend to survive and prosper. Companies that fail to meet this challenge are likely to be acquired by other companies or to play insignificant roles in the global market. Take, for example, a mature industry such as tire manufacturing. The world's tire market is currently dominated by three major companies, Goodyear, Michelin, and Bridgestone. In the past 15 years, tire companies such as Firestone and Goodrich were taken over by Bridgestone and Michelin. In the photo film industry, three brands, Kodak, Fuji, and Agfa dominate the world market. The global athletic shoe market is dominated by a few companies such as Reebok and Nike.

Even in those industries that are more culturally-sensitive and local-specific, such as clothing, cosmetics, consumer packaged goods, distribution, insurance, and consumer finance, companies with globally-recognizable brand names will do much better than those without such recognition. For example, service industries in Korea such as fast foods, banking, insurance, and retailing are threatened by the invasion of foreign competitors. So, the globalization of Korean firms is not an option; it is more of a "do or die" proposition. In the increasingly competitive world of global business, Korean firms are faced with basically three options: globalization, strategic alliance, or localization.

4.5.1 Becoming Global Companies

Industries that are dominated by only a few competitors in the world market are commonly called *global industries* and require economies of scale in production, marketing, and R&D. In global industries that produce and sell globally-standardized products, there is a certain strategic advantage of maintaining economies of scale in production because standardization allows low-cost mass production. Economies of scale essential for running a company at a profitable level is called minimum efficiency scale (MES) (Chandler, 1986). In the case of the automobile industry, for example, the minimum efficiency scale (MES) in production is estimated to be around 250,000 units per year to cover the fixed investment costs. But, the MES in production is not enough to bring a company to global prominence. Marketing and R&D costs also need to be considered.

Rapidly changing technologies require firms to make large R&D expenditures. In order to gain a competitive advantage, global companies must spend a large percentage of their sales on R&D. For example, in the cellular phone industry, global leaders such as Motorola and Ericsson spend as much as 20 to 25 percent of their sales on R&D, making it hard for other companies to compete in that industry. As R&D expenditures increase, so does the MES. In the case of the automotive industry, R&D expenditures should not be as high as those required in a newly emerging industry such as cellular phones. However, global automakers are likely to spend at least three to five percent of their sales on R&D, pushing a combined MES of production and R&D to be as much as one million cars a year. This explains why Mercedes and BMW, which currently produce 600,000 units per year, are expanding their product lines as well as the production capacities (Taylor, 1996).

Marketing expenditures also drive up the MES. As consumer tastes become more similar due to the proliferation of mass media and mass consumption, standardized products with global brands tend to take over the global market. McDonald's hamburger chain is a prime example. Nike, Coca Cola, Disney, Levi, and P&G are other American brands, taking advantage of the popularity of American culture and expanding their marketing arms throughout the world. Global companies spend a large amount of money on marketing to increase global awareness of their products and brand names. When one considers economies of scale in terms of production, marketing, and R&D, it is not unreasonable to project the MES in the automobile industry will be well over one million units a year.

Successful global companies are outperforming competitors both in cost leadership and product differentiation (Dess and Davis, 1984; White, 1986; Kim and Lim, 1988). Porter (1986) suggested that companies follow one of three generic strategies: cost leadership, product differentiation, and focus strategies. His assertion may be appropriate in a fragmented industry such as apparel or service industries. In such industries, a firm can pursue one of these three strategies because of some locational advantages that serve as entry barriers for new comers. However, in global industries, one cannot sustain locational advantages for long because competitors can easily duplicate such advantages by changing their configuration. For example, low-cost labor and raw materials can provide a firm with cost advantages in the short run. But, since global companies have easy access to such input factors, any locational advantages can be easily gained and eroded.

One way to develop a sustainable competitive advantage is through a product-focused hybrid strategy of achieving cost leadership and product differentiation. Since a company has to be efficient and innovative at the same time, it has to develop a whole new approach to product development and process engineering. To gain a product-focused competitive advantage, global companies have to develop innovative products that are attractively designed, show excellent performance, and are easy to produce. Manufacturing operations also must be performed almost defect-free so that high and consistent product quality is maintained. Japanese automakers, for example, are known for gaining such a product-focused competitive advantage by producing high quality products at affordable prices.

Another way to gain a sustainable competitive advantage is to disperse a firm's value-chain activities globally (Porter, 1986). Global companies requiring heavy capital investment tend to be concentrated their manufacturing operations in one location, usually in home their country, to gain economies of scale. And then they disperse marketing activities globally. For example, Japanese automobile and consumer electronic companies used to follow such a concentrated global strategy. U.S. global companies, on the other hand, have been following the dispersed global strategy--dispersing both manufacturing and marketing functions globally. The dispersed global strategy tends to yield a competitive advantage over the concentrated strategy because it allows the firm to reconfigure its value-chain activities in response to the changing conditions in global labor costs, taxes, exchange rates, and others to achieve optimum results. For this reason, even Japanese global companies now follow the dispersed global strategy.

4.5.2 Collaborating with MNCs

Does that mean that all companies must gain global prominence? The answer is no. In a global industry, even a super global company needs a collaboration of small companies abroad. For example, a super global automaker needs at least several hundred suppliers of parts and components and a large number of dealers, service stations, repair shops, and other service industries. Globally, it also need partners in manufacturing, marketing, distribution, and other related services. In other words, even a super company cannot perform all value-chain activities in all countries by itself.

As noted previously, many global companies disperse various value-chain activities overseas for various reasons. Certainly, taking advantage of low-cost labor and raw materials is an important reason. But, other reasons such as having access to the local distribution network, governmental relations, and product specialization can also be legitimate. For example, in the automobile industry, parts manufacturing can be specialized according to the differing expertise available in different countries. Even final assembly or manufacturing operations can be specialized. For example, luxury cars are produced in advanced countries, whereas economy cars are produced in newly developed countries.

What it all mean is that a company can survive and prosper as a collaborator with a super global company. Many Chinese-origin companies in Southeast Asia rely on this strategy. For example, Salim Business Group, the largest business group in Indonesia, explicitly follows such a collaboration strategy. This business group does not make heavy R&D expenditures on high-tech or product development but concentrates its resources in creating local expertise in retailing, financing, and customer services. For technology and product development, it has developed a wide range of joint ventures or alliances with global super companies such as Nissan, Volvo, NEC, Siemens, CNN, and others. This type of strategy is called a *market-focused* or *location-focused* strategy because it derives its competitive advantages from expertise and networks in local markets. The local market could be one country or a region depending on the networks that a company has developed. Salim, for example, has developed business networks in Indonesia and other countries in Southeast Asia.

In the case of the Korean automotive industry, Ssangyong Motors seems to pursue such a location-focused strategy. Rather than attempting to become a global super company, it has developed a strategic alliance with super global companies such as Mercedes-Benz in order to have access to advanced automotive technology and developed a niche in high-quality four-wheel drive vehicles. By collaborating with Mercedes, it should be able to reduce major investment requirements in R&D and marketing and concentrate on developing the MES in production. Since the Korean domestic market is relatively small for such luxury cars, Ssangyong needs to cultivate the regional market in East and Southeast Asia as well as in North America and Europe. Ssangyong is looking for an equity partner to achieve this end.

4.5.3 Remaining as Local Firms

Another way for non-global companies to survive in the global economy is to find a niche in localized industries. Many firms remain as locals in that the market is limited to a small region and there are only a limited number of local companies to compete with each other. There are several reasons why an industry remains local: First, because the market is small and fragmented, global companies might not be interested in entering. Second, the high cost of transportation prevents an industry from becoming global. For example, steelmaking and cement manufacturing tend to remain as local industries despite the large economies of scale. Third, culturally-sensitive and location-specific industries such as restaurants, packaged goods, insurance, distribution, and retailing tend to remain as local. Additionally, government may protect certain industries such as defense-related, medical, and educational to remain as local.

Local industries are not inherently immune from foreign competition. Global companies may standardize products in traditionally fragmented industries. For example, McDonald's turned a local industry into a global industry by standardizing products and services on a global basis and became a super global company with the collaboration of thousands of franchises. Steelmaking remains as a local or regional industry despite a fairly large economies of scale and high transportation costs. However, if a breakthrough can be made in transportation and/or process technology, it too can become a global industry.

Furthermore, localized industries such as insurance, banking, retailing, and construction can also be invaded by foreign multidomestic companies (Porter, 1986). Similar to global companies, multidomestic companies have presence in various countries and regions of the world. But the difference is that multidomestic companies do not standardize their products and services. Instead, they allow local partners to develop their own products and services responding to local needs. The benefit of having local partners is that they have access to the technology and managerial expertise of their international partners. What this implies is that even in localized industries foreign competition has become a way of life.

4.5.4 Strategic Options for *Chaebols*

Traditionally, Korean business groups have pursued a location/market-focused strategy by taking advantage of low production costs and a protected domestic market. As discussed earlier, these locational advantages are no longer available. This means that they need to find new competitive strategies. The choice that they have now is either to pursue a product-focused or a market-focused strategy. If they want to become a global company, they have to pursue a product-focused strategy by increasing economies of scale, R&D, and marketing expenditures. To achieve this end, they need to concentrate their resources in one or a few industries where they can gain and maintain competitive advantages. This means that the current high level of diversification, especially unrelated diversification, is not productive in pursuing a product-focused strategy. It is essential for large business groups to restructure their business portfolio by divesting marginal businesses, especially those that are not related to their core competences.

On the other hand, if they want to pursue the market-focused strategy and remain in the Korean market, they have to lower their expectations and become local collaborators of super global companies. Local collaborators may want to expand the scope of their market to Northeast and Southeast Asia, but this would be difficult because global super companies are already in those markets and are finding local collaborators in those regions. Furthermore, Korean firms have not yet developed localized expertise there to give them some locational advantages.

Currently, Korean firms are pursuing a combination of product-focused and market-focused strategies simultaneously. On one hand, they are trying to catch up with the technology and managerial know-how of super global companies in such industries as automobiles, memory chips, consumer electronics, multimedia, and telecommunications. At the same time, they are expanding their production and distribution bases to certain less developed and developing countries while attempting to develop local expertise. They have yet to achieve competitiveness in either strategy and are running into a danger of being "stuck in the middle."

It is, however, possible that a company may focus its resources on a very narrow product lines and markets to develop product-related as well as market-related expertise. For example, a business group may specialize in a limited number of related industries such as construction, resort development, and hospitality industries and develop expertise in managing such an enterprise. The key to success for them is to focus their resources on a limited number of related industries and to develop competitive advantages in both product and market in a narrowly defined area.

4.6 Summary

Large business groups in Korea have achieved their current size and status by pursuing a high degree of diversification. A protected domestic market, relatively small market size, market imperfections, and motives of owner-managers have contributed to the diversification of Korean firms. The business environment in the 1990s is quite different from that of the last three decades. After the collapse of the Soviet Union in the late 1980s, most developing or former socialist countries have adopted capitalism in forms of liberal policies toward international trade and foreign direct investment. As a result, locational advantages have emerged in East Asia (China), Southeast Asia, and Eastern Europe. At the same time, labor and other input costs have increased rapidly in Korea, making Korea a less attractive production base. In addition, measures for opening domestic market taken by the Korean government have forced Korean companies to face foreign competition in the domestic market.

One response of Korean companies to the deteriorating business environment at home is to move their manufacturing operations abroad. Outward foreign direct investment has increased substantially in the 1990s. Asia and North American account for the major share of Korean FDI. In particular, Asian developing countries have become major destinations for Korean FDI. Compared to earlier FDI projects in Asia whose primary motive was to take advantage of cheap labor for exports, recent investments seem to target host country markets. These host-market oriented projects tend to be bigger in size and tend to have a bigger impact on host countries in terms of technology transfer and employment.

Another response of Korean firms, especially large automotive and electronics companies, has been to become aggressive investors in both advanced and developing countries. Advanced countries are targeted for market access and technology acquisition, whereas developing countries in Asia and Eastern Europe are targeted for market access and locational advantages. The globalization of Korean firms is relatively new. It remains to be seen how fast and how well Korean multinationals learn the skills of managing complex global operations and develop managerial systems to support them. Most importantly, the development of human resources management skills required for global operations will be the major challenge for Korean firms.

In global industries, a few super companies dominate the world market. By achieving competitive advantages in both cost and technology, a limited number of super global companies are developing an oligopolistic structure in many industries. Other companies then collaborate with super global companies to survive. Under these circumstances, a firm has to choose between two alternative strategies: product-focused and market-focused. Product-focused strategy refers to gaining cost leadership and product differentiation; market-focused strategy means collaborating with super global companies in a country or region.

Some large Korean business groups intend to become global companies in such industries as automobiles, consumer electronics, memory chips, multimedia, telecommunications, petrochemicals, and heavy industries. To do so will require them to focus their resources on one or a few industries that will give them competitive advantages. It is suggested that the current level of diversification is a handicap in light of such requirements and that a major restructuring is needed to achieve the economies of scale needed to be competitive in the global market. So far, the progress has been slow, but there is an indication that Korean *chaebols* are in the phase of restructuring. Korean *chaebols* such as Hyundai, Samsung, LG, Kolon, and others are selling off some of their marginal businesses (Sohn, 1996b).

References

Aaker, D.A. (1995): *Strategic Market Management*. New York: John Wiley.

Ansoff, H.I. (1965): *Corporate Strategy*. New York: McGraw-Hill.

Caves, R.E. (1982): *Multinational Enterprise and Economic Analysis*. Cambridge, MA: Cambridge University Press.

Chandler, A.D. (1986): "The Evolution of Modern Global Competition," in M.E. Porter (ed.), *Competition in Global Industries,* Boston: Harvard Business School Press, pp. 405-448.

Dess, G.G. and Davis, P.S. (1984): "Porter's Generic Strategies as Determinants of Strategic Group Membership and Organizational Performance," *Academy of Management Journal*, 27:465-488.

Dubin, M. (1980): *Foreign Acquisitions and the Spread of the Multinational Firm*, New York: Arno Press.

Halsey, D. (1996): "Going Global: From Rhetoric to Reality," *Business Korea*, 13(6):12-13.

Holmes, K.R. and Kirkpatrick, M. (1996): "Freedom and Growth," *Wall Street Journal,* December 16:A16.

Jung, K.H. (1991): *Diversification and International Competitiveness of Korean Business.* Seoul: Korea Economic Research Institute.

Kang, S.Y. (1994): "Korea's International Competitiveness Plunges," *Business Korea*, 12(4):26-27.

Kim, W.C., Hwang, P., and Burgers, W.P. (1989): "Global Diversification Strategy and Corporate Profit Performance," *Strategic Management Journal*, 10:45-57.

Kim, D.K. and Kim, C.W. (1989): "Korean Value Systems and Managerial Practices," in K.H. Chung and H.C. Lee (eds.), *Korean Managerial Dynamics*, New York: Praeger, pp. 207-216.

Kim, L. and Lim, Y. (1988): Environment, Generic Strategies, and Performance in a Rapidly Developing Country: A Taxonomic Approach," *Academy of Management Journal*, 31:802-827.

Kim, Y.S. (1994): "Koreans! Please Treat Us as Human Beings," *Shin Don Ah*, 37(7):492-507.

Porter, M.E. (1986): *Competition in Global Industries*. Boston: Harvard Business School Press.

Rugman, A.M. (1979): *International Diversification and Multinational Enterprise*. Lexington, MA: Lexington Books.

Rumelt, R.P. (1974): *Strategy, Structure and Economic Performance.* Boston: Harvard Business Press.

Sherman, H. (1996): *Investments by Multinational Companies*. Munich, Germany: IFO Institute (Unpublished Report).

Sohn, Y.J. (1996a): "Taking on the Big Boys," *Business Korea*, 13(9):30-41.

Sohn, Y.J. (1996b): "Trimming the Fat," *Business Korea*, 13(10):43-44.

Taylor, A. (1996): "Speed! Power! Status!" *Fortune*, June 10:47-58.

White, R.E. (1986): "Generic Business Strategies, Organizational Context and Performance: An Empirical Investigation," *Strategic Management Journal*, 7:217-231.

Chapter 5
Technological Transformation

5.1 Introduction

Korea has come a long way from an agrarian society to a technologically-oriented society in a short period. Starting in the mid-1960s, Korea emerged as an exporter of textiles, apparel, plywood, and other labor-intensive manufacturing products. Ten years later, it became a major exporter of ships, steel, and construction services. By the mid-1980s, automobiles, computers, semiconductor memory chips were added to the list of Korea's major export items. Then by the mid-1990s, it positioned itself to become a top tier high-tech country by advancing automobile, semiconductor, information processing, telecommunications, and nuclear technologies.

Countries acquire technical capacities over long periods of time. In advanced countries, it has taken centuries to achieve current levels of technological development. As technological pioneers, these countries had to achieve technological advancements through trial and error without the benefit of learning from others. Developing countries have the benefits of learning from pioneers. For most developing countries, it usually takes more than a half-century for them to learn and assimilate advanced technologies. In the case of Korea, however, it has taken only a few decades to achieve its current level of technological capacities.

What accounts for such a rapid technological transformation in Korea? There are many factors that have contributed to such a technological change. Among them are education and human resource development, government technology policy, foreign technology importation, and indigenous research and development (R&D) efforts, and so forth. This chapter reviews the evolutionary processes by which Korean firms have achieved technological transformation, the role of government in preparing for a foundation for technological development (technological infrastructure), and the technological strategies of Korean firms. Additionally, this chapter will look at the technological challenges that lie ahead for Korean firms.

5.2 Patterns of Technological Development

The patterns of technological development in Korea coincided with its economic development plans (Ahn, 1995; Hahn, 1989). At the initial stage of economic development, Korea focused its energies on developing low-tech industries (e.g., food processing, textiles, cement, oil refinery) for import substitution and export. The development of low-tech industries was followed by the development of mid-tech industries (e.g., automobile, steel, chemical, and machinery), which in turn was followed by the introduction of high-tech industries (e.g., consumer electronics, computers, and precision tools). Currently, Korea aspires to become a top tier high-tech country by challenging other industrially advanced nations in automobiles, semiconductors, information processing, telecommunications, and nuclear energy (Holstein and Nakarmi, 1995). Its industrial structure moved from labor-intensive low-tech industries to capital-intensive mid-tech and then on to technology-intensive high-tech industries (Exhibit 5.1).

Exhibit 5.1: Patterns of Technological Transformation

Technology	Inducement	Improvement	Domestication
Low-tech industries	1950s and early 1960s	Mid 1960s and 1970s	1980s
Mid-tech industries	Mid 1970s	1980s	1980s
High-tech industries	Early 1980s	Mid 1980s	1990s
Future-tech industries	Early 1990s	Late 1990s	2000

Source: Adapted from Hahn, C.H. (1989): "Korean Manufacturing Strategy," in K.H. Chung and H.C. Lee (eds.), *Korean Managerial Dynamics*. New York: Praeger, p. 136.

5.2.1 Low-Tech Industries

During the first and second five-year economic planning periods (1962-1971), the policy-makers were primarily concerned with the development of basic industries (e.g., cement, oil refinery, fertilizer, and food processing) and light manufacturing industries (e.g., textiles, footwear, and plywood). Basic industries were needed for import substitution and to prepare for the nation's industrialization programs. Light manufacturing industries were for domestic consumption and for exporting goods to earn foreign currencies. Technological infrastructure was also needed to prepare the population for an age of technological transformation. Since Korea lacked indigenous technological capacity, capital, and managerial know-how, it had to rely on foreign sources. Because required technologies for basic and light-manufacturing industries were already standardized, reaching the maturity or declining stage, it was relatively easy for Koreans to acquire them from various foreign sources. During the initial technology-inducement period, the quality of light manufactured goods was relatively inferior in quality due to a lack of experience in manufacturing. Consequently, most manufactured goods were initially used for domestic consumption. The quality of these goods gradually improved and became a major source of exports. During this technology improvement period, Korean manufacturers learned to design their own products and improve production technologies.

Light-manufactured goods constituted more than 77.2 percent of Korea's exports in 1965, peaking at almost 80 percent in 1970 (Petri, 1990). The figures fell to 55.4, 42.9, and mere 35 percents in 1980, 1985, and 1990 respectively. Two factors contributed to the declining importance of light-manufactured goods. First, heavy investment in mid-tech industries in the 1970s led to the decline in the relative importance of light-manufactured goods in Korea's exports. Secondly, the increase of wages in the 1970s and 1980s made the labor-intensive light-manufactured goods less competitive in the international market. Low-tech industries, producing light-manufactured goods, gradually moved out of Korea to newly developing countries during this period.

5.2.2 Mid-Tech Industries

The Korean government launched a heavy and chemical industries (HCI) promotional drive during the third and fourth economic planning periods (1972-1981), changing the technological landscape of Korea. Once this HCI drive was completed, Korea was no longer a developing country relying on low wages for its economic development. By the early 1980s, Korea had become an industrial nation whose economy depended on capital-intensive mid-tech industries such as automobile, chemical, metal, machinery, steel and Iron, and shipbuilding (Lee, 1991). The relative importance of HCI in Korea's manufacturing structure changed from 26.3 percent of the total values of manufactured goods in 1961 to 64.9 percent in 1991. The share of HCI industries in Korea's exports increased from 11.7 percent in 1961 to 59.9 percent in 1991 (KFTA, various years).

In developing technological capacities, Korea relied on national firms rather than on foreign multinational firms (MNCs). The decision to build national firms was an important factor in Korea's technological transformation. Countries such as Singapore and Taiwan induced MNCs to gain access to advanced technologies and global markets. The strategy of relying on MNCs is often adopted by countries that possess a factor cost advantage in labor or raw materials. However, the problem with relying on MNCs has been that host countries often lose control over the management of MNC subsidiaries. More importantly, this strategy fosters a dependency on MNCs for technology development (Doz, 1986). Korea, in order to minimize foreign dependency and to establish national brand recognition, pursued a strategy of building national firms.

Lacking indigenous technological capacity, Korea depended on the importation of foreign technology. There are several ways in which technologies can be transferred: foreign direct investment, foreign technology licensing, technical consultancy, and capital goods importation. Korea preferred capital goods importation over other means of technology transfer to maintain control over imported technologies. Foreign direct investment (FDI) and foreign technology licensing (FTL) would be under the control of MNCs. During the third and fourth five-year planning periods (1972-81), Korea acquired mature technologies in mid-tech industries through capital goods imports, amounting to 94 percent of total technology imports, compared to a mere 5.5 percent of FDI and FTL. The proportion of capital goods imports to the total technology transfer was the highest among newly industrialized countries (Kim, 1989). The proportion of FDI and FTL, however, increased in the 1980s, when the acquisition of advanced technologies became increasingly difficult by means of capital goods imports.

5.2.3 High-Tech Industries

The Korean economy grew at an annual rate of more than ten percent during the 1960s and 1970s. But the contribution of technology to economic growth was only about 14 percent, compared to 63 and 52 percents for Japan and the U.S. respectively during the same period (MOST, 1988). Most of Korea's economic growth during that period came from labor and capital. During the fifth and sixth economic planning periods (1982-91), the policy-makers in both the private and public sectors shifted their emphasis from capital-intensive HCI to technology-intensive industries such as computers, precision tools, electronics and telecommunications. As a result, the share of exports by high-tech industries went up from less than 10 percent in 1970 to 41 percent in 1985 (Petri, 1990).

Unlike the HCI development drive, initiated and controlled by government, the development of high-tech industries was largely initiated and promoted by the private sector with the encouragement of the public sector. The economic development efforts in the 1960s and 1970s produced a cadre of big business groups which gained sufficient capital, technology, and managerial know-how. Building on the seeds of R&D investment by the government in the initial phase, the private sector expanded R&D activities with commercial applications. The government focused its resources on funding basic research and leading-edge technologies and at the same time encouraged R&D activities by the private sector through tax incentives and regulatory changes. As a result, the private sector's contribution to the total R&D investment increased by about 15 percent annually in the 1980s (Ahn, 1995). The ratio between government and private investments to R&D changed from 97:3 in 1963 to 18:82 in 1993 (MOST, 1994). This point will be further elaborated later.

5.2.4 Advanced Technologies

In the 1990s, Korea is emerging as a top tier high-tech nation. Korea has moved away from being a low-tech, low-wage country that exported shoes, textiles, small television, and cheap cars in the 1970s and early 1980s to become a producer of mid-tech capital-intensive products such as medium-priced cars, ships, steel, and chemicals in the late 1980s and early 1990s. Korea now is bidding to become one of the world's leading producers of technology-intensive goods. Korea is already a major player in the global market in the areas of technology-driven autos, megabyte DRAM semiconductors, high-speed CD-ROMS, liquid-crystal-display screens, fiber-optics, HDTV, and multimedia technology. It is also becoming a world-class participant in nuclear energy, telecommunications, and aerospace. To quote *Business Week*: "Korea could become the first nation to truly establish itself as an advanced industrial power since the emergence of Japan" (Holstein and Nakarmi, 1995).

As noted earlier, the impetus for technological pursuit in recent years is coming from the private sector (*Hankook Ilbo*, August 20, 1996, p. 10). Large Korean firms currently spend as high as 8 percent of their revenues for R&D, aggressively recruit foreign-educated scientists, and forge technological alliances with technologically-oriented foreign companies. For examples, LG Electronics (Lucky Goldstar) plans to spent $2.5 billion in multimedia, display screens, and information-delivery technologies over the second-half of the 1990s. It spent $350 million to acquire Zenith Electric to purse HDTV and multimedia technology. Additionally, Samsung took a 40 percent stake of PC maker AST Research, and Hyundai Electric invested in semiconductor facilities in the U.S.

How realistic is the Korea's drive to become a top-tier advanced industrial nation? Korea has achieved economic success through labor-intensive (factor-driven) and capital-intensive (investment-driven) technologies (Porter, 1990). Korean firms have heavily invested in large-scale process (manufacturing) technologies, largely based on imported technologies, to compete on costs in the global market and have established their own brand names such as Hyundai, Samsung, and Goldstar. The challenge that lies ahead for Korea, if it wants to become an advanced industrial nation, is to move beyond the factor and investment-driven strategies and make the transition to a more innovation-driven strategy. Making such a transition is a formidable task because it requires the development of a large number of technologically-oriented human capital (technological infrastructure) and a major cultural transformation from that which stresses tradition and social acceptance by means of imitating others to that which stresses innovation by means of taking initiative and being different from others.

Koreans are keenly aware of the difficulty of catching-up with advanced nations in cutting edge technologies and the need for transforming its cultural value systems so that it can become an innovation-driven society. They are nevertheless driven by a fierce desire to become an advanced industrial power. More importantly, the new technological push is led by the private sector, and the desire to become a top-tier advanced nation is shared by the entire society including government, labor, and the general public (Holstein and Narkami, 1995). Issues related to cultural transformation are presented in Chapter 9. In the meantime, the issues that involve technological infrastructure are discussed in the following sections.

5.3 Technological Infrastructure

In the absence of indigenous technological capacity, the Korean government had to play an important role in preparing the infrastructure for technological transformation. In order to plan and coordinate the nation's technological development policies and activities, the government established the Ministry of Science and Technology (MOST) in the early 1960s. Initially, MOST placed a heavy emphasis on importation of foreign technologies from industrialized nations. Subsequently, emphasis was placed upon concerted efforts between government, industry, and educational sectors in developing indigenous technology development. The following items illustrate how Korea has prepared itself for its technological transformation.

5.3.1 Human Resource Development

Korea lacks natural resources. It has to import most fuels and minerals from abroad. The only plentiful resource is its people. If any local advantage is to be gained, it should from the development of its people. Modern education was first introduced to Korea by American missionaries and expanded by the Japanese colonial government. But at the end of the Japanese colonial rule, only two percent of the Korean population over fourteen years of age had completed secondary education and the illiteracy rate stood at 78 percent. After World War II, the Korean government placed a heavy emphasis on education. The share of education in the total government budget rose from 2.5 percent in 1951 to over 22 percent in the 1980s. Government expenditures, however, accounted for only one-third of the total educational expenditures; the remainder came from the private sector and parents.

As a result of encouraging education, enrollment at various educational levels increased rapidly since the early 1950s. Elementary school enrollment increased over five times. Even faster growth was seen in the secondary and tertiary educational levels. Secondary school enrollment increased more than 28 times between 1945 and 1986, while enrollment in colleges and universities increased almost 15 time during the same period. The rate of increase in school enrollment stabilized in the 1980s. Other developing nations have achieved rapid growth in elementary education as Korea has, but Korea has shown a well-balanced expansion in all levels of education.

Additionally, overseas education and training has become an important element in Korea's human resource developmental effort. Overseas training goes back to the period of foreign aid in the 1950s, when a high proportion of graduate students, government officials, business executives, and academics were sent to the U.S. under the economic assistance program (Mason et al., 1980). This tradition of overseas education and training continues today in response to the growing need for globalizing the Korean economy in the age of unlimited global competition. In the 1980s, the ratio of college and graduate students training abroad was twice as many in Korea as it was in other newly industrializing countries in Argentina, Brazil, India, and Mexico (Kim, 1989).

In comparative terms, by the mid-1980s, Korea surpassed other newly industrializing countries in all indices of educational attainment. Korea had the highest number of secondary students as a percentage of the total secondary-education age population (90 percent) and the highest number of scientists and engineers per million people (360,000). Korean junior high students usually rank at the top in annual international competitions in mathematics and science.The rapid expansion of education resulted in serious unemployment problems for the educated population in the 1950s and 1960s. However, the formation of educated human capital laid an important foundation for adapting to imported technology and subsequent development of indigenous technology.

5.3.2 Foreign Technology Importation

In developing its economy, Korea had options for developing local industries for domestic consumption, relying on multinational companies (MNCs) to enter the global marketplace, and/or developing its own national firms to compete globally. As noted elsewhere, Korea early on decided to develop its own national firms that are able to compete in the global market. This decision had an impact on the selection of imported technology. Rather than receiving foreign direct investment (FDI), foreign technology licensing (FTL), and technical consultancy (TC), Korea promoted technology transfer though capital goods importation. For example, chemical, cement, steel, shipbuilding, and to some extent automobile industries all resorted to a turnkey mode of technology transfer.

During the developmental phases of Korean economy (1962-86), the amount of capital goods far surpassed other modes of technology transfer. Capital goods imports were worth 22 times the value of other forms of technology transfer ($126 billion vs. $5.8 billion) (Kim, 1989). The proportion of capital goods imports to the total technology transfer was the highest in Korea among newly developing countries (NICs) during the period. In the same vein, the size of DFI to the total technology transfer, indicating the dependency on MNCs, was significantly lower in Korea than in other NICs, including Brazil, Hong Kong, Singapore, and Taiwan (Kim, 1988).

Massive importation of capital goods accelerated the development of internationally competitive national firms in Korea and their capacities to manufacture and export. Furthermore, capital goods import became a major source of learning through reverse engineering by Korean firms. The Korean national firms, once they gained a foothold in the international market, started to rely on DFI, FTL, and TC to upgrade their existing technological capacities. This technology transfer strategy not only helped Korean firms to maintain independence from foreign MNCs but also was effective in upgrading technological capacities.

5.3.3 Indigenous R&D Efforts

Korea has been a latecomer in technological development. As a technological follower, Korea has developed its economy by investing in economies of scale (process engineering) in manufacturing goods in technologically well-established industries such as automobile, consumer electronics, chemicals, steelmaking, shipbuilding, and so forth. As a result, Korea has been behind other industrialized nations in product development. The overall level of technology development in Korea is estimated to be at about 50 percent of the level of advanced countries such as Japan and the U.S. (*Hankook Ilbo*, June 13, 1996, p. 2). Except for industries such as automobile, consumer electronics, shipbuilding, textile, and footwear, other industries are falling behind foreign competitors. Even in those competitive industries, Korean firms are at least five year behind in product innovation and development in comparison to Japan and the U.S.

As global industrial competition heats up, Koreans are keenly aware of the need for not only maintaining economies of scale but also for developing product innovation and development. To meet this challenge, Korea has made major efforts in indigenous research and development (R&D) efforts. As noted earlier, the Korean government has established a number of research institutes of its own and also assists universities to increase human stock in science and technology. As shown in Exhibit 5.2, the number of researchers in Korea has increased from 18,434 in 1980 to 117,446 in 1994. R&D expenditures also have increased substantially. The total R&D expenditures in 1980 were $321 million (0.58 percent of GNP), compared to $10.9 billion in 1995 (2.71 percent). The government plans to increase the R&D expenditures to 5 percent of its GNP by year 2000 (STC, 1992; NSO, 1994).

Exhibit 5.2: Major R&D Indicators in Korea

	R&D Dollars (in million $)	% of GNP	Researchers (in million $
1980	321	0.58	18,434
1985	1,390	1.56	41,473
1990	4,676	1.88	70,503
1995	10,953	2.71	117,446*

* 1994

Source: Ministry of Science and Technology (various years): *Science and Technology Annual*.

There has been a structural change in R&D investment also. In the 1960s and 1970s, the public sector assumed the primary responsibility in the nation's R&D efforts. But in the 1980s and early 1990s, the private sector has gradually assumed a bigger role in R&D efforts in response to increasing international competition and partly in response to conducive government policy for private R&D activities. The public sector accounted for 68 percent of the nation's total R&D expenditures in 1971, but by 1986 its share declined to only 19 percent and it currently remains at this level. There are several reasons for the increase in private sector R&D activities in the 1980s (Ahn, 1995). First, Korean firms, especially large ones, have gained enough financial resources to support their own R&D activities during the first four economic planning periods (1962-1982). Second, as Korean firms become increasingly competitive in the global market, developed nations became more cautious about transferring technology to Korea. Third, the recognition of intellectual rights has also limited the flow of technology transfer into Korea. What used to be readily available intellectual properties now must be respected and compensated for. Fourth, the shortening of product cycles and the importance of technology-intensive products made Korean businesses aware of the crucial role of R&D in formulating competitive strategy. Finally, as the Korean domestic markets opened up to foreign competition, formerly protected domestic manufacturers have to catch up with newer technology.

5.3.4 Research Institutions

In order to build the nation's technological capacities, the Ministry of Science and Technology (MOST) established a number of research and educational institutes. In 1966, the Korea Institute of Science and Technology (KIST) was established as multi-disciplinary industrial research institute to forge a linkage between academia and industry. KIST was initially set up to pursue basic sciences and technologies, but it gradually moved toward research in applied fields. A noticeable contribution of KIST has been aiding industries in adapting foreign technology and transforming basic sciences into commercial applications. Currently, its main function is to conduct research projects that have commercial applications. Much of these research projects are supported by industry. As a result, currently about one-half of its operating budget is derived from the private sector.

KIST's primary constituents are the government and large businesses, leaving small and medium-size companies unassisted. To remedy this situation, the government established the Korea Academy of Industrial Technology (KAITECH) in 1989; its new name is Intelligent Manufacturing

Systems Secretariat (IMSS). Unlike KIST, which conducts basic and applied research projects for commercial uses, KAITECH's primary mission is to assist small and medium-size companies in commercializing existing technologies. Its function is more diverse than is KIST's; its function includes technological information, technical training, process technology, quality assurance, and product development. KIATECH is also partially supported by its industrial clients.

In addition to KIST and KAITECH, the government also assisted in creating a number of private and public research institutes. For example, the Daeduck Science Complex was established in the early 1970s; it houses a dozen or more private and public industrial research institutes. This complex is designed to serve as a center for the nation's science and technology development. In the 1980s, the government actively promoted R&D projects in industry by establishing the Korea Technology Development Corporation (KTDC) in 1981, Korea Development Investment Corporation (KDIC) in 1982, and Korea Technology Finance Corporation (KTFC) in 1984.

These institutions provide industries with capital for technological development projects which cannot be funded by industry alone. The government also provided tax and financial incentives for establishing industrial research institutes by industry. As a result, the number of industrial research institutes increased from 152 in 1984 to 1949 in 1993; the amount of R&D expenditures by industry increased 10-20 percent annually during the same period (Ahn, 1995).

5.3.5 Technological Education

The creation of research institutions would be a futile exercise unless they could be adequately staffed. To meet this challenge, the government took the initiative in providing trained scientists and engineers. In 1971, the Korea Advanced Institute of Science and Technology (KAIST) was established to train scientists and engineers. At KAIST, industrial R&D personnel are allowed to pursue masters and doctoral degrees under the direction of KAIST professors and industrial supervisors. These candidates are often sent to KAIST with research projects relevant to the sponsoring institutions, creating built-in collaborative research endeavors. While KAIST efforts were significant in promoting collaborative research efforts between academics and industries, they were limited to a relatively few participating organizations.

In 1996, a new Advanced Science Institute (ASI) was established as a basic science research arm within KAIST. Its primary mission is to promote basic research in four basic sciences (biology, chemistry, mathematics, and physics) in order to bring Korea within the ranks of the 10 most scientifically-advanced nations. To achieve this end, the ASI created 15 chaired professorships to staff key positions with world renown scientists, including some Noble prize winners. Additionally, more than 50 professors will be recruited overseas and another 100 professors domestically. Once fully staffed, its annual budget will be about $150 million by year 2000 and its costs will be shared by both private and public sectors.

As the nation's economic activities expanded, the need for trained technical manpower increased. To alleviate the shortage of qualified technical personnel, the government (MOST) established the Korea Science and Engineering Foundation (KOSEF) in 1977 to support university science and engineering activities. Since its inception, KOSEF supported universities and colleges in carrying out various science and engineering projects that are designed to accelerate science and engineering education and collaboration between academia and industries. The government expanded its support for universities and colleges in the late 1980s. Through the KOSEF program, universities and colleges in Korea established science research centers (SRCs) to promote basic research and science education and engineering research centers (ERCs) to undertake applied science and engineering projects (Ahn, 1995).

KOSEF also initiated a new model of research funding in 1987 to support those basic research areas that are jointly identified by industry and academia as being vital to the development of new technologies. This program, named the Mission-oriented Basic Research Program, brought together science professors and industrial R&D managers to prepare a detailed list of basic research areas vital to the development of new technologies. For example, applied generic research is identified as one of the vital areas that requires collaboration between academia and industry.

In summary, the government played a major role in developing and preparing for the technological transformation in Korea. Its main focus has been on the development of science and technological capacities by means of education and institutional development. Once such infrastructure is prepared and assisted by the government, it is up to the private sector to carry out the task of technological advancement of Korean firms.

5.4 Technology Development Strategy

Korean firms followed a predictable pattern of developing technological capacities--importation, imitation, and innovation. In the absence of indigenous technologies, they first imported foreign technologies. This importation strategy was primarily pursued by large firms (Kim and Utterback, 1983; Kim and Kim, 1985; Kim, 1989). Large firms aggressively imported foreign technologies that were already developed in advanced countries. The immediate task for these firms at that stage was the implementation of imported technologies to produce exportable products that had been produced and marketed around the world. Small firms, on the other hand, adopted a strategy of imitating foreign products through repair work and reverse engineering. Both technology importers and imitators, upon gaining technological knowledge, assimilated foreign technology into their indigenous technology developmental effort to upgrade the quality of their products and the efficiency of production systems.

5.4.1 Technology Importers

Technological importers were large intermediate and finished good manufacturers (e.g., automobile, consumer electronics, chemicals, fertilizers, steelmaking, and shipbuilding), established at various times during the 1960s and 1970s. They heavily relied on foreign technology in forms of capital goods imports, technology licensing, and consultancy. Given the large size of the financial investment required and the lack of technological experience and capacity, these firms heavily relied on foreign technology to ensure swift plant construction and problem-free start-up. All that was needed at this stage was the engineering effort to implement the adopted technology. Foreign technical assistance was most significant in implementing foreign technology and in debugging problems associated with such implementation.

The initial acquisition of foreign technology by Korean engineers and technicians took place through on-the-job as well as off-the-job training provided by foreign technology suppliers. More importantly, Korean engineers and technicians made deliberate efforts to acquire technological capacities and experiences in an "apprenticeship manner." For example, the initial installation of Pohang Steel Company (POSCO) was accomplished almost entirely on a turnkey basis by the Japanese. The unique aspect was the degree to which POSCO actively prepared human resources and participated from the beginning in assimilating production and engineering technologies. Over 500 engineers and technicians had received overseas training prior to start-up. POSCO engineers also worked closely with their Japanese counterparts in constructing plants to gain practical experience (Juhn, 1991).

As a result, when operations commenced in 1973, POSCO reached the desired level of steel production in 80 days, an unprecedented record in the history of the steel industry. The venture was profitable from the beginning and became one of the most price-competitive steelmakers in the world. In the subsequent three expansions, POSCO engineers had steadily substituted foreign engineering input, reducing costs substantially. Ultimately, when the second steel works were built in Kwangyang in the early 1990s, plant construction could be done entirely by Korean engineering know-how. The Kwangyang plant is one of the most technologically advanced integrated steel mills in the world.

The relatively successful assimilation of imported technologies, combined with increased indigenous technological capacities, led to the gradual transformation of technology in Korea. Technological transformation occurred not only in process engineering but also in product development and innovative research and development. For example, POSCO, on one hand, entered into licensing agreements with several foreign firms to develop new products and to ensure the quality of its products. At the same time, it also exerted its own technological efforts to upgrade its technological capacities. To this end, it established an R&D center in 1977, only four years after the initial production of steel.

5.4.2 Technology Imitators

Technology imitators tended to be small companies, which established production systems with primitive technologies that they had developed themselves or they imitated from others (Kim, 1989). They then gradually upgraded both products and production processes through repair and reverse engineering of locally available foreign products. These small companies lacked financial resources and organizational capacities to identify and negotiate with foreign technology suppliers. They, however, had technically competent individuals who managed to improve or develop products and production processes through reverse engineering and by reading technological information available on technical publications.

For example, Korea Steel Pipe (KSP) initially developed a primitive steel-pipe manufacturing process based on the observations of an imported steel-pipe manufacturing process used by a local bicycle producer. An engineer at KPS was able to imitate, and make an improvement on, foreign technology and eventually develop new steel-pipe-making processes. Each subsequent process had more sophisticated features than the previous one. As KPS gained financial resources, it imported a more advanced line from Japan. It soon duplicated the imported technology and then developed improved versions of the Japanese model for subsequent expansions. KPS now exported steel-pipe plants to other countries including Bangladesh, Kenya, and Saudi Arabia.

Both technology importers and imitators heavily relied on foreign technology. The former initially relied on formal transfers of technology (turnkey plants, direct foreign investment, and licensing), whereas the latter on informal transfers (reverse engineering, subscribing technical journals, and temporary hiring of foreign engineers). They, however, changed the mode of foreign technology transfer over time in response to changes in their environments and their capacities. Technology importers, which heavily relied on formal methods, reduced their dependency on foreign technology as they gained technological expertise. Any technological shortcoming could be overcome by informal technology transfers or through indigenous R&D efforts. A case in point is the aforementioned POSCO, which substantially reduced its dependency on formal technology transfers in its capacity expansion programs.

On the other hand, as small companies became successful in imitating foreign technology, they turned to formal technology transfers to make a major jump in their technological capacities. Financial successes allowed them to rely on formal technology transfers. This technological leapfrog was needed for them to compete in more sophisticated domestic and foreign markets that they had previously served. For example, KPS formed technical alliances with several Japanese and German firms to become a formidable exporter.

5.4.3 Technology Innovators

Korean firms as technological latecomers (importers and imitators) have several advantages over technology innovators (Schnaars, 1994). First, technology innovators as first-movers are forced to spend heavily on R&D for new product development. Latecomers can acquire such technology at a fraction of the cost as do product innovators. Second, latecomers may trade R&D expenditures for production capacities (economies of scale) to reduce production costs. Third, first-movers spend heavily on developing new markets for their products. Latecomers do not need to pay for such market development costs. Finally, latecomers also can trade R&D expenditures for promotional spending. In a well-established industry, spending on marketing tends to be more effective in gaining market share than does spending on R&D (Cooper, 1982).

For these reasons, Korean firms would rather import technologies than developing them internally. However, in recent years, it has become increasingly difficult for them to import technologies because former technology providers are reluctant to lend hands. As Koreans become formidable competitors in the international market, they are seen as potential adversaries. As foreign technology transfer becomes increasingly difficult, Koreans do not have much choice but to become technology innovators themselves. Although Koreans are relatively new in technological innovation, they are nevertheless making some headway. For example, Hyundai Motors invested heavily in developing its own car-making technologies including engines and transmissions. As a result, its technology licensing fees fell from over 1 percent of its sales in 1991 to 0.2 percent in 1995 (Weinberg, 1996). Another example is the information technology. Although Korea is a latecomer in the telecommunications industry, its CDMA (code division multiple access) technology is ahead of Japan and the U.S. (Sohn, 1996). As a result, this industry has emerged as a major exporter for the Korean economy.

Korea's efforts to introduce technological innovation are directed towards in three areas. First, Korea has increased the level of R&D expenditures by both private and public sectors. As noted earlier, the Korean government has been increasing R&D expenditures from less than one percent of its GNP in 1991 to 2.09 percent in 1992, and expenditures are expected to increase 5 percent by 2001. The private sector has also stepped up its R&D expenditures. Major business groups such as Samsung, LG, and Hyundai, and Daewoo spend as high as 7.7 percent of their sales for R&D (*Hankook Ilbo*, August 20, 1996, p.10). In comparative terms, Korea's R&D expenditures are still behind those of advanced nations in their R&D efforts, but Korea is likely to follow the lead of other industrialized nations in such efforts.

Second, the level of technological alliance within particular industries have been increasing. As technology importers, Korean firms are more accustomed to working with foreign technology providers than with other Korean firms. In fact, as Korean firms compete with each other in their domestic market, it has been natural for them to see each other as adversaries rather than as cooperators. This attitude still prevails. However, as Korean firms collectively encounter the difficulties of foreign technology transfer, they are beginning to collaborate on R&D. Such collaboration mostly occurs between private and public sectors and between suppliers and industrial buyers (Yoon and Kim, 1995).

Finally, Korea's technology development efforts are primarily focused on innovating existing product lines and production processes. Developing new products and inventing new production processes are probably the ultimate goals of technologically-oriented societies. Advanced industrial countries such as the U.S., Japan, and Western European countries pursue such technology development strategies. However, newly industrialized countries such as Korea and Taiwan seem to find such strategies to be too expensive and risky. Because their domestic markets are limited, they have to produce goods to export. Promoting new products to overseas markets becomes an expensive and risky venture. It would be safer for them to improve the quality of globally-recognized products and produce and sell them at low costs by improving production processes and economies of scale. This point will be further elaborated on in the following section.

5.4.4 Future Challenges

Technology is generally divided into product and process categories. Product-oriented technology refers to the knowledge associated with product development and design. Process-oriented technology refers to the know-how related to production of goods and services. Furthermore, a nation's technological capacities can be measured by three elements: production, investment, and innovation (Dahlman and Westphal, 1983). Production capacity is the technological ability required to produce products and to operate productive facilities efficiently. Investment capacity refers to the ability to establish new production facilities and expand existing ones in order to achieve economies of scale. Innovation capacity refers to the ability to develop new products and production processes.

Korea's economic success has been primarily based on the investment-driven process technology. Korean firms heavily invested in large-scale manufacturing processes to produce globally-accepted products (e.g., automobiles, consumer electronics, steel, ships, and so forth). Industries that they have selected tended to be mature and growth industries that have already been successfully tested in the marketplace. This strategy tended to reduce any risk involved in introducing a new product and to encounter minimal resistance when marketed. Once industries were chosen, Korean firms were able to lower production costs by reducing the project implementation processes and relying on a highly trained and disciplined workforce. For example, Samsung completed its first 64K DRAM chip manufacturing facility in just six months. The average construction period for such project in the U.S. is 18 months. Another example is the construction of Pohang Steel's Kwangyang Plant, which was completed in two years, some sixth months ahead of an already ambitious schedule.

This process-driven technology helped Korean firms gain cost leadership in the international market. However, as the Korean economy prospered, some of the cost advantages disappeared. First, wages of Korean workers have increased substantially and workers have demanded more leisure time in recent years. Newly developing countries such as China, India, Indonesia, and other Southeast Asian countries have replaced Korea as low cost producers. As a result, many of the labor-intensive industries such as clothing, footwear, and plywood have moved out of Korea to these newly developing countries. Second, other developing countries such as Taiwan and Singapore can easily adopt the investment-driven process technology to challenge Korea in mid and high-tech industries.

There are two challenges that lie ahead for Korea. The first is to move away from its low-cost leadership strategy, which is based purely on economies of scale. Investment-driven process technology is still a viable option for Korean firms in gaining and maintaining mid and high-tech industries, such as automobiles, consumer electronics, semiconductors, and telecommunications. Such process technology also cannot be easily imitated by newly developing economies. However, such a strategy can easily be undermined by advanced economies such as the U.S., Japan, and Western European countries if they choose to compete in investment-driven strategy. A case in point is Samsung's effort to lead the memory chip manufacturing by means of economies of scale. As soon as Samsung showed the possibility of dominating the world's memory chip market, other memory chip manufacturers in the U.S. and Japan stepped up their chip manufacturing to cut the Samsung's lead. Therefore, to be effective, process technology should be based on innovation. The Japanese have been very effective in using this innovation-driven process technology by adopting just-in-time, total quality, and flexible manufacturing systems.

The second challenge for Korea is to improve the quality of product-oriented technology. Traditionally, Korean firms have not been the first mover in new product development and design. As a newcomer in the global market scene, one cannot expect Koreans to become new product developers or designers overnight. At the moment, what we can reasonably expect from Korean firms is to see Koreans becoming innovators in improving product quality and design of globally accepted products. This is the challenge that Korea faces now and in which it must succeed. Eventually, however, Korean firms must learn to become new product developers and designers and to promote them successfully in the global market if they wish to move into the ranks of advanced nations.

5.5 Summary

Several factors have contributed to the successful transformation of technology in Korea. First, Korea invested heavily in education well before it launched its economic development plans. Had it not been for the formation of trained human resources, Korea's economic development would have been much slower. A relatively well-educated and disciplined labor force has contributed to the rapid acquisition of technological capacities. Second, Korea has relied on formal and informal technological transfer rather than on foreign direct investment or foreign technology licensing. Had Korea relied on foreign direct investment or technological licensing, Korea still would be dependent on foreign multinational firms. Technology transfer made it possible for Korean firms to become independent from the control of multinationals. Third, in the absence of indigenous technological know-how, the government played a crucial role in preparing for technological infrastructure (technical training, foreign technology importation, and technology-supporting institutions). Finally, the government's export-driven economic policy stimulated Korean firms to focus their energies and resources on acquiring the technological capacities needed to successfully compete in the international market.

Korea's economic success is primarily based on an investment-driven manufacturing strategy aimed at gaining cost leadership in the international market. The industries and products they have chosen have tended to be those that have been well-established and were in their mature and declining stages. By choosing such products, Korean firms were able to avoid the major risks associated with new product and market development. With the combination of economies of scale, superb human resources, low labor costs, and government supports, Korean firms have been able to establish overall cost leadership in the international market.

Korean firms are facing new realities domestically and internationally. First, as the Korean economy advances, the role of government in providing technical supports for industries diminishes. Government can play an important role in preparing technological infrastructure. Once infrastructure is prepared, it is up to the private sector to build technological capacities of their own. Second, as the economy advances, so do the costs of labor. Industries that have maintained cost leadership by means of low labor costs are now unable to sustain such leadership. If an industry wants to maintain cost leadership, such leadership will have to come from other sources such as process improvement and labor productivity gain rather than from low wages.

Third, Korean firms now face tremendous competitive pressures from such newly developing countries as China, Indonesia, Malaysia, and others East Asian nations. These countries have adopted economic developmental strategies similar to those used by Korea. As a result, Korea's ability to compete in cost leadership has eroded. Finally, as Koreans become increasingly competitive internationally, former technology providers are becoming increasingly reluctant to transfer their advanced technologies to

Koreans for fear of a boomerang effect. Koreans do not have much choice but to rely on their own resources to develop technological capacities.

The challenge that lies ahead for Korean firms are for them to become technological innovators in both product and process developments. Developing and marketing new products for international markets is a very expensive and risky proposition. Viable strategies for Korean firms are two-fold: The first is to improve existing products in function, quality and design to differentiate them from their competitors and to produce goods efficiently enough to maintain cost leadership. In other words, the combination of investment and innovation-driven technology strategies needs to be pursued to achieve both cost leadership and product differentiation. The second is to become product and process innovators in order to become a global industry leader. It is a long-term goal for Korea, for which its resources must be directed.

References

Ahn, S.I. (1995): "A New Program in Cooperative Research Between Academia and Industry in Korea, Involving Centers of Excellence," *Technovation*, 15(4):241-257.

Cooper, R.G. (1982): "New Product Success in Industrial Firms," *Industrial Market Management*, 11(3):215-233.

Dahlman, C.J. and Westphal, L.E. (1983): *Conceptualization of Technology and Technological Capacity*. Washington, DC: The World Bank.

Doz, Y.L. (1986): "Government Policies and Global Industries," in M.E. Porter (ed.), *Competition in Global Industries*. Boston: Harvard Business School Press, pp. 225-265.

Hahn, C.K. (1989): "Korean Manufacturing Strategy," in K.H. Chung and H.C. Lee (eds.), *Korean Managerial Dynamics*. New York: Praeger, pp. 131-146.

Holstein, W.J. and Nakarmi, L. (1995): "Korea: Headed for High Tech's Top Tier," *Business Week*, July 31:56-63.

Juhn, S.I. (1991): "Challenge of Latecomer: The Case of the Korean Steel Industry References to POSCO," in E. Abe and Y. Suzuki (eds.), *Changing Pattern of International Rivalry: Some Lessons from the Steel Industry*. Tokyo: University of Tokyo Press, pp. 269-293.

KFTA (various years): *Foreign Trade Yearbook*. Seoul: Korea Foreign Trade Association.

Kim, I.S. (1988): "The Pros and Cons of International Technology Transfer," *The International Conference on Technology Transfer*. Los Angeles, University of Southern California.

Kim, I.S. (1989): "Technological Transformation of Korean Firms," in K.H. Chung and H.C. Lee (eds.), *Korean Managerial Dynamics*. New York: Praeger, pp. 113-130.

Kim, I.S. and Kim, Y.B. (1985): "Innovation in a Newly Industrializing Country: A Multiple Discriminant Analysis," *Management Science*, 31(3):312-322.

Kim, I.S. and Utterback, J.M. (1983): "The Evolution of Organizational Technology and Structure in a Developing Country," *Management Science*, 29(10):1185-97.

Klebnikov, P. (1995): "Chairman Lee is a Very Young Man," *Forbes*, September 25:66-70.

Lee, S.C. (1991): "The Heavy and Chemical Industries Promotion Plan (1973-79)," in L.J. Cho and Y.H. Kim (eds.), *Economic Development in the Republic of Korea: A Policy Perspective*. Honolulu: East-West Center, pp. 431-471.

Lee, S.Y. (1994): "Science and Technology Policy for Improving International Competitiveness," *Federation of Korean Industries Monthly*, 1994(7):34-39.

Mason, E.S., Perkins, D.H., Kim, K.S., Cole, D.C., and Kim, M.J. (1980): *The Economic and Social Modernization of the Republic of Korea*. Cambridge, MA: Council on East Asian Studies, Harvard University.

MOST (1988): *Introduction to Science and Technology in Korea*. Seoul: Ministry of Science and Technology, Republic of Korea.

MOST (1994): *Science and Technology Annual*. Seoul: Ministry of Science and Technology, Republic of Korea.

National Statistics Office (NSO)(1994): *Major Statistics of Foreign Economy*. Seoul: National Statistics Office, ROK.

Petri, P.A. (1990): "Korea Trade as Outlier: An Economic Anatomy," in J.K. Kwon (ed.), *Korean Economic Development*. New York: Greenwood Press, pp. 53-78.

Porter, M.E. (1990): *The Competitive Advantage of Nations*. New York: Free Press.

Science and Technology Consortium (STC)(1992): *White Paper on Korean Science and Technology Development*. Seoul: Pulensan Press.

Schnaars, S.P. (1994): *Managing Imitation Strategies*. New York: The Free Press.

Sohn, Y.J. (1996): "New Players in the Information Revolution," *Business Korea*, 13(12):32-35.

Weinberg, N. (1996): "Move Over, Japan," *Forbes*, September 23:84-86.

Westphal, L.E., Kim, L.S., and Dahlman, C.J. (1985): "Reflections on the Republic of Korea's Acquisition of Technological Capability," in N. Rosenberg and C. Frischtak (eds.), *International Technology Transfer: Concept, Measures, Comparisons*. New York: Praeger, pp. 167-221.

Yoon, S.J. and Kim, S.P. (1995): "Institutionalization of Technology Development in Korean Automotive Parts Industry," *Yonsei Business Review*, 32(58):5-42.

Chapter 6
Corporate Culture of Korean Business

6.1 Introduction

Culture is generally defined as a set of values, beliefs, and habits that are shared by the people in a society or nation, influencing their attitudes and behaviors (Schein, 1985; Harris and Moran, 1987). Within this national culture, people in an organization also share a set of values, beliefs, and attitudes, which is called *corporate culture*. Studies suggest that corporate culture is closely related to organizational performance (Peters and Waterman, 1982; Kotter and Haskett, 1991; Collins and Porras, 1994). A strong corporate culture that nurtures customers, employees, and other stakeholders is said to enhance corporate performance.

This chapter studies the influences of value systems on the managerial practices and employee behavior in Korean firms. More specifically, it reviews the Korean national culture and its effect on corporate culture, which in turn influences employee behavior and managerial practices. Since the Korean national culture has been modified over the years by industrialization, we need to look at this change in a longitudinal manner. To this end, we will first look at the traditional culture and its influence on corporate culture and then see how the newly emerging value systems modify employee behavior and managerial practices.

6.2 Traditional National Culture

The dominant influence on Korean culture has been Confucianism. Religions such as Buddhism, Shamanism, Taoism, and more recently Christianity have all played an important role in Korean culture. But Confucianism has had the most profound influence on Korean culture. Confucianism came to Korea from China in the 5th century and dominated the customs, traditions, value systems, and everyday lives of Korean people for centuries. Although Korean culture has changed because of various cultural influences, especially from the U.S.A. and Japan in the 20th century, the Confucian heritage still remains strong, providing the basis for moral standards and social norms.

6.2.1 Confucian Ethical Codes

It is difficult to summarize Confucianism in a few words, but its essence can be stated in its ethical codes, harmony-oriented group culture, and education-based social status systems. Confucian ethical codes define the five cardinal human relations between the king and his subjects, between father and son, between husband and wife, the young and old, and friends. These relationships are to be governed by five appropriate rules:

(1) filial piety to parents;
(2) loyalty to the king;
(3) respect for the elder;
(4) obedience to husband and warmth toward wife;
(5) trust among friends (Ryu, 1980).

Confucianism places heavy emphasis on harmony. Harmony is to be maintained by observing the five Confucian cardinal rules, which stress authoritarianism and paternalism. That means people with lower social status respect the authority of people with higher status. In return, people with higher status have an obligation to take care of people with lower status. Furthermore, in the Confucian culture, individuals are required to accept group norms to maintain harmony in their group.

Confucianism also places a heavy emphasis on education. In the Confucian culture, education is seen as an instrument for gaining social acceptance. Confucianism believes that the capacity for goodness and harmony of an individual and society can be cultivated by education. The importance of education is reflected in the way it bestows social status in Korea. The traditional Confucian culture placed scholars and government officers at the top of the ladder of social status, followed by farmers, artisans (engineers), and merchants. To become a government officer, one had to pass the civil service examination. Modern industrialization in Korea has opened up vast new opportunities in business and technical professions that have their own version of social status. But educational achievement is still the most important factor determining one's occupation and social status.

Confucian values permeate every aspect of a Korean's behavior in the society: family, work organization, and social interactions. In the family, the father plays the decisive role in maintaining harmony among family members. In work organizations, the traditional values are reflected in a subordinate's loyalty to the superior (or to the company) and in the latter's benevolence and paternalism toward the former. Trust among friends is reflected in peer relations and in informal interactions. In these manners, Confucian values reinforce centralized authority, vertical hierarchical order, harmony among employees, diligence and hard work, and seniority-based reward system in Korean society.

6.2.2 Confucian Family Values

One of the most important cultural dimensions affecting employee behavior in organizations has been the importance of the family. The family is considered the most important social unit, and family value have a direct effect upon an employee's work values. Four important concepts emerge from Confucian family values: extended family, paternalism, blood-based succession, and gender roles (Janelli, 1993; Kim, 1992).

Extended Family. Under Confucianism, traditional family values are maintained and reinforced through the extended family system. Filial piety to one's parents is extended to grandparents through ancestor worship. Parental love of younger generations serve as role models for children. Brotherly love is extended not only to siblings but also to relatives. In this way, the concept of family in Korea is not limited to a nuclear family unit. As a result, it is not uncommon to see several generations live together under one roof in a Korean family. Moreover, work organizations are often considered to be extended families by many Koreans. Although organization members do not live together, it is common for them to share such family events as children' birthday celebrations, weddings, and funeral services with co-workers. Likewise, ethical codes that govern relationships between family members also apply to relationships between organization members.

Paternalism. Confucianism sees the father as the central figure in the family. The father is expected to lead the family with authority and respect. He should be the role model for his wife and children by leading them with authority on one hand and love and affection on the other. Similarly, the owner is expected to take the role of father in leading his company and its employees with authority while at the same time fulfilling the employees' needs. In return, employees should respect the owner's authority to lead them. The same kind of relationship exists between superiors and subordinates. In this manner, Confucianism reinforces the hierarchical, authoritarian, and paternalistic corporate culture in Korea.

Blood-based Succession. In Confucianism, the eldest son occupies a particularly important place in the family. His relationship to his siblings is like that of the father to the family. The eldest son is expected to inherit the family assets and succeed his father in taking over responsibility for the family. The system in which only the elder son inherits family assets has been modified in recent years to include other siblings in the inheritance process, but the blood-based system remains in force. This inheritance system is also applied to managerial succession. Koreans generally believe that the ownership of a business should be kept in the family. The ownership of many of Korean large businesses (*chaebols*) has been passed on to the founder's children. In those *chaebols* where the founder is still active, his children are placed in heir-apparent positions. Thus, the blood-based succession system contributes to the preservation of family ownership and a centralized power structure in Korean firms.

Gender Roles. In Confucian culture, the roles of males and females are differentiated. Traditionally, Korean society has been male-dominated. Under Confucian ethical codes, the man leads the family as a economic provider while the wife manages the household and nurtures children. In employment, although the law guarantees equal employment for women, discrimination against female employees still exists. Female workers are generally paid less than their male counterparts and are expected to resign upon getting married.

6.2.3 *Yon-go* Relations

Another traditional value in Korean culture is the *yon-go* relation, meaning "relation-based behavior." This relation-based behavior is promoted to foster trust and closeness that people have for others. A sense of closeness and trust is first extended to one's immediate family members and relatives and then to people with common educational backgrounds and regional origin (usually birthplace). Having attended the same school or having been born and raised in the same region promotes a sense of belongingness and trust.

The *yon-go* relationship is deeply rooted in Korean culture and is pervasive in every aspect of Koreans' lives. For example, Korea's major political parties for the past three decades were organized not on ideological but along regional lines. Many of the core leaders of the ruling party were from the southeast region of Korea; the leaders of one of the opposition parties were mostly from the southwest region; and the leaders from the other opposition party were mainly from the central region of Korea. In many business organizations, power is concentrated among members of the owner's family, school alumni, and friends from the same geographical region (Chang and Chang, 1994).

While this sense of belongingness promotes harmony within the close-knit group, it fosters a sense of exclusion toward others. In work organizations, such inclusion fosters a closely-knit relation-oriented group culture. But the sense of exclusion leads to nepotism and favoritism in managerial decision-making. At the societal level, a sense of inclusion promotes strong nationalism while at the same time creates an antagonistic attitude toward foreigners.

6.2.4 Education-based Social Status

As noted earlier, Confucianism defines a person's social status by his or her occupation and education. The most important criterion for obtaining government positions has been the earning of advanced degrees and the passing of the rigorous civil service examination. In business firms, employees are often selected and promoted on the basis of academic achievement and knowledge-based written examinations. This is why Koreans have such strong motivation for a good education. This emphasis on education is also seen in the emphasis placed on management training and development in Korean businesses.

We have briefly reviewed the influence of Confucianism on Korean culture. In the following section, we will see how Korean culture has changed over the years with the influence of Western culture and industrialization. Subsequently, we will examine how this change in national culture has affected the value systems and shared values of Korean workers and management in Korean firms.

6.3 Changing National Culture

Although Chinese culture had a dominant influence on Korean culture for centuries, its influence has been steadily weakening in the 20th century. Korea was under the Japanese control for 36 years (1910-1945). After World War II, Korea established a democratic form of government by modeling after Western systems. This system of government had derailed by the military dictatorship in the early 1960s, which launched a series of successful economic development plans. As Korean people prospered, they demanded political democratization, which resulted in the creation of a freely elected civilian government in the late 1980s. The effects of industrialization and democratization have been spreading throughout the society. The recent emphasis on globalization and regionalization (localization) has further accelerated the pace of change. All these changes seem to have had a profound impact on the newly emerging Korean national culture.

6.3.1 Changing Family Values

As Korea has been transformed into a rapidly urbanizing industrial society, the traditional extended family system has given way to a nuclear family system. Accommodating aging parents in a small apartment is extremely difficult and impractical for a young or growing family. Additionally, the preference for the nuclear family system is rapidly increasing. A study that the authors conducted at the Tonyang Nylon Company (TNC) in 1995 indicated that a large percentage of 300 employees surveyed (200 production workers and 100 managers) prefer a nuclear family over an extended family (71 percent of managers and 43 percent of workers). The shift of preference toward the nuclear family system implies that many traditional family values are changing: the concept of filial piety is weakening; ancestor worship is becoming less prevalent; respect for elders is becoming less evident; and the importance of harmony within a family is decreasing.

In work organizations, paternalistic authoritarianism is now being questioned. Most workers today feel that they should follow formal work-related directives form their superiors, but they do not feel obligated to comply with personal demands of their supervisors. The survey at TNC found that only 17 percent of the workers surveyed said that they would comply with the personal demands of their superiors, while 44 percent said they would reject. Asked about their willingness to follow the opinions of their elders, only 21 percent of the TNC employees showed their willingness to follow, while 52 percent were unwilling and 27 had no opinion. These findings suggest that superiors and senior employees no longer command obedience from their subordinates without legitimate causes.

6.3.2 Changing Gender Roles

Gender roles are gradually changing too. Recent economic and social changes have affected traditional gender roles, opening job opportunities for women and increasing the number of working couples. However, employment opportunities for woman in Korean businesses are still limited. Not only is Korea's chauvinistic culture a major hindrance, but also the attitude toward work on the part of Korean women limits employment opportunities. A recent survey by Korea Employers Federation reveals that Korean women generally lack commitment to their job. The average tenure of female workers is 3.8 years, compared to 6.2 years for male counterparts (KEF, 1995). One reason for the short tenure of women employees is that once married they are unable to continue working. Another reason is that Korean employers are unwilling to accept married women as workers. Seventy percent of over 300 Korean firms surveyed cited the short tenure of women workers and the reluctance of Korean employers to hire married women as the two most important factors in limiting job opportunities for women (*Korea Economic Daily*, January 10, 1995, p. 15).

The general attitude of Korean employees toward women managers is also changing. The TNC study revealed that forty percent of TNC employees surveyed (40 percent of managers and 40 percent of workers) were willing to accept a woman superior, while 24 percent (25 percent of managers and 24 percent of workers) rejected the idea and 36 percent (35 percent of managers and 36 percent of workers) had no opinion. Considering the fact that Korea is still a male-dominated society, the acceptance of female supervisory authority, although not overwhelming, is an encouraging development. A Korean Chamber of Commerce and Industry (KCCI) study revealed somewhat more positive results in regard to women's roles in Korean businesses. According to the KCCI study, 64 percent of Korean workers think that women should work if they can find a job, and 75 percent of them do not mind working for a woman superior (Shin, 1991, pp. 55-56, 74-75). These findings suggest that, although Korean companies are still very much male-dominated, women's roles in Korean businesses are gaining acceptance.

6.3.3 Changing *Yon-go* Relations

The *yon-go* relation is still strong in Korean society as well as work organizations. But attitude towards the *yon-go* relation and its effect on nepotism and favoritism is questioned. One study reported that 52 percent of Korean workers are willing to tolerate the *yon-go* relationship, while the rest reject it (Shin, 1991). Older workers are more willing to accept it than younger employees. People generally reject nepotism and favoritism, but they tolerate the *yon-go* relationship because it has been part of their cultural tradition. The most important *yon-go* bases are still family, alumni, and region.

Yon-go relations are commonly accepted in Korean society because people feel close and psychologically secure when they are with people they know as family members or friends. These relations can be easily seen in hiring and promoting people. However, such managerial practices are likely to decline in the future because of the increasing need for hiring capable individuals in an age of unlimited competition. The survival instinct will force Korean companies to seek capable individuals over people who provide a psychological comfort zone. Korean *chaebols* have been making efforts to avoid relation-based managerial practices (see Chapter 7).

Efforts to avoid relation-based managerial practices seem to be paying off. The TNC study showed that TNC employees do not consider *yon-go* relationships based on school and region as decisive factors for career success. Only 16 percent of the TNC employees surveyed (8 percent of managers and 20 percent of workers) cited *yon-go* as the most important or the second most important factor of career success. Most TNC employees surveyed cited individual ability, effort, and interpersonal competence as major factors determining one's career success.

6.3.4 Ability-based Career Success

As noted earlier, educational achievement has been considered the most important factor leading to career success in a traditional Confucian culture. However, the importance that Koreans place upon education for career success is not as strong as it used to be. For example, fifty eight percent of the employees surveyed at TNC agreed that education was critical to career success, while 22 percent disagreed. Twenty percent of TNC employees showed only a lukewarm attitude toward education. About 70 percent of the TNC employees surveyed cited ability and effort as either the most important or the second most important factor for career success. Thirty-nine percent also cited interpersonal competence as the most important or the next most important career success factor.

The TNC research findings are generally consistent with other studies. The KCCI study found that 62 percent of Korean workers rated individual ability more important than luck and opportunity, and 54 percent of them cited individual effort as the most important factor for career success. This study also revealed that 30 percent of Korean workers rated interpersonal competencies the most important factor, and only 13 percent cited luck as the most important factor to career success (Shin, 1991, pp. 32-34). On the other hand, the study found that only 29 percent of Korean workers rated education as the most critical success factor, compared to 58 percent of the TNC employees in our study.

These studies generally indicate that Korean employees recognize the importance of education and *yon-go* relationships as important career success factors, but they consider individual factors such as ability, effort, and interpersonal competence more important. While managers and workers in the industry emphasize individual attributes over the *yon-go* relationship for career success, university students think differently. A recent study of 3,500 students at a major Korean university revealed that 47 percent of the students think that the *yon-go* relationship is still the most important factor to career success. Thirty seven percent cited individual ability; seven percent gave education as the most important success factor (*Hankook Ilbo*, March 8, 1995, p. 29).

6.4 Value Systems of Korean Workers

In previous sections, we reviewed the influence of Confucianism on Korean culture and how this Confucian culture has changed in recent decades in response to the influence of industrialization and rapid economic growth. In the following sections, we will examine the effects of these economical, political, and social changes on employee attitudes toward their work, work ethics, co-workers, company, corporate culture, and managerial practices.

6.4.1 Concept of Work and Work Ethics

The concept of work among Korean employees has undergone changes during the past three decades. In the 1960s and 1970s, there was a strong consensus among Koreans for economic development and improving the standard of living. Korean employees were willing to work hard for long hours to achieve the national goal. However, in the 1980s when per capita income approached the $4,000 level and higher, the motivation of Korean employees for hard work declined markedly while their desire for leisure increased. One study reveals that in the 1960s and 1970s nearly 60 percent of Korean employees were willing to work hard regardless of their earnings, but, in the 1980s, less than 30 percent showed strong motivation to work (Shin, 1991).

Not only did the motivation of Korean employees to work hard decline, but they also began to avoid dirty, dangerous, and difficult work altogether. This avoidance is commonly known as the "3-D syndrome." It became extremely difficult for Korean firms to fill jobs that demand hard work under strenuous conditions. Small and medium-sized business firms, requiring intensive labor, were particularly hard hit by the 3-D syndrome. To fill the void, more than 50,000 workers from developing countries like China, Vietnam, Sri Lanka, Pakistan, and Philippines were working in Korea by 1995 (*Hankook Ilbo*, April 13, 1995, p. 2). The number of imported laborers, both legal and illegal, is estimated to be about 100,000 workers in 1996.

Changes in work ethic of Korean employees are also evident in their desire for shorter work hours and more leisure time. As late as 1978, Korean workers worked an average of 54 hours a week (KEF, 1995, p. 659). Working long hours was no doubt a competitive advantage for Korean businesses in the world market. But, the number of hours worked began to decline in the late 1980s was down to 45 hours per week by 1994. Korean employees are now reluctant to stay for a few more hours to complete unfinished work, and factory supervisors have to beg workers to work overtime. Koreans have been working half-days on Saturday, but the number of Korean firms taking every other or every third Saturday off has been increasing in recent years.

Work hours are also being adjusted to better suit workers' personal lives. Samsung led the way with the implementation of a new work hour schedule (7:00 am to 4:00 pm) in 1993. They contend that a strict enforcement of the 7-4 work hour schedule would increase quality as well as productivity, and would also enhance workers' quality of living. Flexible work hours are another change, being adopted by an increasing number of Korean firms in recent years. LG (Lucky Goldstar) Electronics recently instituted a flexible work hour system, which allows office workers to begin work between 7:00 and 10:00 am in the morning and to leave for home between 4:00 to 7:00 pm in the evening after completing eight hours of work.

The changing work ethic is also evident in occupational preferences of Korean people. Job seekers generally preferred employment in manufacturing industries, especially in large reputable firms, during the period of rapid economic growth in the 1960s and the 1970s. Since then, manufacturing jobs have lost their appeal and have been replaced by jobs in service organizations and financial institutions as desirable occupations. According to a recent survey by Recruit, an employment information service organization in Korea, the jobs most preferred by prospective college graduates are in broadcasting, computer/software engineering, and strategic planning in large businesses (*Moonwha Daily*, March 4, 1995, p. 21). Jobs in state-owned public enterprises, foreign trade, public accounting, public relations, security analysis, and government are also highly preferred.

The change in work values and work ethics also defy traditional Confucianism. Scholars (professors), civil service officials, doctors, and lawyers are still respected, but they are no longer the most preferred occupations nor do they command the highest social status. Jobs in commerce (management), engineering, art, and entertainment used to have low social status in the traditional Confucian culture, but they now have emerged as highly preferred professions.

6.4.2 Attitudes Toward Company

The organization where one works occupies an important part in one's life. An employee's attitude toward an organization, his or her expectation of the organization, and his or her behavior are affected by how the employee sees and identifies with the organization. The survey at TNC suggests that Korean workers closely identify with their company. Eighty-one percent of the TNC employees surveyed perceived their company as "a second home;" only 4 percent rejected the second home concept, and 15 percent did not feel strongly one way or the other. TNC employees also closely related the company's growth directly with their own individual progress. Sixty-four percent of TNC employees surveyed agreed that the company's growth would enhance their own growth; 9 percent disagreed, and 26 percent showed a lukewarm attitude. Managers generally showed a stronger identification with the company than did production workers.

The TNC study is generally consistent with the KCCI study which reveals over 90 percent of Korean workers perceive their workplace as "a second home." The KCCI study, however, pointed out that the psychological closeness of Korean employees toward their company has weakened over the years (Shin, 1991, pp. 193-195). It appears that the strong tendency of Korean employees to see their work place as "a second home" came from the traditional Confucian concept of the extended family. But, that strong bond has been modified by the rapid economic, social, and technological changes in recent decades. The weakening bond between employees and their company is particularly important, as it affects the employees' loyalty and commitment to their company and work.

6.4.3 Employee Loyalty and Commitment

Although Korean employees strongly identify themselves with the company and perceive their work place as "a second home," their loyalty and lifetime commitment to their company appear to be less strong than in the past. The survey at TNC showed that only 15 percent of the employees surveyed were willing to put the company ahead of their personal life; 53 percent were not willing to sacrifice their personal life for the company, and 32 percent had no opinion. As expected, the reluctance to sacrifice for the company was greater among production workers than among managers; only 10 percent of workers as opposed to 26 percent of managers were willing to sacrifice their personal life, and 61 percent of workers as compared to 33 percent of managers were unwilling. The KCCI study also found that 68 percent of Korean workers put their family ahead of the company (Shin, 1991, pp. 30, 157-162).

Life-time commitment to the company is also weaker now than in the past. Fifty-four percent of the employees surveyed were prepared to leave the company if better offers were made to them, while only 18 percent expressed a life-time commitment to the company. Again, workers showed greater willingness to leave the company than managers. Sixty-two percent of workers, compared to 38 percent of managers, were prepared to leave, while only 14 percent of workers and 25 percent of managers expressed life-time commitment. The lack of life-time commitment to the company was not the result of employee dissatisfaction or low morale. TNC is one of the 15 largest Korean *chaebols*. As such, it is one of the more respected and well-paying employers (Kim, 1992).

Although Korean employees do not show strong loyalty to their company, they show a strong willingness to work hard and work late if it is required. Eighty-one percent of TNC employees (94 percent of managers and 73 percent of workers) expressed their willingness to work overtime, while 6 percent (2 percent of managers and 8 percent of workers) expressed their reluctance. Thirteen percent (4 percent of managers and 19 percent of workers) had no opinion. The KCCI study found that 76 percent of Korean workers expressed their willingness to work overtime (Shin, 1991, pp. 193-197).

These findings indicate that loyalty and life-time commitment of Korean employees to their company are on the decline. It appears that the lack of loyalty and life-time commitment are more prevalent among younger workers than among their elders. It also can be speculated that young Korean employees do not expect or wish to remain employed in the same company until their retirement. Most Korean college students expect to change their job several times during their career. Loyalty and life-commitment, which have been traditionally associated with Korean employees, are no longer strong social norms.

6.4.4 Group Norms and Conformity

It is generally understood that Korean employees have strongly group-oriented values. For example, Hofstede's study on national cultures categorizes Korea as a collectively oriented culture, more so than Japan (Hofstede, 1983). However, a number of studies point out that Koreans tend to be more individualistic than Japanese (Kusayanagi, 1980; Kim, 1982; Chang and Chang, 1994, pp. 45-46). The study at TNC revealed that TNC employees generally respect group opinions and are generally willing to comply with group decisions. They also feel compelled to help out their co-workers at times of increased workload. Sixty-five percent of TNC employees stated that they are willing to go along with the group opinion even though they might not agree with it. Only 11 percent said they would oppose the group opinion, if they did not like it; 24 percent were reluctant to respond in one way or another.

The fact that only 11 percent of TNC employees reject group opinion suggests a strong group orientation among Korean employees. Conforming to a group opinion, however, does not necessarily mean that one agrees with it. For example, TNC employees are generally willing to conform to group opinions, but as many as one third of them desire opportunities to express their own opinions. The KCCI study also found that 85 percent of Korean workers are willing to go along with group opinion, but as many as 43 percent of them desire opportunities to voice their own views different from group opinion (Shin, 1991, pp. 70-71).

These findings suggest that individual opinions of Korean employees are in many times suppressed, either because not enough opportunities to participate are allowed or because they are simply submissive to authority. Or, they may be willing to suppress their own opinion for the sake of group harmony. Whatever the reason, the group orientation of Korean employees, shown through their conformity to group opinions, is not a genuine consensus. In the absence of a real group consensus, there is room for individualistic attitude and behavior.

The high level of conformity of Korean employees to group opinion indicates that they are not oriented toward "Jeffersonian" individualism. Group conformity without strong group consensus is not necessarily the "melting-pot" type of group either. The melting pot group implies a strong common identity. Rather, Koreans are oriented toward what Chang and Chang call a "salad bowl" type of group, in which each of the group members shows his or her own identity (Chang and Chang, 1994, pp. 47-49).

The "salad bowl" phenomenon directly relates to the individualistic attitude and behavior of Korean employees in group situations. In the absence of a clear superordinate goal, individual members seek their own individual interests. As a result, teamwork and cooperation among group members are weak and unpredictable. *Yon-go* relations are adopted in Korean firms to promote the "melting pot" work group. But since group members who are not a part of *yon-go* relations are likely to be excluded, *yon-go* can work against group cohesiveness.

So far we have discussed how Korean culture has been changing and how the value orientation of Korean employees is being affected by it. Rapid industrialization, massive urbanization, democratization and liberalization, globalization and the information revolution have all contributed to a weakening of traditional Confucianism in Korea. The traditional extended family system is giving way to the nuclear family system; obedience to superiors and elders is diminishing; the work ethic is disappearing; and rigidly fixed gender roles are slowly loosening.

While most Koreans tolerate *yon-go* relations, they still believe that individual ability and effort are the most important career success factors. Although most Korean employees identify themselves with the company and perceive the company as "a second home," they do not show strong loyalty or life-time commitment to the company. While most Korean employees are willing to obey their superiors and elders on formal work-related matters, they are unwilling to obey them on other matters. While Korean employees are willing to conform to a group opinion, they want to have opportunities to voice their own views.

Such behavioral patterns of Korean employees indicate that their value orientation reflects both traditional Confucianism and new Western values. The co-existence of Confucian and Western cultures in the value orientation of Korean employees means that traditional Confucianism is weakening or is being modified by the newly emerging values of industrialism and democracy. We will see in the next section how both traditional and new values co-exist in formulating and maintaining the corporate culture of Korean firms.

6.5 Corporate Culture: Shared Values

A convenient starting point for understanding the corporate culture of Korean firms is to study the *sahoon*, which can be translated "company credos." Basically, a *sahoon* could be called a company motto or slogan. It could be called management ideology or core value and beliefs. A *Sahoon* generally consists of a few words or short phrases which best express the company's most important values and beliefs. In Korean firms, the *sahoon* is often written with beautifully crafted calligraphy, nicely framed, and hung on the walls of executive offices, conference rooms, training centers, and major work areas. It also appears on the first pages of company brochures, operating manuals, training texts, diaries, directories, and important company publications.

Thus, the *sahoon* is the formal statement of managerial values that a Korean firm considers most important. It corresponds to basic values in American firms: "customer service" in IBM, MBWA (Managing By Wandering Around) in Hewlett Packard, and "innovation" in 3M Company. In many Korean firms, the *sahoon* reflects the personal values, beliefs, and philosophies of their founders. It serves as a general guide for company management and a "guiding spirit" for employee behaviors. It is especially important in indoctrination training of new employees and in shaping their attitudes. Thus, the *sahoon* plays an important role in shaping the corporate culture of Korean business.

6.5.1 *Sahoon* in Korean Firms

As pointed out earlier, *sahoon* reflects the cultural values, personal values and beliefs of the founder and top management. Until recently, *inhwa* (meaning harmony) and unity were the most common values emphasized in the *sahoon* in Korean firms. Sincerity and diligence, and entrepreneurship and development were also frequently emphasized. Other values reflected in a typical *sahoon,* but with much less frequency, were credibility, work responsibility, and productivity and quality. Only a few Korean firms included such values as rationality, sacrifice, and service in their *sahoon.*

Unlike American companies, which generally emphasize their values in terms of functional and technical performance such as customer service, innovation, and product excellence, the *sahoon* in Korean firms traditionally emphasize the attitude and behavior expected of employees among themselves, toward the company, and to society. This is one of the reasons why traditional cultural values (collectivism and loyalty) are frequently stated in the *sahoon* of Korean firms. In small and medium-size Korean firms which are more traditionally managed, such values as *inhwa*, sincerity and diligence tend to appear more often in their *sahoon* than in large Korean firms where modern management methods are practiced. The *inhwa*-oriented values also tend to predominate in *sahoon* of low performance Korean companies as compared to relatively high performing Korean companies (Lee, 1989, pp. 113-116).

Economic development, democratization, and globalization, in recent years have brought about changes in the value orientations of Korean business employees as well as in shared values and *sahoon*. Although *inhwa* oriented values are still most widely emphasized, performance oriented values such as customer service, challenge, and innovation are increasingly emphasized in *sahoon*. The more the company is future and globally oriented, the greater the emphasis placed upon the new values. Here are some illustrations of shared values and *sahoon* in major Korean *chaebols* (Exhibit 6.1).

Exhibit 6.1: Shared Values of Korean *Chaebols*

Chaebol Group	Shared Values or Official *Sahoon*
Samsung	Respect for individual, pursuit of technology, and empowerment
Hyundai	Diligence, thriftiness, trust, and affection
LG	Value creation for customers, respect for individual, and empowerment
Daewoo	Creativity, challenge, and sacrifice
Sunkyong	Humanism, rationalism, and realism
Ssangyong	Trust, credibility, innovativeness, and *inhwa*
Hanjin	Service, credibility, and progressiveness
Hyosung	Service, sincerity, innovativeness, and unity
Hanwha	Trust, credibility, modesty, and excellence
Lotte	Honesty, integrity, service, and passion
Daelim	Creativity, cooperation, and responsibility

Source: Company brochures of various business groups in Korea.

Samsung Group. With 180,000 employees, Samsung is the Korea's largest *chaebol* group. Since its incorporation in 1938, Samsung's shared values were built around *cheil-joo-ee*, meaning "firstism" or "being the best." The traditional Samsung *sahoon* consisted of principle which stressed responsibility to the nation through business, respect for human resources, and pursuit of rational management. It was Samsung's ideal to be in the business that people want, to recognize that employees themselves are the company, and to become the best company in Korea in terms of organization, management, and manpower. The core values behind the Samsung's *sahoon* were: entrepreneurial spirit, ethical mind, excellence, perfection, and spirit of co-existence (prosperity shared with employees). Samsung's *sahoon* were taken from the personal values and beliefs of the founder, B.C. Lee, and they had guided Samsung's management until recently.

As Samsung became more globalized in an increasingly competitive world market, Chairman K.H. Lee, the successor to the founder, initiated a drastic change in the overall orientation of Samsung's core values. After taking over the Group in 1987, Chairman Lee instituted Samsung's "New Management" and declared the new core values to be "respect for the individual, pursuit of technology, and empowerment." He also stated that Samsung's new corporate ethos would be built around the slogans of "together with the customer," "challenge to the world," and "orientation toward the future." He changed the Samsung Group's logo to stress its global outlook, and declared "Quality Management" as the first principle needed for Samsung to become a "super first class" business.

Hyundai Group. Hyundai employs 160,000 people and is the Korea's second largest *chaebol* group. Hyundai's *sahoon* are diligence, thriftiness, and mutual trust and affection. It also reflects the personal values and beliefs of the founder, J.Y. Chung. Chung also instituted in Hyundai employees a "Can-Do" spirit and a positive attitude of "creating something from nothing." Hyundai's positive attitudes and can-do spirit were amply demonstrated in the firm's construction of a huge shipbuilding dock on barren land in Ulsan and its building of a ship even before the dock was completed all in a matter of few years. Other accomplishments were construction work in the Middle East desert where nobody had previously attempted and the successful exporting Excel automobiles to North America in 1986 when Korea was still a developing country. While challenge, entrepreneurial risk-taking, aggressiveness, and positive attitude are visible characteristics of Hyundai employees, Hyundai's management emphasizes sincerity, thriftiness, and collectivism.

LG Group. LG (Lucky-Goldstar) Group is the third largest *chaebol* group in Korea. It has 100,000 employees in the areas of chemicals, electric, communications, electronics, trade, and others. LG has been particularly well known in Korea for its *inhwa* oriented culture. *Inhwa* was the personal philosophy of the founder, I.H. Koo, and it has served as the guiding principle among the family members whom he had brought into management since the business was established in 1947. The traditional LG *sahoon* also emphasized research/development and entrepreneurial spirit, but *inhwa* has been the most important value for the past three decades.

However, in the late 1980s, LG's *inhwa* oriented culture was not contributing to the unity among its employees needed for the company to successfully compete in the globalizing business environment. Rather, *inhwa* was promoting a conservative, complacent, and inward-looking culture. In order to change LG's corporate culture, Chairman C.K. Koo, son of the founder, began a bold cultural revolution in 1987 by making sweeping changes in organizational structure and management practices. Many senior family members were relieved of major executive responsibilities. LG then adopted the concepts of "value creation for customers," "respect for the individual," and "empowerment" as new core corporate core values. It took several years for the new values to be accepted by LG employees and the new corporate culture to become firmly established.

Daewoo Group. Established in 1967, the Daewoo Group has achieved spectacular growth, emerging as the fourth largest *chaebol* group in Korea. In fact, Daewoo may best symbolize Korea's rapid economic and industrial growth. Daewoo's core values are entrepreneurial spirit, challenge, and sacrifice. Again, these are all personal values and beliefs of the founder, W.C. Kim. These values were evident in a series of daring moves by the founder in the 1970s and 1980s. In these moves, W.C. Kim took over bankrupt companies in strategic industries, and turned them into profitable businesses. Daewoo Motors, Daewoo Heavy Industries, Ockpo Shipbuilding, and Daewoo Electronics were all near bankrupt at one time before being acquired by the Group. Daewoo's commitment to challenge and entrepreneurial spirit have led it to become one of the most active *chaebol* groups in international joint ventures and business alliances. Many bright and highly educated executives and managers have helped Daewoo's rapid growth and globalization. W.C. Kim is known as the busiest and most "workaholic" of all *chaebol* group chairmen.

Sunkyong Group. The corporate ethos of Sunkyong, Korea's fifth largest *chaebol* group, stresses management practices that reflect humanistic values, rationality, and business realism. But, the most important shared value at Sunkyong is vitality, which is central to a concept sometimes called "Sunkyongmanship." "SK Manship" emphasizes creative and progressive thinking, positive and tenacious effort, and drive for perfection. It has become a model for the training and socialization of new employees and in shaping their basic attitude and behavior.

Ssangyong Group. In Ssangyong, Korea's sixth largest *chaebol* group, traditional core values were national service, *inhwa*, and *chung-doh* (meaning `right way'). These values came from the founder, S.K. Kim. As Ssangyong diversified its businesses not only in cement, oil, and paper manufacturing but into such high technological areas as automobile, engineering, machineries, and computer services, a new corporate culture to match the diversification strategy was needed. Under the leadership of S.W. Kim, son of the founder, Ssangyong adopted a new corporate culture in 1986. The new core values include trust and credibility, innovation and change, and *inhwa*. The movement toward this new corporate *sahoon* is still going strong under the new leadership of S.J. Kim, another son of the founder. S.J. Kim has recently added a new emphasis on globalization.

Hyosung Group. Hyosung, another leading *chaebol* group, has also modified its core values in recent years to better adapt itself to the changing business environment. The core values stressed in the original *sahoon* were sincerity, diligence, and service responsibility. These reflected the beliefs of the founder, H.J. Cho. As Hyosung diversified its businesses from textile to heavy industries, high-tech chemicals, and computers, the traditional values proved to be not very conducive to success in the new ventures. Therefore, in an attempt to transform the Group into a more innovative and outward-looking culture, S.R. Cho, the founder's son, has been modifying Hyosung's *sahoon* by putting heavy emphasis on creativity and developing positive attitude.

6.5.2 *Sahoon* and Corporate Culture

We have looked at the official *sahoon* of major Korean *chaebol* groups. How much these *chaebol* groups strictly observe their official values in daily management practices is debatable. Evidence thus far suggests that Korean firms are making a honest effort to instill their core management values and beliefs in their employees. *Sahoon* values are used as a guide for training and supervising employees as well as evaluating their performance. Samsung's "being the best," Hyundai's "Can-Do" spirit, and Daewoo's entrepreneurial spirit are all derived from their *sahoons* and reflect their distinct corporate cultures.

Although the specific values emphasized in a corporation's *sahoon* are different, the *sahoons* themselves have some common characteristics. First, as explained earlier, the *sahoon* reflects the personal values, beliefs, and philosophies of the founder or his successors. This concept is similar to the corporate values found in American companies. IBM's management creed (respect for the individual, customer service, and excellence) were originally formulated by the founder, Thomas Watson, Sr. (Rodgers, 1986). Hewlett Packard's 'HP Way'(MBWA) was originally articulated by the founders, William Hewlett and David Packard (Hewlett and Packard, 1980). But, in Korean firms, the *sahoon* carries a much deeper meaning for employees; it goes beyond the mere articulation of management philosophies. In Korea, a firm's *sahoon* is analogous to a family's creed.

Second, the values expressed in a *sahoon* are generally congruent with the values of the national culture. Therefore, changes in the national culture bring about changes in values reflected in the *sahoon*. Because of the influence of traditional Confucian culture, a *sahoon* typically emphasized such values as *inhwa*, sincerity and diligence. Such a *sahoon* basically dealt with employee attitudes and behavior related to collectivism, harmony, and order. However, cultural changes and increasing global competition in recent years have caused changes in *sahoon* values in many Korean business firms. The general direction of change is toward more performance-oriented values such as customer service, respect for the individual, and empowerment.

Changes in *sahoon* in Korean business have an especially significant implications. As much as a *sahoon* reflects the personal values and beliefs of the founder, the successor makes utmost efforts to preserve it out of respect for the founder. If the successor attempts to change the company's *sahoon,* he or she should have compelling reasons for and commitment toward new management direction. In this respect, the changes in corporate values in recent years have significant implications for the new direction of corporate culture in Korean businesses. Many Korean firms are already undertaking changes in their *sahoon*, similar to those of Samsung and LG, placing greater emphasis upon performance-oriented values and de-emphasizing traditional *inhwa*-oriented values.

6.6 Management Style

Thus far we have discussed the value orientation of Korean employees and the shared values of Korean business. In this section, we will study the management style of Korean firms, influenced by the Korean corporate culture. The characteristics of Korean management are management by owner-managers, centralized organization and management, and authoritarian leadership. We will discuss each one of these characteristics in conjunction with Korean national and corporate cultures.

6.6.1 Management by Owner-Managers

One of the unique features of Korean businesses is that owners actively participate in management. In Western societies, as a business firm grows, ownership and management are separated, and management is left to professional managers. This has not yet occurred in Korean *chaebols*. In Korean businesses, the founders and their families are directly involved with day-to-day managerial responsibilities. In Hyundai, for example, the founder's family, his brother (S.Y. Chung) and his seven sons have taken charge of the Group. In LG, a few dozens of members of the founder's family hold executive positions, including the Group Chairmanship. In Samsung and Daewoo, there are not as many of owner's family members actively participating in the management of the Groups as there are in Hyundai and LG, but the founder's family members are able to exert just as powerful control over internal management as do family members in Hyundai or LG.

Business expansion requires additional capital and human resources, and it becomes increasingly difficult for the owner to meet the financial and executive manpower requirements internally with his own and family resources. As a result, the owner begins to depend on the outside capital market by issuing stocks and also begins to put hired managers in charge of management. As business expansion with equity financing continues, ownership is dispersed among many stockholders, and management is gradually delegated to professional managers. Intense competition and pressure to meet the demands of all stakeholders (customers, employees, labor unions, creditors, suppliers, governments and others) will further increase the need of capable professional managers.

However, in Korean firms, there has been no separation between ownership and management or professionalization of management. The ownership of most Korean businesses, large and small, is not only concentrated in the hands of founder's family, but the family also controls management. Even in the largest *chaebol* groups, the owner and his family have a substantial share of ownership control. As shown in Chapter 3, in 1995 the owner families of the 30 largest Korean business groups possessed on the average 10.5 percent of the total outstanding stock and group member companies owned 32.4 percent through cross-shareholdings, making the effective controlling share 43.3 percent.

There are some cultural and economic factors underlying the owner-manager management system in Korean businesses. First, as explained earlier, the Korean family system is based on strict blood-lineage and a system of inheritance favoring the eldest son tend to preserve the ownership and management control within the family (Hattori, 1989). Koreans strongly feel that business ownership should be preserved within the owner family, and inability to do so is thought of as a disgrace and dishonor to the family and to older generations who built the business.

Second, until recently Korea did not have a private capital market with which to finance business expansion. Banks were the only major source of funds. Hence, debt-financing was the traditional method of additional funding in Korean businesses, and the owners were able to maintain their ownership share through debt financing. This partially explains why most Korean businesses have a very high debt-equity ratio, over 10:1 in some cases.

Third, the Korean government protected Korean firms from foreign competition and provided them with financial and administrative support. In this sheltered environment, the need for capable professional managers for successful business management was not as great as it would have been under open competition. As a result, the owners were able to manage their growing business without professional management. However, globalization and trade liberalization have brought increased competition to Korean businesses in recent years, and capable professional managers are now becoming critical to business success.

Finally, *chaebols* are defended on the basis of their contribution to Korea's economic success. *Chaebols* have provided vast employment opportunities to Korean people and have contributed immensely to economic development. Korea's impressive economic performance was attributed partially to the family ownership of Korean businesses, which promoted stability and continuity, and protected *chaebol* companies from a hostile takeovers. These companies have also been free from any pressure from conflicting stockholder interests, and have not been pressed for quick short-term performance as in the case of many U.S. corporations. Consequently, they have been able to concentrate their energies on long-term survival strategies. Also, *chaebol* groups have been able to mobilize large resources for big and audacious business projects that a single firm would have been unable to undertake.

6.6.2 Centralized Managerial Structure

One of the most striking features of Korean organizations is the high degree of centralization and formalization of their managerial practices. Centralization means the degree of authority concentrated at upper levels of organizational hierarchies. Formalization means the degree of explicit rules and regulations governing employee's work behavior, roles, and role relations with others (Scott, 1992, pp. 18, 23-24). In most Korean firms, decision-making power and authority are concentrated in the higher echelons of managerial hierarchies. The strong "power distance" and "uncertainty avoidance" of Korean culture as observed by Hofstede (1983) seem to foster centralization and formalization of Korean firms.

The degree of concentration of authority among owner-managers varies form firm to firm. One study of 108 Korean business groups in 1987 found that as many as 8.8 percent of top executives were members of the owner's family. The proportion of owner-managers in the ten largest *chaebol* groups was 2.7 percent, as compared to 10.9 percent in smallest groups (Jung, 1989, pp. 126-127). It is estimated that the proportion of owner-managers in Korean business groups has decreased somewhat because businesses have expanded substantially since the study was conducted. However, the concentration of owner-managers in comparatively smaller business groups has not changed.

Major decisions, especially those requiring expenditures, usually go through formal procedures of *kyul-jae,* meaning the "approval from upper levels of management." The formal approval process could provide a mechanism for discussions and consultations among employees and managers throughout the organizational hierarchy, but it has not been used as such. *Kyul-jae* is similar to *ringi* in Japanese firms, but the former is considered to be more of a means for exercising authority and control than asking for consultation and participation that characterizes the latter.

Along with vertical and hierarchical control, Korean firms generally emphasize strong functional control, such as planning, finance, and personnel. Many Korean firms have pursued a policy of "rational management" during business expansion. In the process, they have established specialized staff departments with strong planning and control functions under the direction of the chief executive. The Planning and Coordinating Department under the Chairman (in case of *chaebol* groups) is especially strong.

This department formulates strategic plans and implements by controlling the allocations of internal resources (people, money, technology, information, and others) throughout the group or the company. The vertical concentration of decision-making authority at upper levels, especially on or around the owner-managers and their close associates, and the horizontal concentration of planning and control functions in staff departments lead to a centralized and functionalized bureaucratic organizational structure.

Korean firms generally have a "tall" structure with many hierarchical levels. In a control-oriented structure, the span of control (meaning the number of subordinates under a supervisor) is generally narrow. In addition, Korean firms seldom employ a personal staff with the exception of the Group Chairman or President. For other executives, Korean firms tend to employ deputy or assistant managers in line positions, thus increasing the number of vertical hierarchies and contributing to a tall centralized structure.

6.6.3 Informal Power Groups

Besides the concentration of authority at the upper levels of management, especially around owner-managers, professional managers constitute other power groups in Korean firms. Since the 1970s when many Korean firms began hiring their employees through open competition on the basis of ability and qualification, the number of *tobagi* managers has steadily increased. *Tobagi* means literally a native or a long career employee who joined the company through open competition hiring and has stayed with the company for a long time.

In many business groups, *tobagi* managers form elite power structure, and they are able to exercise significant influence over company management through interpersonal networks they have cultivated with other managers throughout their long tenure within the company. A study of 108 Korean business groups in 1987 revealed that *tobagi* managers constituted about 16 percent of all top management personnel (21 percent in large *chaebols* and about 13 percent in smaller business groups (Jung, 1989, p.27). The percentage of *tobagi* managers is estimated to have increased substantially in the nine years since the survey was conducted.

Yon-go relationships among the *tobagi* managers play an important role in the formation of informal power groups. It is common in Korean firms to find that owners bring in their school friends or home-town friends to management position in addition to bringing in their close family relatives.

In some Korean firms, the top management group is dominated by executives who have graduated from a certain school or by executives who are from a certain geographical area. In Daewoo, a dozen or so of the most powerful group executives are graduates of the elite Kyung-gi High School, which is also Chairman W.C. Kim's alma mater. And in Kumho Group, many executives and managers are from Honam (Chul-la Province), the southwestern region of Korea.

In a *yon-go* group, the relationships among members are largely determined by age. Older employees have the status of *sun-bae* (a senior), and younger ones the status of *hoo-bae* (a junior). In the case of school-related *yon-go* group, the *sun-bae* and *hoo-bae* relationship is determined by the year of entrance to or graduation from the school. Members of the same class share special comradeship among themselves with a strong emotional bond. Thus, *yon-go* relations play an important part in informal relations among employees. These relations are further carried over to the formation of cliques and power groups. Needless to say, *yon-go* relations affect employees' social interactions and personnel decisions and often result in nepotism and favoritism in many Korean organizations.

6.6.4 Leadership and Communication

Another common characteristic of Korean management style isauthoritarian but paternalistic leadership, reinforced by a clear hierarchical order and vertical communication. Authoritarian leadership is an expected managerial behavior in a hierarchy-based Confucian culture. It is further enhanced by the centralized managerial structure found in Korean firms and by the generally obedient and passive attitude of Korean subordinates. The authoritarian behavior of Korean managers is not strictly leader-centered but is more often task-centered to accomplish certain work goals. Authoritarian leadership is also associated with a national culture characterized by a strong "power distance" between superiors and subordinates (Hofstede, 1983).

Although the overall organizational structure is centralized and planning/controlling functions are formalized, individual jobs are not formally structured. Korean firms usually do not have formal job descriptions or job specifications, and work assignments and individual responsibilities are largely determined by supervisors. While the absence of job descriptions often causes such inefficiency as duplication of work or uneven distribution of workloads among employees, it increases flexibility in work assignments, allowing speedy adaptation to changing work conditions. In such an unstructured environment, the performance of a work unit greatly depends on the manager's ability to get things done with the support of his or her superiors and subordinates.

A bureaucratic organization, characterized by centralization and functionalization, requires exceptional leadership. Because most critical decisions are made at the top, top management must possess technical as well as interpersonal competency to get the job done. He or she must work long hours and must be able to withstand persistent stress. The research at TNC revealed that 74 percent of employees cited that ability and performance were more important that seniority and experience as qualifications for leadership. Interestingly, more managers than production workers (87 percent vs. 67 percent) felt that ability and performance were more important leader qualifications than seniority and experience. TNC managers also felt that overcoming a bureaucratic work environment and maintaining good human relations as the two most important problems encountered in the leadership process. Sixty-two percent of managers cited bureaucracy as the most or the second most difficult problem to deal with, and 58 percent of them cited human relations as the most or the second most difficult problem. Managing excessive work loads was also seen as a major problem.

Although many Korean firms have shifted their emphasis from *inhwa* to more performance-oriented corporate culture in recent years, achieving harmony with subordinates and maintaining a harmonious work group are still highly valued leadership attributes. In decision-making, Korea managers try to preserve good relations with subordinates and stability within the work group, even if it means sacrificing the group performance at times. Korean managers try hard to attain a unanimous consensus from subordinates. However, subordinates are usually reluctant to express their opinions, expecting that their manager will understand them and accommodate their feelings in his decision. Therefore, Korean managers pay extra attention to their subordinates to understand them as individuals. They make concerted efforts to provide opportunities for informal interactions with subordinates in order to promote mutual trust, understanding, and harmony in the group.

The passive attitude of Korean employees does not mean their unquestioned acceptance of authoritarian leadership. In fact, they prefer leaders who take a consultative approach. Seventy-one percent of TNC employees prefer a consultative leader, while 29 percent show preference for a task-oriented leader "initiating structure." More production workers than managers seem to favor consultative leadership (73.7 percent vs. 63.7 percent).

Effective leadership behavior is of course contingent upon leadership situations: specific task to be accomplished, abilities and motivation of subordinates, and support from higher levels of management (Fiedler, 1967). In general, the predominant leadership style of Korean managers is authoritarian with an emphasis on harmony. However, changes in the value orientation of Korean employees require managers to use a consultative approach in dealing with subordinates. Since authoritarian and consultative styles of leadership are basically incompatible, Korean managers have to change their behaviors to become more consultative. Change in leadership behavior with an emphasis on participation is already taking place in many Korean firms. Labor unions especially are an important factor contributing to the change in leadership behavior at lower echelons.

6.6.5 Organizational Communications

Communications in Korean firms tend to be top-down. The communication process in Korean firms is very much influenced by hierarchical relations, determined not only by formal authority but also by perceived status based on roles, power, age, and seniority (tenure). Vertical communication involves superiors issuing directives and subordinates implementing them. Directives usually lack specificities. Superiors are reluctant to issue detailed directives because such behavior could be interpreted as supervisors not having confidence in subordinates. Subordinates are supposed to understand the intentions of their superiors and carry them out to the best of their capacities. Failure to do so usually constitutes incompetency on the part of subordinates. When the directives are not clear or specific enough, subordinates should make their own assumptions rather than ask their superiors for clarification. This is especially true in formal meetings.

As one can see, open communication and debate between hierarchical levels does not exist in Korean firms. It is not that Koreans oppose open communication, but rather that it occurs in informal communication settings than in formal meetings. This kind of communication behavior seems to be common in a culture that is characterized by high power distance and feminism (Hofstede, 1983). Out of respect for superiors and elders, subordinates are generally reserved in formal meetings and prefer to communicate with their superiors in informal settings.

The lack of specificities in communications and the perceived psychological distance between superiors and subordinates should have contributed to poor communications in Korean firms. In reality, however, communications have rarely emerged as a major problem in Korean firms. A major contributing factor has been that informal relations and *yon-go* relations promote mutual trust and that the close feelings that exist between superiors and subordinates help overcome potential communication problems. Korean employees spend a great deal of energies in developing interpersonal relations with their superiors, subordinates, and co-workers. They often socialize after work and visit the homes of their supervisors on special occasions such as New Year's Day and birthdays. They use such occasions to get to know each other better and build trust. Essentially, Korean firms overcome deficiencies in formal communications through informal communications.

Modern communication technologies such as computers and telecommunications (electronic mailing, computer conferences, and tele-commuting) have brought about many changes in organizational communications in Korean firms. Many routine face-to-face communications have been replaced by modern communication devices, and even many routine *kyul-jae* (approval) procedures are simplified in many Korean firms. But, the utilization of modern information technologies calls for a greater and better coordination among employees, and the importance of face-to-face informal communication has not been diminished. Although the work values and work ethic of Korean employees are changing, the perceived barriers of organizational hierarchies and status differences still exist, inhibiting their open communication. Overcoming communication barriers between hierarchical levels is an important task for Korean managers.

6.7 Summary

Korean culture has been shaped by Confucianism, which stresses harmonious relationships between father and son, husband and wife, young and old, and the king and his subjects. Harmonious relationships are maintained by observing ethical codes that specify mutual obligations for parties involved. Children are required to respect their parents, while parents are obligated to nurture their children with warmth and support. The same kind of obligatory relations exist in other relationship.

Confucian-based culture has influenced the formation of corporate culture in Korean firms. Employers are expected to play the role of father with their employees. Likewise, superiors are expected to command respect from subordinates. In return, the former protect the latter with warmth and support. The Confucian values have helped to develop cohesive and harmonious work groups in Korean firms. When combined with the emphasis on education, Confucianism became an instrument for developing productive work groups.

While Confucianism played a positive role in creating harmonious and productive work groups, it had some negative impact on corporate culture in Korean firms. The Confucian group-oriented culture suppressed individualism. The *yon-go* relationships often promoted favoritism and nepotism in

Korean firms. Confucian exclusionism became a major hindrance to accommodating outsiders. Less productive family members and friends were usually preferred over productive outsiders in the name of maintaining harmony and trust.

Many changes have occurred in Korea's economic, social, and political environments. In turn, these changes have modified the value orientation and work ethic of Korean employees, further affecting the shared values (corporate culture) of Korean firms. Industrialization of the Korean economy changed the value systems and work ethic of Korean employees. Political reform freed Korean workers from suppression. Workers now demand higher wages and more leisure activities. Labor unions challenge managerial prerogatives. Globalization of the economy necessitates hiring of capable employees, signaling an end of nepotism and favoritism in human resource management.

While most Korean employees strongly identify themselves with their company, their loyalty and life-time commitment to the company are not as strong now as they were in the past. Most Korean employees recognize the importance of loyalty, but they are no longer willing to obey their superiors or elders on non-work-related matters. While most Korean employees respect group opinions, they still desire opportunities to express their own views. The traditional work ethic is giving way to having more leisure time.

The *sahoon*, as a formal statement of employees' shared values and management's core ideology, is changing from traditional *inhwa* (harmony) toward one which stresses performance. Most Koreans seem to accept *yon-go* relations, but they recognize the importance of individual ability as career success factor. While business ownership and management control still remain in the hands of owner-managers, the authoritarian leadership style of Korean managers is being replaced with more of consultative and participatory one.

References

Chang, C.S. and Chang, N.J. (1994): *The Korean Managerial System: Cultural, Political, Economic Foundations*. Westport, CT: Quorum.

Cho, D.S. (1994): *Study of Korean Chaebols*. Seoul: Korea Economic Daily.

Collins, J.C. and Porras, J.I. (1994): *Built to Last: Successful Habits of Visionary Companies*. New York: Harper Business.

Fiedler, F.E. (1967): *A Theory of Leadership Effectiveness*. New York: McGraw-Hill.

Harris, P.R. and Moran, R.T. (1987): *Managing Cultural Differences*. Houston: Gulf Publishing.

Hewlett, W.R. and Packard, D. (1980): *The HP Way*. Palo Alto, CA: Hewlett Packard.

Hofstede, G. (1983): "National Culture in Four Dimensions," *International Studies of Management and Organization*, 13(2):78-85.
Hattori, T. (1989): "Japanese Zaibatsu and Korean Chaebol," in K.H. Chung and H.C. Lee (eds.), *Korean Managerial Dynamics*. New York: Praeger, pp. 79-88.
Janelli, R.L. (1993): *Making Capitalism: The Social and Cultural Construction of a South Korean Conglomerate*. Stanford, CA: Stanford University Press.
Jung, K.H. (1989): *Growth Strategy and Organizational Structure of Korean Firms*. Seoul: Korea Chamber of Commerce and Industry.
Kim, C.S. (1992): *The Culture of Korean Industry*. Tucson, AZ: University of Arizona Press.
Kim, K.D. (1990): "Work Ethics of Korean Workers," *Journal of Labor Relations*, 1(1):63-85.
Kim, K.W. (1992): "The Conditions and Characteristics of Excellent Companies in Korea," *Korean Management Review*, 22(1):83-118.
Kim, T.K. (1982): *A Study of Korean Value Systems*. Seoul: Munumsa.
Korea Employers Federation (KEF)(1995): *Employment Practices of Korean Firms*. Seoul: Korea Employers Federation.
Kotter, J.P. and Haskett, J.L. (1991): *Corporate Culture and Performance*. New York: Free Press.
Kusayanagi, T. (1980): "My Perceptions of Korean," *Dong-A Daily News*, October 18:1-2.
Lee, H.C. (1989): "Managerial Characteristics of Korean Firms," in K.H. Chung and H.C. Lee (eds.), *Korean Managerial Dynamics*. New York: Praeger, pp. 147-162.
Lee, H.C. (1993): *Corporate Culture of Korean Firms*. Seoul: Pakyungsa.
Peters, T.J. and Waterman, R.H. (1982): *In Search of Excellence*. New York: Harper and Row.
Rogers, F.G.B. (1986): *The IBM Way*. New York: Harper and Row.
Ryu, S.G. (1980): *Confucianism in Korea*. Seoul: King Sejong Foundation.
Schein, E.H. (1985): *Organizational Culture and Leadership*. San Francisco: Jossey-Bass.
Scott, R.G. (1992): *Organizations: Rational, Natural, and Open Systems*. Englewood Cliffs, NJ: Prentice-Hall.
Shin, Y.K. (1991): *Value Orientations of Korean Workers*. Seoul: Korea Chamber of Commerce.

Chapter 7
Human Resource Management

7.1 Introduction

The importance of human resources takes a special place in Korea. Korea is poorly endowed with natural resources, but it is plentiful in human stock. Hence, any effort to develop the nation's economy and sustain its growth has to depend on the development of its human resources. Fortunately, Korean people are resourceful and highly motivated to learn and achieve economic success. Korean firms has been taking advantage of such human resources, and they should keep relying on these valuable resources to gain competitive advantages.

This chapter discusses human resource management of Korean firms. There are wide variations in human resource management practices among small, medium, and large firms in Korea. Our discussion will focus on the managerial practices in dealing with human resources of large business firms. In large firms, the nature of human resource management has changed considerably, reflecting the changing economic condition within the country and the changing nature of industrial competition in the global market. The chapter is divided into four major sections: recruitment and selection, training and development, performance evaluation and promotion, and compensation and fringe benefits.

7.2 Recruitment and Selection

Recruitment is the process of attracting potential employees to apply for employment; selection is the process of hiring employees from the pool of job applicants. Recruitment and selection are important personnel management functions for all organizations, but these functions are especially important in Korean firms because they are associated with life-time employment. In Western societies, any mistake associated with recruitment and selection processes can be corrected through replacement (McMillan, 1996, pp. 175-180). Because reappointment is contingent upon the satisfactory performance of employees and the firm's financial health, employers, especially in the private sector, can remedy selection errors. This is not the case in Korea. Although life-time employment has been under attack in recent years, it is generally expected that employees, once hired, keep their jobs for a life time. As a result, Korean firms pay greater attention to recruitment and selection processes.

7.2.1 Recruitment Practices

Traditionally, Korean business firms depended heavily on *yon-go* based recruiting processes (relation-based recruiting). The primary source of recruitment were the owner's owner family members, school alumni, and friends from the employer's birth place. However, as Korean businesses expanded, they were unable to meet increasing manpower needs through *yon-go* sources alone. To meet the increasing demands for manpower, Korean firms had to open and systematize their recruitment processes. Job openings are now widely advertised in newspapers, and applications are sought through active recruitment efforts. According to a study by Korean Employer Federation (KEF), the 50 largest Korean *chaebols* use a variety of recruitment methods: newspapers, magazines, company newsletters, TV commercials, campus visits, and others (KEF, 1994).

Korean firms consider the recruitment of college graduates to be utmost important personnel function and pay greater attention to it. So much so that this function is performed centrally through the Human Resource Team in the Office of Planning and Coordination for the entire business group. Recruitment of college graduates takes place twice a year, in the spring and fall. In the fall of 1996, the top 20 largest *chaebols* recruited about 13,000 college graduates. Samsung, Hyundai, and Daewoo recruited more than 2,000, and LG 1,100 respectively (*Hankook Ilbo*, November 13, 1996, p. 18). As the demand for high quality manpower increases, so does the competition among large *chaebol* groups to recruit the graduates from elite universities (Seoul National, Yonsei, and Korea).

Campus Visits. The most common recruitment activity, next to advertising, is the campus visits made by recruiters. Unlike American companies, which send professional recruiting staff to college campuses, Korean firms usually send executives who are alumni of the university from which graduates are being recruited. They give briefings about the company to prospective graduates and distribute company brochures. They also call on their former professors and ask for their assistance in attracting the interests of qualified students toward their company. Competition is especially fierce in the fields of science, engineering, management and economics, and campus visits are certainly considered to be effective recruitment tools.

Company Tours. Some firms give prospective graduates a tour around their company or plant facilities. For example, Samsung, Hyundai, LG, and Daewoo bring hundreds of students on a two-day tour around their plants in industrial sites such as Ulsan, Koomi, and Changwon. The tour is an eye-opening experience for many students who have not seen an industrial site. The tour is sometimes combined with a study tour of historical sites. This experience not only arouses the students' interest in the company but also provides a learning experience about modern plant operations.

Professorial Contacts. Soliciting recommendations from college professors is another important source of recruitment, especially for identifying high quality candidates. Since professors know both their students and the company, they are in the best position to recommend the students best suited for the company. As demands for high quality employees increase, Korean business firms increasingly depend on professors' recommendations for good students. The Kumho Group has been soliciting a selected number of professors at the best universities to recommend best students, and their recommendations have been Kumho's most important source of recruitment for many years. Those recommended by the designated professors are exempted from employment examinations, and their employment is virtually assured.

Internship Program. Recruitment for college graduates is greatly facilitated by internship programs. Korean companies have been offering internship programs for prospective college graduates for many years. As competition for recruiting high quality college graduates from elite universities became increasingly difficult, so did the popularity of internship programs. Each year, thousands of college graduates go through summer internship programs. This gives employers and graduates the opportunities to learn more about each other before formal employment begins. Internship programs will be discussed in more detail later.

Company Reputation. How many prospective employees are attracted to a company depends not only on the company's recruitment activities but also, to a large extent, on the firm's image and reputation. Among *chaebol* groups, the largest ones (Samsung, Hyundai, LG, Daewoo, Sunkyong, and Ssangyong) are most preferred by college graduates. Obviously the economic performance and the prospective growth of these *chaebol* groups make them the favorites among Korean college graduates. Aside from economic performance, the firm's social responsibility records also affect the student's image of the company. To improve their image, an increasing number of Korean firms participate or contribute to industry-university research projects, scholarship funds, and other university development programs in recent years.

TV Commercials. TV commercials also play an important role in the student's image of the company as a place to work. In order to project favorable images, Korean firms use an increasing number and frequency of TV commercials claiming technological leadership (Samsung), customer satisfaction leadership (LG), quality leadership (Daewoo), and so forth. The Sunkyong Group has been running a TV program called "Scholarship Quiz," something similar to a "College Bowl" in the U.S. Sunkyong's Scholarship Quiz, combined with a commercial message aimed largely toward student viewers, has developed a unique relationship with students who perceive Sunkyong as an enlightened business group. Such a favorable image in the minds of many Korean students has been a big help for Sunkyong's recruitment efforts.

7.2.2 *Yon-go* Versus *Gong-chae* Systems

As noted earlier, Korean firms traditionally hired employees on the base of *yon-go* relations. As businesses have expanded, so has the need for staffing positions. To meet this demand, Korean firms have formalized the employment process on the basis of open competition. Open competition meant that employees were hired on the basis of educational achievements, including performance on written examinations. *Yon-go* relations still played an important part in employment decisions; graduates of elite universities or applicants from certain regions were favored over others (Shin, 1988). In the absence of valid tools to objectively evaluate the qualities of applicants, graduates of elite universities or certain *yon-go* relations had halo effect on employment decisions. As global competition becomes more intense and the needs for high quality manpower increases, the nature of open competition is changing. Korean firms began to explore the use of assessment techniques to improve the effectiveness of the selection process.

Gong-chae system, literally meaning open employment system, was first implemented by Samsung in 1957. Since then, the open system of hiring was widely adopted and practiced by most large Korean firms. An open employment system might not mean much to Westerners who take open competition for granted. But, for Koreans who have been living under the traditional *yon-go* based culture, *gong-chae* means a significant change. Beside formalizing and systemizing the selection process with a clear selection criteria and related review procedures, the open competition system gives an elitist feeling and a special pride to those who have passed the rigorous evaluation process. When Samsung first implemented the open competition system in 1957, over 2,000 applicants took written examinations on English proficiency, a general knowledge test and an essay test on special topics. These 2,000 applicants were competing for 27 job openings (Lee, H.C., 1994, p. 210).

Specific selection procedures under the *gong-chae* system vary among Korean business firms, but the procedures generally consist of the following:

(1) A review of bio-data on the application form;
(2) Written examinations on general and technical knowledge, English or other appropriate foreign language proficiency, an essay on special topics, and/or a psychological test;
(3) Interviews;
(4) Letters of recommendation;
(5) A review of the internship record (for internship trainees);
(6) A physical examination.

These selection procedures are similar to those used by U.S. companies, but the selection criteria and evaluation methods are different. The typical selection process in Korean firms begins with a review of bio-data presented in the application form. For new college recruits, age, schools, academic majors, and grades attained are the main items of evaluation. The entry level age is usually under 29 years old. The age limit is strictly enforced in most Korean firms because too much age difference among the newly hired could be a source of conflict and could disrupt group harmony.

The review of application data generally favors graduates of prestigious colleges, such as Seoul National, Yonsei, Korea, Sogang, and Hanyang Universities. In selecting college graduates, life-time employment is the basic feature in most Korean firms. Consequently, the applicants are evaluated from a life-long career perspective. The potential for high performance throughout an entire career, not just for the entry-level job, is emphasized in evaluating the application data. As a result, the educational experience at an elite university is highly valued. Obviously, the traditional Confucianism reverence of good education has a major influence on favoring elite school graduates (Chang and Chang, 1994).

The impact of traditional Confucianism is also seen clearly in discriminatory hiring with strong preference for male graduates in most Korean firms. Many Korean firms accept only male applicants among new college recruits. Female applicants are usually screened out at the bio-data review phase. In 1994, the 50 largest *chaebols* hired only 2,000 female college graduates, a mere 8 percent of the total hired. Over 170,000 college graduates were in the job market that year, and 40.5 percent of them were female (*Hankook Ilbo*, April 20, 1995, p.39).

The second stage of the selection process is a series of written examinations. Language (usually English) proficiency, general or technical knowledge, essays on special topics, and psychological aptitude tests are administered to the applicants who have passed the bio-data review phase. The applicants spend one whole day in taking the examinations. Generally, twice the number of people to be hired pass the written examinations.

Those who pass the examinations move on to the third stage of the selection process, the interview. The interview is conducted individually or in a group of two to five applicants. A panel of interviewers, usually made up of several executives, conducts the interview. The contents of the interview vary from brief questions and answers on personal hobbies, family background and career interests, to an intensive and in-depth probing of specific subjects related to the applicant's technical backgrounds. Because of a large number of interviewees, long and intensive interviews are rare. On the average, most interviews last less than ten minutes.

The primary objective of the interview is to assess personality traits and job-related knowledge. Appearance, leadership quality, interpersonal skills, attitudes, and job related knowledge are subjectively assessed by interviewers. Because it is a subjective process, many biases enter into the interviewer's judgements, favoring *yon-go* relations and graduates from elite schools. Despite the formalized and systematic procedures comprising the selection process, the end results clearly favor the graduates from prestigious schools. In 1994, 55 percent of 32,000 college graduates hired by 50 largest Korean *chaebols* were graduates of college and universities located in Seoul (KEF, 1995). Considering the fact that the graduates of Seoul-based college and universities accounted for only 27 percent of all graduates nationwide, they were favored twice as much by large business groups over graduates of college and universities located outside of Seoul.

7.2.3 Performance-based Selection

Although the open competition system turned the traditional relation-based hiring practices into a formal and systematic selection process, a lingering question has been whether or not the open system contributes to the selection of performance-oriented applicants. In fact, open competition turned out to be an elaborate system of employee selection based on educational backgrounds. Korean firms have made few attempts to evaluate the effectiveness of open selection procedures. Without an analysis of the selection criteria and testing instruments, most Korean firms do not know whether or not they have been hiring qualified individuals.

Under the pressure of increasing global competition and growing needs for high quality manpower, Korean firms began to shift their emphasis from an education-based to a performance-based selection criteria in recent years. An increasing number of Korean firms are either eliminating or simplifying examinations and are instead devoting more time and effort to assessing job-performance related traits--personality and job-related skills. Korean managers feel that examination results (except for foreign language) are the least credible among the various selection tools (KEF, 1994, p. 33). In the 1995 selection of college graduates, nearly one half of the 50 largest *chaebols* did away with written examinations.

In this new approach, interviews are conducted more like simulated exercises or discussion sessions. A hypothetical problem is given to an applicant or a small group of applicants for analysis and solution. Hyundai Motors use the so-called "blind interview" method, in which the applicant is given a question or a problem requiring creative solutions (Lee, 1994). The interview lasts about 20 minutes and interviewers assess the applicant's responses. The interviewers are not given any bio-data or recommendation letters on the applicant. In this way they will evaluate the applicant on performance alone, unaffected by any bias or halo effect caused by the application data. The blind interview is also intended to eliminate the traditional *yon-go* and elite school biases.

At Samsung Electronics, applicants in a small group are given a topic to discuss for about 40 minutes. Assessors observe and evaluate each applicant's performance on analytical, communication, interpersonal, problem-solving, and leadership skills. In some companies, English speaking ability is also tested.

At Miwon, a major Korean *chaebol*, senior-level employees (usually 4) meet with 6 applicants somewhere away from the work place for 4 to 24 hours in order to assess applicant's qualifications. Although various firms have their own unique forms of assessment, all of these forms are aimed at departing from the traditional forms of assessment and at implementing a new performance-based employee selection process.

Korean firms still value personality traits that promote harmony, but they now add such performance related traits as creativity, positive attitude, and outward-looking perspectives. A KEF study found that the 50 largest *chaebols* place such personality traits as creativity, sincerity and desire to face challenges above human relations on their desired personality list (KEF, 1994). In most Korean firms, the interviewers and assessors now include human resource staff and in some cases line managers in addition to corporate headquarters' executives. Also, in the bio-data review, extra-curricular activities such as sports, student organizations, and social work activities are now highly valued along with academic achievements. In some *chaebol* companies like Samsung and Hansol, the data on education and birthplace are taken out of the records of the applicants.

7.2.4 Pre-employment Internship

Internship programs prior to formal employment greatly supplement the selection process in many Korean firms. The internship program was first started in 1984 by LG Group. Since then, the program has been widely adopted by many *chaebol* groups, with the primary objective of attracting high quality college graduates. In addition to attracting high quality college graduates, the program also provides opportunities for the company to assess the job-related skills and personality traits of the prospective employees and for the interns to assess the working environment and personal growth potential with the firm.

Another benefit of the pre-employment internship is that the internship experience reduces the number of mismatches between employers and new employees. Before the internship program was put into effect at Daewoo, 15 percent of newly hired college graduates left the company within the first year of employment. But, after the implementation of the internship program, this number was reduced to 5-6 percent. These positive experiences led to the widespread adoption of internship programs in Korean firms. Pre-employment internship training is becoming a popular program not only among large *chaebols* groups but also among other Korean businesses. In the spring of 1995, 5,500 prospective college graduates were selected by over 40 Korean business firms to participate in their summer internship programs. These programs were no longer limited to office jobs in the Seoul area but were expanded to manufacturing jobs in industrial sites throughout the country. Some even extended to overseas branches and subsidiaries. Internship trainees are also recruited internationally. Doosan is one of *chaebol* groups which is recruiting overseas college students for summer internship in Korea.

7.3 Employee Training

One of the human resource management functions that Korean business firms emphasize as much as or even more than American firms is employee training and development. The emphasis on training and development is consistent with Korean culture which places a high value on education. Employee training and management development have played an important role in achieving Korea's economic success during the past three decades. This section discusses various training and development methods practiced by Korean *chaebols*, including education-based training, new employee orientation, character building, cultural indoctrination, on-the-job training, overseas training and other new developments in management development.

7.3.1 Education-based Training

One of the unique aspects of training and development in Korean firms is that they occur in a cultural environment that reveres education. As noted in Chapter 6, Korean culture places a high value on education due to the influence of Confucianism. Under the traditional Confucianism, educational achievements were the most important criteria of success and social status throughout Korean history until the twentieth century. In modern Korea, educational achievements are not as critical to one's success as they were before, but they are still considered to be very important. This national culture had influenced the managerial practices of Korean firms. As discussed in the previous section, Korean firms used to hire and promote employees on the basis of educational achievements. Although a major change is occurring in employment practices, education is still an important part of employee training and development in Korean firms.

Within a society that reveres education, it is only natural to see its business firms emphasize employee training and management development. Great efforts made by Korean firms to promote training and development are evidenced by the fact that many Korean *chaebol* groups have their own management training institutes with boarding facilities capable of accommodating hundreds of trainees. Major banks and government-owned organizations also have their own training centers. It is not uncommon to see as much as five percent or more of the employee's work time is spent on formal training each year. In addition, many employees are enrolled in evening MBA programs or foreign language programs on their own. Often these employees receive financial support from their companies.

Korean businesses have been steadily expanding training and development activities as they become aware of the increasing importance of human resources in an age of limited global competition. Globalization especially has made training and development activities all the more important in recent years. In 1995, many Korean firms increased their training and development expenditures (Exhibit 7.1). Samsung spent more than a quarter billion dollars in training and development in 1995, about $1,441 per employee, amounting to 3.5 percent of the payroll. Motorola, one of leading American companies in management development, spends 1.5 percent of its payroll in training and development (Collins and Porras, 1994, p. 193). Other largest *chaebol* groups such as Hyundai, LG, and Daewoo, all significantly increased their training expenditures in 1995.

Exhibit 7.1: Training Expenditures by Korean *Chaebols* (1995) (Unit: $1 million)

Chaebols	Expenditures	*Chaebols*	Expenditures
Samsung	260 (71)	Kia	20 (4)
Hyundai	195 (78)	Kumho	19 (2)
Daewoo	130 (39)	Doosan	14 (8)
LG	130 (20)	Kolon	14 (2)
Sunkyung	58 (19)	Dongboo	14 (8)
POSCO	45 (9)	Halla	14 (3)
Hanhwa	40 (3)	Daelim	12 (6)
Ssangyong	32 (3)	Hyosung	12 (3)
Hanjin	30 (3)	Hanil	7 (5)

Note: Figures in parentheses are overseas training expenditures.

Source: *Korea Economic Daily News*, March 21, 1995, p. 1.

Employee training and development programs in most Korean *chaebols* are well organized and systematically designed, covering all functional areas (production, marketing, accounting/finance, human resource, labor relations, strategic management, and international management). These programs are tailored to serve different managerial (top, middle, low, first-line supervisory) levels. They also have many special training programs such as foreign language, "in-house MBA," overseas training, and so forth. While increasing globalization requires employee training and management development in Korean firms more than ever, the training focus and contents are undergoing significant changes.

In addition to teaching routine knowledge and skill training to improve immediate task performance, many Korean *chaebols* are attempting to change employee values and attitudes. Also, foreign language proficiency and overseas training have become more important than ever to all employees. These are difficult changes, requiring Korean employees to learn many new things throughout their entire career. But, Korean employees are well conditioned to take any kind and any amount of training. They may complain about low wages or poor working conditions, but they never complain about excessive training. Considering the kind of changes Korean firms have to go through, there is no doubt that employee training and management development will play an increasingly important role in human resource management in Korean firms. Let us look at employee training and development programs in Korean firms.

7.3.2 New Employee Orientation

Orientation programs for new employees (college graduates) generally last for about four months. New employees are hired centrally for the entire group by the Office of Planning and Coordination or the Group Chairman's Office. Company managers to whom the new employees will be assigned have little input in the selection process. The new employee orientation also occurs centrally. Only after this initial training, new employees are assigned to specific companies with the business group.

This centralized employment and placement practice accentuates the importance of the selection function, but it also causes some problems. Many new employees are not assigned to the company or to the job in which they want to work. This incompatibility is a source of serious dissatisfaction, and causes many mismatched new employees to quit the firm within the first year. In some cases, the rate of new employees leaving is as high as 20 percent. Therefore, many Korean firms pay extra attention to their orientation programs so that new employees are successfully placed. As pointed out earlier, internship programs facilitate the successful adaptation of new employees to the new job.

At Hyundai, orientation for new hires is decentralized and it begins even before they graduate from colleges. Hyundai Motors, for example, pairs up each new employee with a senior or alumnus employee, usually at the assistant manager level, who helps the prospective new recruit to prepare himself for the new job while still in college. The senior employee gives useful advice to the recruit on computer skills and foreign language skills that he may need later on the job so that he can prepare himself for these skills in the few remaining months in college before the formal employment begins. Hyundai Motors also sends the new employees books on the automobile and auto industries and offers financial assistance to those who want to enroll in computer or language training courses in the evening.

Beside pairing each new employee with a senior employee who gives pre-employment guidance, Hyundai Motors provides a placement information session to new employees toward the end of the orientation program. New employees are exposed to major work units during the formal orientation period, but they may still want to know more about specific jobs in various departments before they decide on which department they would like to be placed. In this session, which is held in a large auditorium for a full day, representatives from 20 major operating departments set up information booths and talk with new employees who are interested in their departments. The numbers of open positions and applicants usually do not match. For example, planning, marketing, and overseas assignments tend to attract more new employees than they can accommodate. Therefore, these departments are more selective in accommodating new recruits. Actual selection is done on the basis of the new employee's performance during the initial assessment and orientation process.

7.3.3 On-the-Job Training

Once new employees are assigned to a specific work unit, they go through on-the-job training for about a year. The main objective of this training is to help the new employee assimilate to the new job. In many Korean firms, not only does the immediate superior pay attention to the newly hired subordinates, but also another manager is assigned to each new employee to give necessary guidance. Hyundai Motors, for example, has a mentoring system called the “Hyundai Brothers (HB)” system, in which a middle manager in another department is assigned to a new employee to oversee his assimilation process on the job during the first year of employment. Under the HB system, the manager is responsible for arranging a formal meeting with the new employee each month, providing necessary guidance and counseling. At the end of the first year, the manager prepares a progress report. This report, along with the report from the immediate superior, is used to evaluate the new employee.

The Doosan Group also operates a similar program. After the initial orientation, which lasts as long as four months depending on the area of work, a newly hired employee is assigned to a senior employee. This senior employee is responsible for helping the new employee to settle satisfactorily into his job. The immediate superior is required to submit a monthly progress report to the Human Resource Department during the on-the-job period. This report recommends, if necessary, appropriate measures to help the new employee make satisfactory progress on his job.

7.3.4 Indoctrination Training

An important characteristic of employee training in Korean firms is the great emphasis placed upon instilling basic management values and beliefs into their employees. Instilling management values and developing strong corporate culture is generally recognized as an important requirement for high business performance (Collins and Porras, 1994, pp. 115-139; Kotter and Haskett, 1991, pp. 25-57). The indoctrination of employees in order to create a strong corporate culture in Japanese business firms is especially well known (Pascale and Athos, 1984, pp. 49-52). Korean firms place as much emphasis on this indoctrination as do Japanese firms. Indoctrination training in Korea firms begins with the orientation program for new employees, and remains as an important part of other training programs. In this way, training continuously reinforces the management values and beliefs throughout the employee's entire career with the firm.

Indoctrination training in Korean firms is based on clearly articulated management values and beliefs, reflecting the personal philosophy and commitment of the founder or the top management. Management values and beliefs, usually stated in the *Sahoon* (company credo), serve as a framework for forming the employee's attitude toward his job and company and for building his character during this indoctrination phase. As much as 50 percent of new employee training time is devoted to building the desired moral character. This training is also devoted to instilling the basic management values and company loyalty, and to cultivating positive attitudes and behaviors.

The Sunkyong Group has been especially well known for articulating its management values and beliefs and instilling them in the minds of new employees during the orientation process. The behavioral pattern called "Sunkyongmanship" (or SKmanship) reflects the basic management values of the current chairman J.H. Chey, and defines the desired attitudes and behavior for Sunkyong employees. The three management values in the Sunkyong *sahoon* are humanism, rationalism, and pragmatism. The central value related to the Sunkyong spirit is *vitality*. This consists of positive thinking, creativity, tenacious effort, and the drive for perfection. The concepts of SKmanship are described in detail in an official booklet, published after numerous revisions over the years by the Chairman's Office of Management and Planning. The booklet is an important instrument not only for indoctrination training but also for the socialization of Sunkyong employees throughout their career within the Group.

Samsung and Ssangyong are other *chaebol* groups with well articulated management values and beliefs which serve as a guide to indoctrination training. The traditional Samsung value systems include entrepreneurial spirit, high ethical standards, eliticism, perfection, and shared prosperity. These values had guided Samsung's training programs in the past until Quality Management was adopted as a new management value in 1993. Indoctrination training for the new "Samsung man" emphasizes a new set of values such as quality orientation, technology orientation, consumer orientation, respect for the individual, and autonomy.

At Ssangyong, indoctrination training is closely coordinated with a new corporate culture that stresses the importance of trust and innovativeness. The Corporate Culture Team in the Group Chairman's Office, which coordinates new corporate culture programs, has conceptualized a behavioral model for the new "Ssangyong man," emphasizing customer-centeredness, honesty, integrity, innovativeness, accommodation to change, respect for the individual, and teamwork. This behavioral model has been used as a guide for training Ssangyong employees on its new corporate culture.

In addition to instilling basic management values and beliefs, indoctrination training in many Korean firms includes hardship training aimed at developing a positive mental attitude and physical strength. Typical hardship training involves a long forced march on rugged mountain trails, often at night. Sometimes, groups of trainees are required to explore the mountain trail to search for certain objects planted in advance by the professional hardship trainers. Such exploration requires a great deal of teamwork. This kind of training helps the trainees not only to strengthen their mental and physical capabilities but also to promote a sense of unity, belongingness, teamwork, and comradeship (Kirk, 1994, pp. 46-47).

Indoctrination training in Korean firms reflects a group-oriented Confucian culture. It aims at transforming the employees into a group culture--Samsung man, Sunkyong man, and Ssangyong man. Traditionally, indoctrination training in Korean firms emphasized building the basic character and attitude of employees toward harmony, unity, and cooperation. Recently, however, as Korean firms have become globalized, they have begun to emphasize performance-oriented values. As a result, the new indoctrination program has shifted toward putting more emphasis on quality, customer, technology, innovation, autonomy, and respect for individualism.

How effective is the indoctrination training? Although indoctrination training has been widely used by many Korean firms, there has not been any clear evidence that it indeed has produced noticeable behavioral changes among the employees who received such training (Lee, H.C., 1994). In order to be effective, such training has to be based on a clear vision and on well-articulated values that inspire the employees. Also, what is taught in training should actually be practiced at work, and it should be continuously reinforced. Although Korean employees accept indoctrination training, they do resent training practices which they feel are unjustified. In some Korean firms, employees felt that some of the hardship training methods were unnecessarily harsh; therefore, in recent years, firms have refocused their training to emphasize mainly group unity and teamwork.

7.4 Management Development

Management training and development have contributed immensely to the growth of Korean business firms in the past three decades. The introduction of advanced management concepts and skills from the U.S. and Japan through management training and development have been particularly helpful to the high performance of Korean firms. Management training and development in most Korean firms began with class-room teaching of basic management concepts or principles by invited lecturers. This was followed by the introduction of modern management methods and case studies.

Management development activities were expanded drastically as many Korean firms established their own training centers in the 1970s and 1980s. In addition to lectures, case studies, role playing, simulation, experiential exercises, and programmed instructions were utilized. Lecture-based training gradually gave way to discussion-based approaches--case discussions, oral presentation, and small group discussions. The training staff at the training centers also began to develop task-oriented training and instruction materials. As management training and development programs became systemized and clarified their objectives and contents, these programs became an important part of the overall human resource management. Many Korean firms measure a trainee's performance in its training program, and incorporate it into the formal performance appraisal. This appraisal is ultimately reflected in an employee's rewards.

Typical management training and development in Korean firms consists of a two-to-three day program at the training center. Training begins at six o'clock in the morning and lasts until ten o'clock at night each day. The schedule includes early morning calisthenics, conversations with top executives, and small group problem discussions in the evening. Therefore, going to the training center is not exactly taking time off to rest. In fact, many trainees return home quite exhausted. Training provides not only the opportunity to learn but also the occasion to reinforce group harmony and unity. Most training centers operate at full capacity throughout the year. In recent years, management training and development in most Korean firms placed special emphasis on developing global managers and behavioral changes to facilitate ongoing corporate transformations (see Chapter 9).

7.4.1 Global Management Training

Globalization of Korean businesses has increased the importance of the international dimension of managerial work. In recent years, topics related to internationalization, global strategies, multi-national collaboration, and international competitive advantage have been scheduled in almost all management development programs. Foreign language training has been substantially expanded. Foreign language ability is becoming an important qualification for global managers, and it is now almost a necessary requirement for career success in Korean firms.

Development of international awareness is not confined to classroom training only. Many business firms are sending their executives on overseas training and study tours. Most large Korean *chaebols* have designed one to three week overseas training programs in cooperation with foreign graduate schools of management. Some Korean firms such as Pohang Steel and Ssangyong are extending overseas training to non-managerial employees. Pohang Steel Company sent over 2,000 employees for one-week overseas training in 1994. The U.S., Europe, Japan, China, and Southeast Asia are common overseas training sites for most Korean firms.

International exposure is also becoming an increasingly important part in training new employees in Korean firms. Daewoo is implementing a new training program, in which new employees go through 1,000 hours of training during the first three years of employment. Included in this training program are several weeks of international work at overseas subsidiaries and training in two to three foreign languages to reach a reasonable proficiency level. Training for new employees at the Hanhwa Group also includes study tours to Japan, China, or Southeast Asia (*Korean Economic Daily News*, May 2, 1995, p. 11).

Developing international area expertise is also an important part of developing global managers in Korean firms. In 1990, Samsung Group initiated a five-year program to develop 2,000 international area experts. Trainees were selected from young employees with three years of work experience in the company. These employees were sent to foreign countries for one year to learn the local language and culture. Samsung budgeted $50,000 per trainee for a total of $100 million for the program (Nakarmi and Neff, 1994). Other *chaebols* including Daewoo, Ssangyong, and Hanjin are also implementing similar international area expert development programs on a smaller scale.

7.4.2 Organizational Development

In recent years, Korean firms, in their management training and development programs, have emphasized behavioral and organizational changes. Faced with increasing global competition, many Korean firms have initiated ambitious corporate transformation programs to strengthen their ability to compete in the open world market with the ultimate objective of becoming a "super world-class company." Many Korean firms re-defined their core ideologies and new values in this endeavor, and have initiated changes in their business strategies, organizational structure, and human resource management. Naturally, employee training and management development play a big role in a successful transformation.

Restructuring, re-engineering, benchmarking, customer satisfaction management, total quality management, and corporate culture development are some of the approaches and methods of change that Korean firms are applying in their corporate transformation processes. Korean firms know that a successful corporate transformation requires a fundamental change in employees' values, perceptions, and way of thinking. Korean top executives are determined to support management training and development to achieve it. Scholars and consultants with expertise in organizational change and corporate transformation are invited by Korean firms to their training programs. Some Korean companies have studied such cases involving successful corporate transformation as GE, Xerox, and ABB. In addition, GE's training methods such as "workouts" and "best practices" are attempted by some Korean companies (Ticky and Sherman, 1993).

7.4.3 In-house MBA Programs

Another major characteristics of management development in Korean *chaebols* is for firms to have their own in-house MBA programs for middle managers and executives in cooperation with Korean or foreign graduate schools of management. An in-house MBA program is not a formal degree program, but the trainees receive a two-year MBA equivalent education plus foreign language training and/or overseas studies. Kumho is one of the first *chaebol* groups to initiate in-house MBA program in cooperation with Korean universities. Under this program, over one hundred executives and managers are being sent to four Korean schools of management (Seoul National, Yonsei, Korea, and Sogang Universities) each semester for 600 hours of full-time studies. The curriculum includes MBA equivalent course work and foreign language training (English and Japanese) tailored to meet Kumho's needs. Over one thousand Kumho executives and managers have been trained under this program since the program began in 1990.

Other *chaebols* have developed similar in-house MBA programs in cooperation with Korean and foreign universities. Samsung has a number of such programs; "21st Century Leadership Program" is designed to give MBA equivalent general management training, "Techno MBA" to train managers in production and other technical areas, "Socio MBA" to develop administrative and human resource management personnel, "Samsung Life Finance Program" to train managers in finance and insurance areas (in New York University), and "Marketing MBA" to train domestic and international marketing managers. Samsung also has a "CEO Development Program" for selected executives. These programs are offered to 30-50 managers at a time for a period of six to twenty-four months; most of these programs include foreign language training and course work at overseas universities.

Other *chaebols* also have their own in-house MBA program in cooperation with foreign universities. Hyundai has a "Global Management Program" and "Leadership Development Program" in cooperation with University of California (Berkeley) and University of Michigan, respectively. Daewoo has a "Global MBA Program" and an "AMP Program" with University of Michigan, Sunkyong with International Graduate School of Management (Thunderbird), and Halla Group with Long Island University. Ssangyong has a series of "Global Manager," "Global Leader," and "Global Executive" Programs at various universities and research institutes in the U.S. and Europe. Ssangyong's programs combine classroom training with industry tours. Overseas training in these programs are usually proceeded by preparatory course work and language training at home training centers and universities.

7.4.4 Executive Development Programs

In addition to in-house MBA programs, many Korean firms send promising managers and executives to the world's top MBA and executive development programs--Harvard, Pennsylvania (Wharton), Stanford, INSEAD, and others. They have been developing managerial and executive talents through special work assignments, executive MBA degrees, or advanced executive development programs at prestigious foreign graduate schools of management.

Sunkyong is one of the first *chaebol* groups to systemize the search and development process of executive talents. Under Sunkyong's Executive Management Development (EMD) Program, promising young low and middle level managers are selected and put through a long period of systematic career development training to prepare them for executive responsibilities. The talented young trainees are identified at an early stage of their careers on the basis of Sunkyong's Skmanship behavioral model. They go through a specially designed development process which includes overseas assignments and training at reputable graduate schools.

Korean business firms make greater efforts toward training and development than toward any other human resource management function. In recent years, the globalization of Korean businesses has caused Korean firms to make even greater efforts toward training and development. In addition to fostering traditional knowledge and skill training, Korean businesses are placing more emphasis on high quality human resource development and organizational development. The eventual goal of such efforts is to facilitate corporate transformation of Korean firms into "super first-class" businesses (see Chapter 9).

7.5 Performance Evaluation

Performance evaluation and promotion are important human resource management functions. How well organizations measure the performance of their employees and reflect it in their reward systems will greatly affect the morale, motivation, and future performance of their employees. Given the important role the performance evaluation system plays in employee motivation, it is expected that an achievement-oriented culture will be conducive to effective performance evaluation and promotion systems. However, contrary to this expectation, employee evaluation and promotion are relatively ineffective human resource management functions in most Korean firms. We will discuss in this section traditional as well as new trends of performance evaluation and promotion practices in Korean firms.

7.5.1 Traditional Performance Evaluation

Most Korean firms have a formal system of performance evaluation. Employee performance is rated on such factors as quantity of work, quality of work, ability, interpersonal skills, leadership skills, and work attitude. Employees are then evaluated on these criteria in three stages. They are first evaluated by their immediate superiors. This first stage evaluation is reviewed by the next higher level manager. Although there are not many cases of serious disagreement, the second stage review is to make sure that the employee is evaluated fairly. Finally, the Human Resource Department adjusts the results of the evaluation to achieve some uniformity in evaluation among the raters. Most Korean firms do not hold appraisal interviews, and most employees do not know how their superiors have evaluated them.

The evaluation systems in most Korean firms are well designed, and the multiple evaluation at two hierarchical levels are intended to ensure fair evaluation. However, these systems are not effectively utilized in Korean firms for two reasons. First, most Korean managers tend to evaluate their subordinates too leniently with little differentiation between high and low performers. The Human Resource Department adjusts the evaluation data in order to convert the skewed distribution with lenient tendency into a normal distribution scale. Second, the results of performance appraisal have not been used in rewarding employees. The traditional reward system (promotion and compensation) is largely based on seniority and is still in use in many Korean companies.

The tendency of Korean managers toward lenient employee evaluation and the use of traditional seniority-based reward systems are no doubt related to the harmony-oriented Korean culture. As explained in the last chapter, harmony is one of the most emphasized values in Korean firms. Most Korean managers are inclined to maintain harmony with lenient appraisal of subordinates than to arouse conflict and tension through critical or negative evaluations. Paternalistic leadership behavior under traditional Confucianism also tends to lead Korean managers to practice generous and lenient rating of subordinates.

7.5.2 New Trend in Performance Evaluation

The absence of effective performance appraisal discourages high performing individuals. Lenient and indiscriminate rating practices fail to recognize individual differences in performance, and the absence of appraisal interviews alienates employee who seek feedback. The seniority-based reward system makes performance evaluation meaningless, and as a result, few managers take performance evaluation seriously. Many of them merely go through the motion of generating evaluation data in order to meet record-keeping requirements.

Recently, however, an increasing number of Korean firms are initiating improvements in the performance evaluation process. Employees are given opportunities to evaluate themselves. The self-evaluation data is taken into consideration not only in performance evaluation by their superiors, but also in training and career development. Some companies let employees know how their supervisors react to their self-evaluation. Others use peer evaluation and even allow evaluation by subordinates. Subordinates are asked to rate their superiors on such criteria as initiative, communication skills, and leadership skills.

Another recent development is the use of the behaviorally anchored rating scales (BARS) method of performance appraisal. This method identifies a set of behaviors considered critical to job performance and develops rating scales for such behaviors. For example, for an office manager's job, punctuality and conflict resolution can be critical behaviors. Being on time for work hundred percent may be rated as five point; being on time ninth-five percent may be rated as four point on a five-point scale. The office manager's actual performance is then rated against this scale. BARS are developed to avoid the subjective judgement of the rater. Korean firms have recently spent great efforts in training managers to be able to make better performance evaluation.

These new developments will certainly improve the effectiveness of performance evaluation systems in Korean firms. Furthermore, they are in tune with changes in organizations that stress the importance of performance-oriented value systems--quality, customer service, innovation, and individualism. These changes are gradual, but they are likely to be successful because the majority of Korean employees seem to desire the use of performance-based reward systems more than the use of traditional seniority-based ones (Lee, H.C., 1994). As the reward system becomes more performance-based, the importance of performance evaluation will increase accordingly. Superiors as well as subordinates will take performance evaluation more seriously, and ultimately, the employee evaluation system will function more effectively in Korean business firms.

7.5.3 Performance and Promotion

Promotion is a very important reward for Korean employees. As noted in Chapter 6, the Korean culture is characterized by authoritarianism, high power distance, and achievement. In such a culture, promotion carries an especially important meaning as a measure of one's power, success and self-actualization. However, promotion practices in Korean firms have been traditionally based on seniority. A study by the Federation of Korean Industries a few years ago revealed that 50 percent of large Korean businesses promote their employees strictly on the basis of seniority (*Korean Economic Daily News*, February 18, 1993). Recently, however, major changes have occurred in promotion practices in many Korean firms. We will examine traditional as well as new trends in promotion practices in Korean firms.

Promotion criteria in most Korean firms generally include seniority, job-related skills, work performance, and personality traits. The most important criteria has been seniority. Normally, an employee has to serve a certain length of time in a rank before being promoted. In most large firms, a newly employed college graduate has to work for four to five years to be eligible for promotion to assistant section manager, another three to five years before being considered for promotion to deputy department manager, and then another four to seven years to be eligible for promotion to department manager.

Eligibility for promotion also involves other criteria. Educational achievements and job-related qualifications such as graduate degrees, major "in-house" training programs, special awards, special certificates, licenses, QC awards, foreign language proficiency, and "in-house MBA" program certainly help positive evaluation for promotion. Performance evaluation includes not only the amount and quality of work done but also personality traits--attitude, harmony, cooperation, and loyalty.

Although seniority has been the most important criterion, the relative importance among various promotion criteria varies depending on hierarchical levels. At the assistant section manager and section manager levels, seniority is the most important factor. However, seniority becomes less important at higher levels. For promotion to the directorate level (executive level) and higher, past performance and work attitude are as important as seniority, if not more important. Chairman W.C. Kim of Daewoo Group, for example, emphasizes as qualifications for an executive not only ability but also complete devotion to work even at the sacrifice of one's personal and family life (Kim, 1992). Likewise, in most Korean firms, promotion to executive level requires complete loyalty and dedication to work along with a proven track record.

It normally takes 12 to 17 years to reach the department manager level; the average age of department managers in Korean firms is 44 years old. The time required for promotion has become longer as the rate of growth in Korean firms has stabilized. But, in recent years, the number of young executives has increased as greater emphasis is being placed on performance than on seniority. In 1995, the average age of 821 newly promoted executives in the 30 largest *chaebols* was 47 years old. The oldest was 60, and the youngest was 36 years old. The youngest executive was a close relative of a *chaebol* founder.

Although a variety of criteria are considered, promotion decisions especially at the directorate level tend to favor education in elite universities. Of the newly promoted executives in 1995, 60 percent were graduates of four well known universities--Seoul National, Yonsei, Korea, and Hanyang. Forty-seven percent were engineers and 28 percent were business/economics majors, reflecting the importance that many Korean *chaebols* are now placing on new technological development (*Korean Economic Daily News*, April 4, 1995).

Elite university graduates hold an equally high proportion of chief executive positions among large Korean businesses. A survey of 85 large Korean firms by the Korean Association of Listed Stock Companies (KALSC) revealed that 64 of their executives were graduates of Seoul National, Yonsei, and Korea Universities (*Korean Economic Daily News*, December 21, 1995). Seoul National University graduates dominated the field with 47 percent. The average age of chief executives was 54 years old, and the average length of work in business was over 20 years including 10 years of executive experience. Unlike newly promoted executives, nearly 80 percent of the chief executive received liberal arts or management degrees.

Fifty-one percent of them have come through the general management track, while 16 and 13 percents through marketing and manufacturing tracks respectively. Over 50 percent were home-grown, 33 percent were from other companies within the same *chaebol* group, and 16 percent were brought in from outside.

In recent years, promotion practices have changed in many Korean firms. The eligibility requirement based on seniority has been less stringent, and employees with proven track records are being promoted even before they would have been eligible for promotion under the old system. Large *Chaebols* like Samsung, Hyundai, LG, and Daewoo have all begun to promote exceptional middle managers to the executive level regardless of age and the length of their service. They are extending performance-based promotion to middle management levels. As pointed out earlier, most chief executives in large *chaebols* are now selected on the basis of ability. A recent survey shows that 69 of 85 chief executives of large Korean businesses appointed in 1994 were professional executives having no kinship relation with the owner family. Only 16 were owner family members (*Korean Economic Daily News*, January 8, 1995, p.8).

7.6 Compensation Systems

Compensation systems have played an important part in Korean management and in the success of Korean businesses. Whereas low wages contributed immensely to the competitive advantage of Korean businesses in the world market in the 1960s and 1970s, the rapid increase in wages in the past decade became the primary reason for the deteriorating competitiveness of Korean businesses, causing them to launch vigorous corporate transformation efforts in recent years. It normally takes many years for a country to double real earnings; in fact it took more than seventy years in the case of English workers (Amsden, 1989, pp. 195-198). But it took less than a decade for Korean workers to more than triple their real wages. Exhibit 7.2 shows the changes in labor costs for Korea and other countries.

As in the case of other human resource management practices, the compensation systems in Korean firms have been largely based on seniority and have been group-oriented, reflecting traditional Korean culture. The rapid growth of Korean firms in the past three decades brought little change in the overall compensation system other than an increase in the wage level. However, an increasing emphasis on employee performance in recent years has brought some change in the compensation system of many Korean firms. This section discusses the general characteristics of wage structure and fringe benefits. Also, new developments in compensation will be explored.

Exhibit 7.2: Changes in Hourly Labor Costs in Manufacturing

Country	1985 ($)	1995 ($)	Increase (%)
Korea	1.23	7.40	501
Taiwan	1.50	5.82	288
Japan	6.34	23.66	273
Germany	6.60	31.88	231
Singapore	2.47	7.28	195
Hong Kong	1.73	4.82	178
France	7.52	19.34	157
Great Britain	6.27	13.77	119
Malaysia	1.08	1.59	47
Indonesia	0.22	0.30	36
Unites States	13.01	17.20	32
China	0.19	0.25	31
Mexico	1.59	1.51	-1
Thailand	0.49	0.46	-6
India	0.35	0.25	-28

Source: *The Economist*, November 2, 1996, p. 77.

7.6.1 Wage Structure

The wage structure of Korean firms is complicated but highly structured. It is composed of base pay, allowances, and bonuses. Base pay, the largest component, is primarily based on one's education and experience. Allowances are intended to compensate for special skills, responsibilities, special task assignments, and hardship. There are also allowances for leaves not taken and family responsibilities. Many types of allowances, which keep increasing as time goes, complicate the overall wage structure.

One of the reasons why Korean firms let allowances continue to increase is to keep down the amount of the base pay on which retirement contributions and severance pay are based. By making allowances and bonuses optional, the firm can theoretically reduce the wage burden at times of extreme financial difficulty. Labor strikes in recent years especially have contributed to the expansion of allowances, serving both management and union as a convenient means for wage settlement. While additional allowances meet union demands for higher wages, they keep down the base pay. But the problem has been that allowances have become fixed costs to the firm. Allowances are supposed to fluctuate reflecting the economic health of the firm. But once they are instituted, they become a permanent fixture to the wage structure.

Bonuses are supposed to compensate employees for outstanding performances. However, in most Korean firms, bonuses are paid to all employees regardless of their performance. As a result, the bonus is actually extra pay in addition to the base pay to Korean employees. Bonuses paid to executives are somewhat performance-based, reflecting the performance of their business units. Bonuses, like allowances, have been increasing in most Korean firms over the years. They are generally equal in amount to the base pay plus allowances, paid twice or four times a year. But, some companies pay nearly every month.

Wage statistics from Korean Employer's Federation show that the average starting monthly salary for department managers in Korean firms, with 100 employees or more, was $2,680 ($32,160 annually) in 1995 (KEF, 1995). The average starting monthly salary for male college graduates and male production workers (mostly high school graduates) were $1,266 ($15,192 annually) and $1,014 ($12,168 annually) respectively. According to the same KEF data, the proportions of base pay, allowance, and bonus in 1995 were 56.3, 14.5, and 29.2 percents respectively (Exhibit 7.3). The proportions differed slightly for different ranks, depending on the frequency of allowance and bonus payments.

Exhibit 7.3: Average Starting Salaries for Korean Employees (1995) (in $)

Position	Base pay	Allowances	Bonuses	Total
Department manager	1,446	464	770	2,680
Assistant dept. manager	1,261	393	668	2,322
Section manager	1,111	331	582	2,024
Assistant section manager	957	255	494	1,706
College graduates:				
Male	737	154	375	1,266
Female	653	130	341	1,124
Vocational school graduates:				
Male	651	148	327	1,126
Female	566	122	302	978
High school graduates:				
Clerical (Male)	593	122	302	1,017
Clerical (Female)	500	104	254	858
Production (Male)	586	129	299	1,014
Production (Female)	491	106	250	847
	56.3%	14.5%	29.2%	100%

Source: Korean Employers Association (1995): *KEF Compensation Quarterly*, 3(4): 132-133.

7.6.2 Cultural Factor Affecting Pay

Traditionally, there had been a clear demarcation in wage levels between college and non-college graduates and between white-collar and blue-collar workers. Better compensation for the educated and white-collar employees is no doubt related to the traditional Confucian culture. However, industrialization has brought tremendous improvement to the economic status of blue-collar production workers, and the wage differential between college and non-college graduates has been substantially reduced. Korean firms have tried to improve the status of blue-collar workers, and the wage differential between white and blue-collar workers has now been virtually eliminated. Some *chaebols* are even consolidating white and blue collar jobs into a single job classification. These are significant changes to the traditional culture preferring white-collar jobs.

However, Korea's Confucian and male-dominated culture is still strongly reflected in discriminatory wages favoring male over female employees. The KEF data show that Korean business firms pay 12.6 percent more to male college-educated employees than to female college-educated employees, 15.1 percent more to male vocational college graduates, and 19.7 percent more to male production workers (KEF, 1995). Wage discrimination by gender is becoming a contested issue in Korea, but this issue is shadowed by the much more pressing issue of discriminatory (male-preference) hiring practices.

Liberal allowances and bonuses paid regardless of performance strongly reflect collectivism and paternalism in Korean society. Although some allowances compensate for special skills and additional responsibilities, other allowances are in large part given for long service, family responsibility, and miscellaneous reasons, all of which are of paternalistic nature. Bonuses are hardly performance-based in Korean firms. All employees are entitled to bonus irrespective of their work performance. Some Korean companies attempt to link a part of the bonus to the employee's work performance, but it is insignificant, and does not change the general perception of Korean employees in seeing bonus as just another part of their basic pay.

The non-performance based wage system fulfills the economic needs of Korean employees, but fails to motivate them. It rather de-motivates high performing employees. The base pay favors the educated, but not high performers. Numerous allowances and bonuses, designed to differentiate the contributions of employees to their the jobs, do not really serve the purpose, and they merely complicate the wage structure. Although the overall wage structure is logically designed, it is not implemented as intended. As a result, Korean wages skyrocketed in recent years without a commensurate increase in productivity. Between 1987 and 1995, real wages increased at an annual rate of 14.9 percent, while productivity increased at an annual rate of 11.0 percent *(Hankook Ilbo*, October 30, 1996, p. 8). Korean firms are initiating changes to simplify the wage structure, and align it more closely to employee performance. These changes in the wage system will be explained later.

7.6.3 Fringe Benefits

Korean business firms provide a wide range of fringe benefits to their employees, again reflecting the paternalistic, group-based, and harmony-oriented culture. Benefit packages include retirement contributions, medical insurance, and paid vacation. In addition to these benefits, which are major fringe benefit items in American companies, most large Korean business firms provide a variety of other fringe benefits. These include child support, free lunch, commuting buses, vacation expenses, dormitory and housing, college tuition support for children, support for various employee activities (clubs, circles, etc.), gifts/donations for special events (marriages, birthdays, deaths in the family, and others), and many more. Revitalization of union activities since 1987 has contributed to a drastic expansion in fringe and welfare benefits in most Korean business firms.

At Tongyang Nylon, for example, free lunch, college tuition supports for employees' children, vacation expense support, and medical insurance expenses are among the largest supplementary fringe and welfare benefit items. Welfare benefits at the TNC Ulsan Plant were $1,847 per employee in 1994, amounting to about 9 percent of the payroll. However, not included in this figure are other major fringe benefit items such as retirement contributions, housing overhead costs, and time not worked. If all these items are taken into account, the total fringe benefits amount to more than 30 percent of the total payroll.

7.6.4 Annual Salary System

Compensation systems of Korean firms are also undergoing major changes. But, unlike other human resource management practices, changes in compensation systems are being implemented slowly and cautiously. The new wage system, called *yonbongjae*, meaning annual wage system, is generally intended to simplify the existing wage structure and set employee wages on the basis of job-related skills and performance.

Doosan is one of the first Korean *chaebol* groups to implement *yonbongjae*. Under the new plan, the wage structure is divided into base pay and merit pay. Base pay is based on job-related skills (ability), and merit pay is based on performance. The existing allowances and bonuses are re-allocated into either base or merit pay (Exhibit 7.4). A new base pay is set on an annual basis for each employee on the basis of the employee's ability, and merit pay is determined based on performance at the year's end. Performance evaluation has been re-designed, utilizing a behaviorally anchored rating scale (BARS) techniques, in order to ensure objective measurements of employee performances. Additionally, all managers are put through intensive training to facilitate successful implementation of the new wage and performance evaluation systems.

Exhibit 7.4: Annual Salary Structure

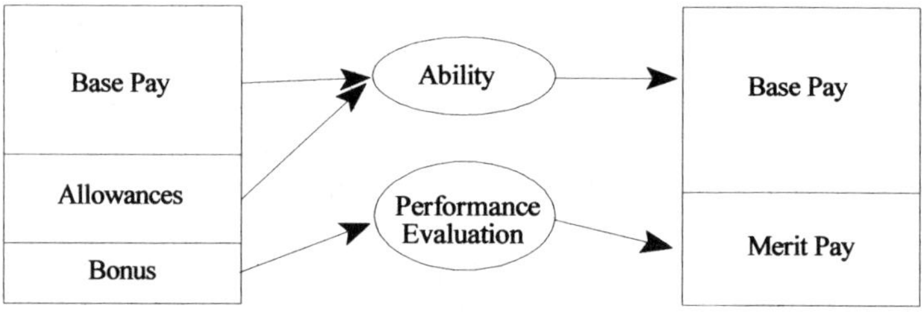

Many Korean business firms are seriously considering or preparing for *yon-bongjae*, and in the meantime, they are watching closely how Doosan is making out with the new wage system. Doosan is widely known for its conservative and traditional harmony-oriented culture. Doosan's implementation of its new revolutionary wage system naturally draws much interest from all Korean businesses. While most Korean business firms recognize a need for drastic changes in the existing wage system, they are apprehensive of the possible negative consequences of change. The current wage system has been in practice for a long time; it is deeply ingrained in the management system of most Korean firms. Korean employees generally support the annual salary system, but they are not sure whether it can be carried out successfully. This is why many Korean firms are waiting to see the outcome of Doosan's experience. If Doosan's new system is implemented successfully, it will have a significant impact not only on the compensation system but also on the overall human resource management of Korean business firms.

7.7 Summary

Human resource management is an integral part of corporate culture, reflecting the shared values of organizational members and management strategies. Under the influence of Confucian culture, the corporate culture in Korean firms had been harmony-oriented and education-based. These cultural traits were reflected in the human resource management practices. Employee recruitment and selection were based on educational achievement and *yon-go* (personal) relations. Training and development focused on the instillation of core management values such as harmony, teamwork, and loyalty.

Performance appraisal and reward systems tended to be group-oriented rather than stressing individual differences in performance. Employee evaluation was also largely education-based and harmony-oriented; promotion was not performance based. Pay was also based on education and seniority based. Bonuses were originally intended to reward performance, but they were paid regardless of performance. Because employees were paid on the basis of education and seniority rather than on their performance, both employees and their supervisors went through the performance appraisal procedures simply to generate required performance data.

However, the globalization of Korean firms in recent years has changed the cores of human resource management practices in Korea. Korean firms, in order to survive in an increasingly competitive global market, have launched vigorous corporate transformation efforts in all areas of human resource management. New values such as quality, consumerism, innovativeness, and individualism are emphasized in building corporate culture. This in turn exerts pressures for changing traditional human resource management practices toward more performance-oriented ones.

While these changes may conflict with Korea's traditional Confucian culture, the urgency felt by Koreans in general in meeting the global challenge has created an environment conducive to major changes in the corporate culture and managerial practices of Korean firms. Inasmuch as changes in human resource management are necessary requirements for a successful corporate transformation, Korean firms will no doubt fully devote their efforts to bringing about these changes in the years ahead.

References

Amsden, A.H. (1989): *Asia's Next Giant: South Korea and Late Industrialization*. Oxford: Oxford University Press.

Chang, C.S. and Chang, N.J. (1994): *The Korean Management System*. Westport, CT: Quorum Books.

Collins, J.C. and Porras, J.I. (1994): *Built to Last: Successful Habits of Visionary Companies*. New York: Harper Business.

Kim, W.C. (1992): *Every Street is Paved with Gold*. New York: William Morrow.

Kirk, D (1994): *Korean Dynasty: Hyundai and Jung Ju Yung*. Armonk, NY: M.E.Sharpe.

Korea Employers Federation (KEF)(1994): *Employment Practices of Korean Businesses*. Seoul: KEF.

Korea Employers Federation (KEF)(1995): *KEF Compensation Quarterly*, Spring Issue.

Kotter, J.P. and Haskett, J.L. (1991): *Corporate Culture and Performance*. New York: Free Press.

Lee, H.C. (1994): *Corporate Transformation of Korean Businesses*. Seoul: Bupmoonsa.

Lee, Y.L. (1994): "More Companies Rely on Employee Interviews," *Business Korea*, 12(5):22-24.

McMillan, C.J. (1996): *The Japanese Industrial System*. Third Revised Edition. Berlin, New York: Walter de Gruyter.

Nakarmi, L. and Neff, R. (1994): "Samsung's Shakeup," *Business Week*, February 28:74-76.

Pascale, R.T. and Athos, A.G. (1984): *The Art of Japanese Management*. New York: Simon and Shuster.

Shin, Y.G. (1988): "Human Resource Management in a Korean Industry," Paper presented at the Korean Human Resource Management Conference, Seoul, June.

Shin, Y.G. (1992): *Korean Management*. Seoul: Barkyoungsa.

Tichy, N.M. and Sherman, S. (1993): *Control Your Destiny or Someone Else Will*. New York: Doubleday.

Chapter 8
Labor-Management Relations

8.1 Introduction

A nation's labor-management system reflects its social, cultural, political, and economic conditions. In the U.S., the labor-management system has taken a confrontational mode, reflecting a history of economic class struggle and the pluralistic nature of American society. In contrast, Japan is a racially homogeneous society, which places a heavy emphasis on harmony among people. Reflecting such a social condition, its labor-management system has developed a cooperative mode of interaction. In Europe, especially Germany, labor-management relations are based on the principle of codetermination, stressing the need for workers to participate in managerial decisions. Codetermination is seen by Europeans as a means of fighting against the class struggles deeply rooted in their societies. In Korea, labor-management relations have taken a confrontational form. This is an unlikely development of Confucian culture, a culture which cherishes harmony.

This chapter reviews the historical roots of labor-management relations in Korea to explain the reason for the confrontational mode in the past. It also examines the new patterns of labor-management relations that are emerging in the new era of political democratization. The political reform process, started in 1987, was the turning point in the Korean labor movement. Prior to 1987, the government played the major role in the determination of wages and working conditions. It is only in recent years that labor and management have become directly involved in negotiating labor-related issues. What form of labor-management relations will emerge in the future is difficult to tell. But the economic necessities in the age of increasing global competition are likely to force labor and management to be more cooperative in the future.

8.2 Historical Roots of Labor Relations

While labor movements in other industrial nations generally started as an effort to enhance the economic well-being of labor, trade unions in Korea started as an anti-Japanese movement during the Japanese occupation of Korea (Kim, 1994; Park and Lee, 1992). Korea's early industrialization was started in the late 19th century by foreign capitalists who began to exert control over the peninsula. In the absence of indigenous capital formation, Korea depended on foreign capital for its industrialization. Consequently, the labor movement in Korea during this period was directed against foreign capitalists. The first strike occurred in 1888 at a foreign-owned gold mine, located in Chosan, Hamgyungdo (Lee, 1989). The first labor union was the Sungjin Dock Workers' union, organized in 1898 with 46 workers (Federation of Korean Trade Union, 1979).

8.2.1 Japanese Colonial Period

The Japanese occupation of Korea (1910-1945) accelerated the introduction of modern production systems, increasing the number of factory workers and labor unions. The first national federation of trade unions (*Chosun Nodong Konjeahyei*) was organized in 1920. It was during this period that Korean workers organized themselves to fight against Japanese colonialism (Park and Lee, 1992). The Japanese colonial economic policy helped to shape the labor movement as a national independence movement (Lee, 1993). Labor disputes were seen as patriotic struggles against the Japanese industrialists. By recognizing the trade labor movement as a threat to Japanese colonialism, the Japanese government enacted the Korea Public Order Maintenance Law in 1923, making union activities especially at the national level illegal. Workers who participated in any union activities without prior approval of Japanese authorities were sentenced to hard labor, lifetime imprisonment, or even death.

During the colonial period, Korean workers' working conditions were inferior to Japanese workers. The wages of Korean workers were about 40 percent of those of their Japanese counterparts. In the 1930s, 47 percent of Korean employees worked twelve hours a day, and 28 percent of factories in Korea operated 365 days a year (Lee, 1989). Naturally, Korean workers demanded improvements in wages and working conditions. The number of unauthorized labor strikes increased substantially from about seven per year in the 1910s to 140 in the early 1930s. To counteract the increase in union activities, Japanese authorities stepped up the enforcement of the Public Order Maintenance Law, resulting in about 40 fewer strikes per year (Lee,

1989). But Japanese suppression stimulated Korean workers' desire to be independent and turned the labor movement into a national independence movement.

Added to this labor movement was the birth of communism in the Soviet Union in 1918. Communistic ideology appealed to Korean workers as well as intellectuals, who perceived the labor movement as a class struggle between the Japanese capitalist and the Korean proletariat. The involvement of intellectuals in the labor movement produced positive as well as negative outcomes. On the positive side, the labor movement brought Korea's intellectuals and workers together to fight against Japanese colonialism. But, on the negative side, the differences in their respective interests weakened the effectiveness of the labor movement. Trade union leaders, especially at the national level, were mostly intellectuals, and they were more interested in their own political ends than in improving the economic and working conditions of workers. Because of this lack of cohesiveness, most labor actions were poorly organized and coordinated between the national and local levels (Kim, 1985).

8.2.2 Aftermath of World War II

At the end of World War II in 1945, Korea was divided into the communist North and the capitalist South. Trade unions were also divided along these ideological lines. Soon after Korea's independence from Japan, a national federation of trade unions, called *Junpyung* (General Council of Korean Labor Unions), was organized by communists in South Korea (Park and Lee, 1994). These communist-led unions staged more than 2,000 labor disputes up until March 1947, when all communist-led unions in South Korea were made illegal by the U.S. military government. Meanwhile, *Daehan Nochong*, the predecessor of the current Federation of Korean Trade Unions (FKTU), was formed in 1946 by pro-American rightist groups to counteract the communist-led *Junpyung*. *Daehan Nochong* gained the dominance in the Korean labor movement with the support of the U.S. military government. This was the genesis of government intervention in Korea's labor movement; an intervention which continued to prevail until recently.

The labor movement during this period could be characterized as a political struggle between communism and capitalism. *Junpyung* supported the political activities of the communist party of North Korea in the South; *Daehan Nochong* was to fight communism in South Korea. With the birth of the Republic of Korea in 1948, *Daehan Nochong* defeated the communist-led labor union and emerged as the sole labor power in South Korea. Once emerged as the dominant labor force, *Daehan Nochong* could have devoted its energy to improve workers' wages and working conditions. But, in reality, its leaders wasted their energies on political infighting rather than serving the needs of their members. Disenchanted rank-and-files workers formed an independent union federation, called *Nohyup* (Council of Labor Unions) in 1959 (Park, 1979), which merged with *Daehan Nochong* the following year.

Although not much progress was made in labor relations during the first Republic, President Syngman Rhee's government enacted four labor-related laws in 1953 during the Korean War: Labor Union Law, Labor Dispute Adjustment Law, Labor Relations Commission Law, and Labor Standards Law. Labor Union Law dealt with the formation of labor unions, regulations of union activities, management of unions, collective bargaining procedures, definition of unfair labor practices, and penal provisions. Labor Dispute Adjustment Law provided mechanisms and procedures for resolving labor disputes--strikes, sabotages, sit-in demonstrations, and lockouts. Labor Relations Commission Law established the Labor Relations Commission within the Ministry of Labor and defined its roles. Finally, Labor Standards Law defined the basic standards of labor management concerning employment discrimination, dismissal, minimum wage, and retirement allowance.

These labor laws were enacted to guarantee labor's rights to organize, negotiate, and strike, to set labor standards to protect labor, and to handle labor disputes. However, actual implementation of these laws never took place because they were unrealistic in the war-torn economy. These laws emulated the Western-style labor relations, but their application to labor-related problems during and immediately after the Korean War was unrealistic. High unemployment, low wages, poor working conditions, and corruption in union leadership contributed to an unproductive labor movement during this period. These laws were amended several times by subsequent military-dominated governments to restrict labor's rights to pursue their economic and political ends.

8.2.3 Military Dictatorship Phase

The military coup led by General Park Chung Hee in 1961 suspended all union activities. Shortly thereafter, the Federation of Korea Trade Unions (FKTU) was formed. With this union restructuring, trade unions were organized into a number of industry-wide national unions affiliated the FKTU. In order to pursue its ambitious economic development plans, the Park Chung Hee Administration decreed the Law Concerning Social Security to suppress the labor movement. The Administration also amended existing labor laws. These amendments allowed stronger government intervention in labor management. Union activities were restricted and political activities by labor unions were also prohibited. These new laws strengthened industry-wide unions while restricting the autonomy of enterprise unions. Arbitration and emergency adjustment of labor disputes were placed under the control of the government's Labor Relations Commission, denying the workers' right to strike. Additionally, these amendments prohibited the formation of new labor unions.

In the first-half of the 1960s, Korean workers generally accepted the government policy of controlling labor costs and movements so that the country could pursue an export-driven economic development strategy. The export-driven economic policy brought enough economic prosperity in Korea to relax labor movement restrictions in the second-half of the 1960s (Ogle, 1981). Subsequently, labor began to demand high wages and improved working conditions. The number of labor disputes increased in the late 1960s. The number of local unions grew from 1,526 in 1962 to 3,063 in 1970; union membership increased from less than two hundred thousands to nearly a half-million (Lee, 1993, p. 255).

As the number of labor disputes increased, so did the government's resolution to control them. The authoritarian government declared a state of emergency and issued the Special Law on National Security in 1971. This decree suspended the Labor Dispute Adjustment Law. It prohibited labor disputes and required unions to obtain government approval prior to wage negotiations. Additionally, in 1972, President Park introduced the Yooshin Constitution, which allowed presidential decrees to dictate all labor-related activities. With these changes, the government became directly involved in all labor disputes.

The restrictive labor laws were somewhat relaxed after the death of President Park in 1979, but not for long. In the early 1980s, Korea plunged into severe economic stagnation and social confusion due to the world-wide recession after the second energy crisis and the political turmoil following President Park's death. The Fifth Republic headed by President Chun Doo Whan, perceived the labor movement as a potential threat to his power. President Chun amended the Labor Union Law and the Labor Dispute Adjustment Laws to suppress the labor movement. The union shop provision was deleted, third party intervention was prohibited, the cooling-off period was extended, and the arbitration power of the Labor Administration was strengthened. The government also enacted the Labor-Management Council Act in 1980 to further weaken the power of labor unions and at the same time to strengthen the power of management in labor relations.

Labor-Management Council Law required all business enterprises with more than 50 employees, union or nonunion, to form a labor-management council to promote labor-management cooperation. The law required employee representation in the council to deal with employee-related matters such as employee education and training, productivity improvement, wage settlement, grievance handling, prevention of labor disputes, safety and health, and others. Employers were also required to report to the council regarding overall business plans and actual results: capital investment, production, manpower, and financial performance. Labor-management councils, if functioning properly, were to replace or supplement the roles of unions.

As union activities were suppressed, disgruntled workers went underground. The underground labor movement grew rapidly in large part because of the participation of students and intellectuals in union activities. Students and intellectuals saw their involvement in labor affairs as a way of furthering the democratization movement. Students and intellectuals joined the labor force to organize labor unions and led the labor and democratization movement in the workplace (Park and Lee, 1994). These student labor leaders staged a series of strikes in the mid-1980s, eventually leading to the downfall of President Chun and the enactment of political reforms in 1987.

8.2.4 Political Reform Phase

The political reform declaration in June 1987 removed government intervention in labor-management relations and restored the rights of workers to organize, negotiate, and take collective actions (Lee, 1988). Under the newly amended Labor Union Law (1987), union shops became legal provided that more than two-thirds of the employees were union members, and workers were free to establish industry-based national unions. This law also protected workers from unfair labor practices by employers, including

(1) dismissal of, or discrimination against, workers who join or attempt to organize a union;
(2) rejection of a collective bargaining agreement;
(3) harassing workers in the formation and operation of a labor union.

The newly amended Labor Dispute Adjustment Law shortened the cooling-off period during labor disputes, forced arbitration on only those labor disputes involving "businesses vital to the public welfare," and reduced the length of time for withdrawing from a dispute after an emergency adjustment had been announced. In the case of the Labor Standards Law, the amendments called for an expansion of the Law's coverage: priority payment of wages, severance pay, and accident compensation; a reduction of standard work hours from 48 to 44 hours per week; an increase in annual paid leave from a maximum of 8 days and minimum of 3 days to 10 and 8 days respectively; and so forth. Additionally, the government enacted the

Minimum Wage Law, the Gender-free Equal Opportunity Employment Law, and the Industrial Safety and Occupational Health Law.

With their new-found freedom, workers started to reorganize and take collective actions, demanding high wages and improved working conditions. However, due to the lack of any well-established collective bargaining mechanisms and labor-management bargaining experience, workers were taking their grievances to the street to mobilize public opinion against management. As a result, in the second-half of 1987, soon after the political reform declaration, Korea experienced almost 4,000 labor disputes, compared to fewer than 300 in 1986 (National Statistical Office, 1994b, p. 46). The Roh Tae Woo Administration, unlike its predecessors, took a hands-off policy, insisting that labor disputes should be resolved by employers and employees themselves.

During the Roh Administration, more than three thousand new labor unions were formed. Both newly formed unions and previously existing unions, disillusioned with the *Nochong* (FKTU), formed the Korea Trade Union Congress (KTUC), or *Chunnohyup*, in 1990. *Chunnohyup* was especially favored by workers in small companies as an alternative to *Nochong*. Government and business, however, perceived it as a radical labor movement and did not recognize it as a lawful union federation (lee, 1993). Another major union federation, formed during this period, was *Chonkyocho* (Korean Teachers' Union). It too was branded as a radical labor movement, operating outside the government's legal framework.

8.2.5 Civilian Government Phase

The civilian-led government under President Kim Young Sam pressed forward with the labor liberalization movement started by its immediate predecessor. As a long-time fighter for workers' rights and democratic reforms, President Kim garnered the support of labor unions in the presidential election and was perceived to be fair by Korean workers as well as by the general public in dealing with labor-related issues. As a result, the widespread perception that the government only represented the interests of management has been revised. Labor disputes have subsequently become less frequent and violent (Sohn, 1994). Labor disputes still occur, but they receive less sympathy and support from the public, as seen in the labor strike staged by subway and railroad workers in 1994 and the general labor strike in 1996.

Another factor contributing to labor peace was the improved wages and working conditions for Korean workers. As noted in the previous chapter, Korean workers' wages have increased more than 500 percent between 1985 and 1995, making Korean worker wages the second highest in Asia. The income gap between blue and white collar workers has narrowed. Average weekly work hours have been reduced to 44 hours from more than 60 hours a decade ago. Annual paid leaves have grown substantially, and fringe benefits are now comparable to those of workers in advanced nations. Furthermore, Korean workers realized that constant wage increases, without an increase of productivity, could weaken the nation's industrial competitiveness, which in turn would jeopardize their economic well-being (Sohn, 1994).

The observation noted above does not imply that the Kim's government has been totally free from intervention and that labor unrest has been a thing of the past. The government required prior approval of a union's formation, prohibited the formation of a teachers' union in private educational institutions, failed to recognize *Chunnohyup* (Korea Trade Union Congress) and *Chunkyocho* (Korean Teachers' Union) as legal entities, and prohibits political activities of labor unions. These restrictions were contrary to international labor law standards. As a member of the International Labor Organization (ILO), Korea had to revise its labor laws to meet international standards (*Hankook Ilbo*, December 4, 1996, p. 3).

In the absence of the suppression of labor movement, workers have gained freedom to exercise their rights. However, much needed cooperation between labor and management has not been achieved because they both have not gained experience in negotiation and labor still has not removed a deep-seated mistrust in management and government. As a result, any element in the society that causes labor discomfort can lead to labor disputes. A case in point was the massive general labor strike launched against the government's effort to revise the labor laws in 1996. While the new laws would legalize multiple unions at the workplace, third party intervention, and teachers unions, they would make it easier for employers to layoff employees in times of economic distress. There are many latent factors in Korean society that could touch off another round of labor disputes: slow economic growth, high inflation, land speculation, and uneven income distribution.

8.3 Labor Movement and Its Consequences

The Korean government's involvement in labor-management relations, especially during the period of military-led government, was thorough and extensive. The government controlled the entire process of the labor movement, including union formation, wage negotiations, the setting of work hours, labor strikes, and dispute adjustment. Given this historical background, the labor movement in Korea was characterized by labor-government relations rather than labor-management relations (Kim, 1994). The government's labor policy was to develop the nation's economy first and then distribute its wealth later. This policy undoubtedly contributed to the high growth of Korean economy, an average about ten percent annually during the past three decades, and benefitted the economic welfare of the populace. Economic growth, however, stimulated the growth of the middle-class, a group which demanded political freedom. Political democratization was accompanied by the liberalization of labor movement, which in turn adversely affected the nation's international competitiveness. In the following section, we will study the effects of labor movement on the nation's economic performance.

8.3.1 Labor Policy and Economic Performance

Being a country endowed with fewer natural resources, Korea had to rely on human resources for its industrial development. In the developmental process, the government exploited labor to accumulate the capital needed to acquire foreign technology and raw materials. Military-dominated governments justified labor suppression as a means of achieving their economic goals--international competitiveness, full employment, and price stability--and relentlessly pursued these economic goals to legitimize their existence.

The government's economic developmental strategy proved to be positive in achieving its economic goals. During the developmental phase, Korea's economy grew at an annual rate of 10 percent; its exports grew at 30 percent per year; its share of the world trade increased from less than one to 4.5 percent; employment grew at 3.4 percent annually; the unemployment rate dropped from 8.2 to less than 3 percent; the inflation rate dropped from more than 25 to less than 10 percent, and real income grew at an annual rate of 7.6 percent (Park and Lee, 1994; International Monetary Fund, various years; National Statistical Office, various years). Additionally, the Gini coefficient, an income distribution measure, improved from 0.402 in 1970 to 0.368 in 1980 and then to 0.288 in 1990, and wage differentials among varying sectors of the labor market also have narrowed. In short, the government has largely achieved its economic objectives--increased employment opportunity, global industrial competitiveness, and price stability.

The above economic objectives were, however, achieved at the expense of the labor's economic welfare and the development of sound labor-management relations. Although workers benefitted economically from the expanding economy, these gains were achieved through long working hours, poor working conditions, and high industrial accidents. Working hours averaged more than 50 hours per week; fatal accident rates were one out of two thousands annually. These figures represented the highest of this kind among industrial nations (National Statistical Office, various years).

Management, protected by the government in dealing with labor-related problems, failed to develop sound labor relation policies and bargaining procedures. As noted earlier, whenever labor disputes erupted, the government was called in to settle the disputes; disputes were settled mostly in favor of management. The involvement of the state in labor relations left little room for employers to play any major role. The Korean Employers' Federation (KEF) was formed in 1971 to deal with labor-related issues. However, because autonomous collective bargaining between labor and management was prohibited for the most part of the 1970s and 1980s, the KEF was ineffective. It was only after 1987 that the KEF begun to play a proper role. The KEF serves as the employers' counterpart of the FKTU in dealing with labor-related issues.

Workers, disenchanted by the lack of free labor movement, increasingly turned to the radical underground union activities. In the absence of well-established collective bargaining mechanisms, workers took their grievances to the streets and often resorted to radical subversive activities. Workers and labor leaders were not satisfied with dispute settlement packages offered by government officials, no matter how good they were, because they felt that they would have gained better deals had they exercised their rights to negotiate and take collective actions (Kim, 1994). In 1987, workers joined with student demonstrators to overthrow the authoritarian government, ushering in the political reform process. Ironically, the national economic expansion that was in large part derived from the repression of labor rights by the government strengthened the political power of workers.

8.3.2 Labor and International Competitiveness

Since the political reforms in 1987, the labor movement has expanded. The number of labor union units (enterprise unions) increased from 2,534 in 1986 to 7,698 in 1990, doubling membership from 1,036 thousands to 1,887 thousands (Ministry of Labor, various years). The impact of the new development in labor movement on economy is far-reaching. Wages of Korean workers have increased substantially in the late 1980s and early 1990s, making their wages the second highest in Asia. More importantly, workers have gained their rights to organize, negotiate, and strike.

These changes in labor relations have had a significant impact on the nation's international competitiveness and industrial structure. Cost-push inflationary pressures have been severe as wages increased at a double-digit rate annually. According to the Korea Development Institute's study, between 1987 and 1995, Korean workers' wages increased 14.5 percent annually, compared to an increase of 11 percent in productivity (*Hankook Ilbo*, October 30, 1996, p. 8). This rapid increase in wages undoubtedly contributed to high inflation and weakened international competitiveness. Consumer prices went up by 6.6 percent annually for 1988-95; producer prices rose by 3.2 percent during the same period. The trade surplus, which had been increasing since 1986, recorded its highest level at $8.9 billion in 1988, dropped substantially. Since 1990 Korea's trade balance turned into trade deficit, reaching the level of nearly $20 in 1996. The growth rate of Korea's GNP also slowed to 5.1 percent level in 1992, the lowest in recent years (National Statistical Office, 1994).

In the first-half of the 1990s, the Korean economy, despite rising wages, expanded, although it did so at a slower rate. Two factors accounted for the steady growth of the economy. The increased wages of Korean workers stimulated domestic consumption, and the over-valued Japanese yens helped Korean exports. To deal with labor shortages and rising labor costs, large firms contracted out labor intensive work to small firms to avoid high union wages. Small and medium-size firms in turn employed foreign workers at low wages, or relocated their production facilities overseas for cheap labor. By 1996, nearly 100,000 foreign workers were employed by small firms in Korea. In 1992, 73.6 percent of the foreign direct investment by Korean firms was done by small companies mostly in Southeast Asian countries (Park and Lee, 1994). As noted in Chapter 4, large Korean firms also increased their foreign direct investment in order to deal with raising labor costs in Korea.

Since Korea no longer is a low-wage country, it has to sustain its economic growth by promoting high value-added industries. Changes in the industrial structure from labor-intensive low-tech industries to capital-intensive high-tech are normal in an industrialization process. In the case of Korea, the structural change has had to occur rapidly due to the rapid increase in wages. As shown in Chapter 5, Korea has made great strides in this direction by heavily investing in such capital-intensive high-tech industries as consumer electronics, semiconductors, information processing, telecommunications, and nuclear energy (*Business Week*, July 31, 1995; *Business Korea*, February 1995, 18-20). This point has been elaborated on in Chapter 5.

8.4 Patterns of Industrial Relations

Labor-management relations in Korea have entered a new era in which employers and employees themselves deal with labor-related issues without government interference. Most disputes are now settled through negotiation between labor and management. However, due to the lack of well-established collective bargaining procedures and experiences, negotiations quickly break down into sit-ins and work-slow-downs. Adding to these problems is the role of government in this new era. Can the government afford to be totally neutral and use a hands-off policy in dealing with the nation's labor problems? Should the government use the police force to deal with violent labor disputes as a last resort? Also the labor laws are presently unclear about the scope and structure of collective bargaining. To what extent should workers be allowed to participate in managerial decision making processes? We will review these issues in the following section.

8.4.1 Union Organization and Bargaining Structure

In Korea, a labor union is basically formed at the enterprise level, and workers at a company regardless of their job categories join the same union. Local unions in the same industry establish an industrial federation. Twenty-one federations constitute the Korea Federation of Trade Unions (KFTU). There were 7,698 local unions with a membership of 1.8 million in 1990, compared to 2,658 local unions with a total member of about one million prior to the political democratization in 1987. Union membership stabilized in the first-half of the 1990s.

The KFTU has been the sole national union organization authorized by the government since the 1960s. There is a rival organization, the Korea Trade Union Congress (KTUC), or *Chunnohyup*, but it has not been recognized as a legal entity by the government. There are other non-affiliated independent industrial federations, such as the Korean Clerical and Financial Workers' Union and the Korean Teachers and Educational Workers' Union, which are mainly composed of white-collar workers. In some unorganized companies, labor-management councils play the role of union under the Labor-Management Council Law.

By law, collective bargaining is carried out at the enterprise level, and the FKTU and *Chunnohyup* propose the general guideline for their affiliated unions. Because of this in-house structure of labor unions, the influence of these national centers is limited to general economic and political issues, and firm-specific issues are negotiated by local unions. The national and industrial federations can assist local unions in organizing and educating workers in the process of developing bargaining strategies.

Related to the enterprise unionism has been the prohibition of multiple unions at a plant. In order to prevent the confusion and conflict of multiple unions in a single plant, the Labor Union Law prohibited the establishment of two or more unions. Once a union complete its registration with the government, it has been entitled to demand collective bargaining and negotiation. The labor law used to require a union be formed with a minimum of 30 workers or one-fifth of the total workforce. An amendment of the law in 1989 abolished this requirement. As a result, two or more workers can organize a labor union, provided its application is approved by the government. The new amendment of the labor law in 1996 would allow multiple unions in the workplace.

The exclusiveness of a single local union could create serious problems for the labor movement. A small management-favored union, commonly known as *sweetheart union*, could exclude a competing union, even one with a large membership, in collective bargaining (Kim, 1994). A case in point was the labor dispute at the Hyundai shipyard in 1987. A small labor union at the shipyard was organized in July 21, 1987 upon the successful completion of its registration. A week later, a large group of workers at the plant, claiming that the union was a sweetheart union, demanded that Hyundai to expel the small union. The employer, under the pressure, agreed to do so, but the union resisted by charging management with interfering in the normal activities of a legally-constituted union. Because the employer was unable to expel the existing union, thousands of workers from eleven Hyundai member companies engaged in violent demonstrations for several days. These discords eventually led to a long and violent strikes in 1988. To avoid such pitfalls, the law was revised in 1996 to allow multiple unions at a plant or select one on a majority vote.

8.4.2 Labor Dispute and Conflict Resolution

The number of labor disputes skyrocketed in 1987, following the declaration of political reform. The apparent chaos in labor-management relations during this period was largely due to the lack of well-established bargaining procedures and direct negotiation experiences without government involvement. The most popular forms of dispute were sit-ins, refusal to work, and demonstrations. In 1980, about half of labor disputes were in the form of sit-ins. The proportion increased to about 65 percent in 1987, and decreased to 13 percent by 1990. Refusal to work was also popular; it becam more frequent than sit-ins in the early 1990s (National Statistical Office, 1994a, p.97).

About one-third of labor disputes arose from disputes over wage negotiations and working conditions, another third over wage delinquencies, and the rest from other causes such as plant closures, layoffs, and unfair labor practices. More than 85 percent of labor disputes in 1987 were aimed at improving wages and working conditions. Kim (1994), however, cautioned that many labor strikes occur, not as a result of a single cause, but because of multiple reasons.

The labor disputes in the late 1980s were not an exclusive phenomenon of unionized firms. In 1987, more disputes occurred in nonunionized companies than in unionized ones: 1,356 vs. 599. This abnormal phenomenon illustrates the unhealthy state of Korean industrial relations during the decades of military dictatorship. During this period, official unions did not represent the interests of workers, and frustrated workers had to rely on unlawful acts of protest (Lee, 1993). Freedom in the labor movement brought these nonunionized workers to unionization. As a result, more than 95 percent of labor disputes in 1990 occurred in unionized firms (Korea Labor Institute, 1991, p. 61).

Once labor disputes occur, the concerned parties can bring the issues to the Labor Relations Commission for resolution. The Commission has the authority to rule on matters related to unfair labor practices. It may order a relief, dismiss the case, or reject consideration. It also provides conciliation, mediation, and arbitration on matters related to wage disputes and working conditions. The number of cases brought to the Commission increased steadily from 528 in 1987 to 1,887 cases in 1989. A dramatic jump in the number of unfair labor practices charges reflected the increase in the number of unions and their intensified activities. However, the proportion of relief orders has declined from 35 percent in 1983 to 11 percent in 1990. At the same time, the dismissal rates ran about 25 percent. The proportion of voluntary withdrawals by unions was 55 percent in 1989 and 39 percent in 1990 (Lee, 1993). Probably some of the charges, brought to the Commission, were frivolous in nature.

Labor disputes could be legally resolved by following the conflict resolution procedures, stipulated in the Labor Dispute Adjustment Law, such as notifying the administrative authorities, seeking conciliation and mediation, and not agreeing to bring the dispute to arbitration. However, both labor and management often failed to adopt such procedures. Unions have taken the tactics of "act first, and negotiate later," in which workers engaged in sit-ins and work-slow-downs even the before official bargaining processes started (Kim, 1990). Employers also avoided lawful collective bargaining actions for fear of getting involved in lengthy, costly negotiations. They would rather invite government intervention or make concessions to labor than engage in collective bargaining.

Since 1990, the number of labor disputes has declined significantly to what might be considered a normal level of 235 in 1992 and 144 in 1993. Labor relations in Korea seemed to enter a new era of labor stability in the first-half of the 1990s. The relative stability in labor-management relations had been achieved for several reasons: First, the civilian government under President Kim Young Sam maintained neutrality in labor-management relations. It appeared that labor accepted the legitimacy of Kim's government. Second, management took union demands seriously and dealt with them sincerely. Finally, workers enjoyed a higher standard of living due to wage gains in the past few years. They also seemed to fear the likelihood of lay-offs if the nation loses its industrial competitiveness (*Business Korea*, 1994).

As noted earlier, however, there still are latent problems that could easily touch off labor problems (Sohn, 1994). If workers lose the economic gains they have achieved in recent years to inflation, job security, job scarcity, and/or managerial insensitivity, they would not hesitate to return to the old confrontational modes of industrial relations. The widespread labor strike, in response to the government's effort to easy management's burdens, already has proved this point.

8.4.3 Wage Negotiation and Settlement

The ways in which wage increases have been negotiated and settled typify the labor-management interactions in Korea. Prior to 1987, unions played a limited role in wage determination. The extent to which labor unions could force management to accept their demands for wage increases, called the union effect, was relatively small due to labor movement restriction (Kim, 1994). In the late 1970s and early 1980s, during the high inflationary period, union demands for wage increases ranged from 48 percent to 58 percent. Employers' initial offers were much less than half of the union demands, and actual wage increases were settled closer to employer offers than to union demands. The gaps between union demands and employer offers was narrowed somewhat during the price stabilization period (1982-87), but actual wage increases were still closer to employers' initial offers.

The union effect on wage increases became evident only after labor gained its basic rights to organize, negotiate, and strike in 1987. As noted early, actual wage increases were much closer to union demands than to employers' initial offers. In the early 1990s, actual wage increases were even higher than union demands. Employers in nonunionized companies, for fear of unionization of their firms, granted higher wage increases.

Although wages are negotiated at the enterprise level, FKTU and KEF appear to have a significant impact on wage settlements. Despite their limited roles, these national organizations have been influential in wage determinations because labor as well as management use the wage increase guidelines suggested by FKTU and KEF in their initial bids (Park and Lee, 1994). The differences in wage increases suggested by FKTU and KEF have been wide, but FKTU has been more effective than the KEF in influencing wage determinations.

Prior to 1987, the government played a decisive role in wage determination. As noted earlier, the government used to intervene in labor disputes mostly in favor of management. Following the political reform in 1987, the government promised a hands-off policy in labor-management relations. However, as the rapid wage increases threatened the price stability and international competitiveness, the government began to intervene in an indirect manner. In the early 1990s, the government advised, with little success, labor and management to settle their wage increases to less than a single-digit figure. Actual wage increases, however, far exceeded the single-digit guideline. In order to deal with the problems of rising wages, the government has amended the labor law to make it easier for employers to layoff employees in times of economic downturn.

8.4.4 Labor Management Practices

Korean employers, like their counterparts elsewhere, have resisted unionization in their plants. Various tactics have been adopted to discourage unionization. While some firms resort to unfair, often violent, labor practices, others take more conciliatory and proactive approaches (Lee, 1993). Unfair labor practices by employers include: dismissing employees for unionization activities, forcing yellow dog contracts, not bargaining with labor union leaders, interfering in normal union operations, subsidizing union expenses, and punishing employees for participating in collective actions. More proactive approaches would involve higher wages, better working conditions, better employee and managerial training, and other personnel management practices.

Chung and Lie (1989) found that companies with fewer labor disputes in the late 1980s tended to be nonunionized but adopted proactive labor management approaches. In contrast, companies with frequent labor disputes were unionized and lacked such positive management practices. Even in unionized firms, those which adopted proactive approaches experienced few labor disputes. It would have cost more for employers to adopt proactive management practices, but there was a payoff in maintaining labor peace. Also, the employees in those companies with fewer labor disputes felt more positive about their jobs, compensation, human relations, communications, and labor-management relations than those in dispute-prone companies.

Samsung Business Group is a prime example of adopting proactive labor management programs. Since its inception, Samsung has maintained the "no union at any cost" policy. To prevent unions, Samsung has adopted a set of sophisticated human resource management practices including a rigorous selection process, employee training and development, merit-based promotions and compensation, and better than industry average pay. While practicing such proactive labor management programs, Samsung has been accused of using both legal and illegal union-busting tactics, such as encouraging pro-company employees to submit a union formation report to the government to preempt the formation of a bonafide union with the majority of employee support. As a result, only four out of twenty-seven Samsung-affiliated companies are unionized, and among these companies only one union, at Central Daily Newspapers, is active.

8.5 Options for Korean Industrial Relations

Much progress has been made in recent years in dealing with labor-related problems in Korea. Employers no longer see union leaders as socialistic radicals who undermine management's prerogatives; workers do not see their employers as capitalistic exploiters. However, the basic tenet of labor-management relations in Korea is still confrontational, deeply rooted in the history of industrial relations in Korea. As long as management attempts to maximize efficiency and profitability and labor seeks better wages and working conditions, conflicts between labor and management will continue. In the past, such conflicts were resolved by government intervention. As the government becomes increasingly reluctant to intervene, labor and management must find a way in which their conflict can be productively resolved. Since it is a relatively new experience for labor and management to become directly involved in collective bargaining and conflict resolution, it will be beneficial for them to review and learn from the experiences of other nations in dealing with labor relations. Of particular interest are the industrial relations in the U.S., Japan, and Germany.

8.5.1 Industrial Relations in U.S.A.

The history of labor-management relations in the U.S. has been wrought with endless struggles between labor and management. In the initial stage of economic development in the 19th and early 20th centuries, workers were exploited by capitalists (Leap, 1991). The exploitation of children, African slaves, and new immigrants was common; substantial wage cuts and massive layoffs were also common. Workers fought back with unionization efforts, sabotage, and strikes. Employers responded with such anti-union tactics as yellow dog contacts (forcing new employees to pledge nonunion activities), industrial spies (monitoring union activities), blacklisting (circulating the names of labor activists among employers), and sweetheart unions (unions set up by employers). During this period, government officials, judges, and legislators were supportive of employers. Federal and state police forces were deployed to protect employers' interests, and courts readily issued injunctions against striking workers.

It was only after the Great Depression of the 1930s that workers gained their rights to organize, negotiate, and strike. Recognizing the lack of purchasing power on the part of workers as a reason for the depression, the government enacted the National Labor Relations Act (Wagner Act) and instituted the National Labor Relations Board (NLRB) in 1935 to enforce the Act. This law protected workers from unfair labor practices by employers. It prohibited employers from interfering with employees in exercising their rights in unionizing, interfering with the formation or administration of unions, encouraging or discouraging membership in any union, discriminating against employees who filed unfair labor practice charges, and refusing good faith bargaining with duly elected union representative. With the passage of this Act, unions enjoyed a phenomenal growth between 1935 and 1947, increasing their members from approximately 4 million to 16 million. It was during this period that the two national union organizations--the American Federation of Labor (AFL), established in 1881, and Congress of Industrial Organizations (CIO), established in 1935--expanded their power bases.

In spite of their growing popularity, unions restrained themselves from collective bargaining activities during World War II for the sake of winning the war. The end of the war brought a period of labor unrest. Once the war ended, workers demanded higher wages, which were frozen during the war, and improved working conditions. Unrestrained collective bargaining led to a large number of labor disputes involving strikes, sabotages, and lockouts. In order to curb labor unrest, the Labor-Management Relations Act (the Taft-Hartley Act) was enacted in 1947. This Act protected employers and individual workers from unfair labor practices by unions. It prohibited unions from restricting employees in exercising their rights, causing employers to discriminate against employees engaged in unionization, refusing to bargain in good faith with employers, engaging in unlawful strikes or boycotts, charging employees excessive union initiation fees and dues, and engaging in featherbedding.

Although the Taft-Hartley Act restricted union activities, the power of unions still grew due to the expanding post-war economy in the 1950s and 1960s. The U.S. was the major producers of the world's goods. During this expansionary period, unions gained strength. Unions were successful in gaining increased wages and benefits. Unfortunately, this eroded the U.S. industrial competitiveness in an increasing competitive world. Recovering from their war-torn economies, Germany and Japan challenged the U.S. in economic warfare. Other latecomers, such as Taiwan, Singapore, Hong Kong, and Korea, emerged as formidable competitors. As a result, workers in the industrial sector experienced layoffs, plant closings, and wage concessions. Throughout the 1970s and 1980s, union membership dwindled from approximately 35 percent of the workforce in the 1950s to less than 15 per-cent in the 1990s. Furthermore, improved labor-oriented legislation (e.g., the Civil Rights Act, health and safety regulations, and minimum wage law) and human resource management techniques (e.g., job enlargement, job enrichment, quality circles, and employee empowerment) reduced the need for union protection.

Currently, the issues at bargaining tables center around job security and skill training rather than around issues related to traditional union demands--higher wages, increased benefits, and improved working conditions. Jobs are not expanding much in the industrial sector; wages are not increasing as fast as they did in past decades. Unions have become more cooperative in implementing organizational and technological changes. As union power declines, employers are becoming increasingly assertive in determining wage increases, resulting in improved profitability (Craver, 1993). As a result, Corporate America is getting healthier, but workers' economic welfare is threatened. At the moment, unions are cooperative with management. But, if Corporate America continues to undermine employees' economic and psychological well-being, it will destroy the capacity of workers to compete in the increasingly competitive global market.

Korea and the U.S. differ greatly in their economic, political, and cultural experiences. And yet, the two economies share many similar experiences in labor-management relations. First, workers were exploited during the initial stages of economic development. Second, management fought hard to keep unions out. Third, both governments were pro-management, intervening in favor of management. Finally, industrial relations in both countries were marked by violent labor disputes. As Korea shares similar experiences, it can learn some lessons from its American counterparts. An important lesson is that the confrontational mode of labor-management relations leads to a zero-sum game in which one party can win at the expense of the other. Such a zero-sum game can weaken the industrial competitiveness of the entire economy. Labor-management cooperation is urgently needed to sustain the economic growth and labor peace.

8.5.2 Industrial Relations in Japan

Before World War II, the labor movement was severely restricted by the imperial government as a measure in its pursuit of wartime activities (Taira, 1993). In fact, labor unions were dissolved by the government as part of its wartime resource mobilization efforts. The end of the war opened the floodgate for unionization of Japanese workers. General Douglas MacArthur, the Supreme Commander of the Allied Forces (SCAP), directed the Japanese government to eliminate all obstacles to the labor movement. During this period, workers spontaneously organized themselves in an effort to correct past unfair labor practices by management and to deal with such economic hardships as low wages and runaway inflation in the aftermath of the war. It was the most violent period in the history of Japan's industrial relations. In 1949, the unionization rate reached an all-time high of 55.7 percent of the Japanese labor force.

In order to promote unionization, SCAP enacted the first Japanese labor legislation, the Labor Union Law, in 1945. This law emulated the pro-labor provisions of the Wagner Act of the Unites States. Under this law, any group of workers could organize a labor union, provided that certain documentary requirements were met. It further stated that workers could demand collective bargaining with the employer, and be protected from unfair labor practices. The Japanese Constitution, adopted in 1947, also guarantees the workers' rights to organize union, engage in collective bargaining, and take collective action. These constitutional rights were implemented through the Labor Union Law, Labor Dispute Adjustment Law, and Labor Standards Law, and Labor Relations Commission Law. The Labor Union Law defined the workers' basic rights; Labor Dispute Adjustment Law provided mechanisms for resolving labor disputes; Labor Standards Law stipulated standards for wages, working hours, and other working conditions; Labor Relations Commission Law defined the role of the Labor Relations Commission in labor disputes.

Despite the pro-union constitution and legislation, Japanese unions are not as powerful as their counterparts in the U.S. and Western Europe for several reasons (Kochan, 1994; Taira, 1993). First, unlike national and industrial labor unions in Western societies that are powerful enough to shape their national industrial relations policies, Japanese labor unions emerged as enterprise unions. Enterprise unions are organized at the enterprise level with little help from outside organizers, and they include both blue and white collar workers. Although enterprise unions belong to the national labor union center (Japanese Trade Union Confederation), actual collective bargaining occurs at the enterprise level. An exception to this enterprise collective bargaining is the annual round of business, labor, and government consultations and subsequent labor-management negotiations during the Spring Wage Offensive.

Second, in many non-unionized firms, employee associations play the role of labor unions in terms of representing workers' interests to management and consulting with management on matters related to management plans, production schedules, wages and benefits, layoffs, and other aspects of labor-management relations. In principle, employee associations have as much rights as do unions in collective bargaining processes, guaranteed by the Japanese Constitution. If employee associations want to be protected by the labor law, they can always register themselves as labor unions with the labor administration.

Third, Japanese employers early on, recognizing the importance of labor peace, adopted progressive human resource management strategies (e.g., lifetime employment, promotion within, extensive training, and quality circles) that encourage institutional loyalty and work motivation (McMillan, 1996). Faced with labor unrest and labor shortages during the post-war period, Japanese employers made a decision to make employees as major stakeholders of their firms by letting them to play part in influencing managerial decisions and sharing economic gains. The cooperative relationship between labor and management is further reinforced by promoting union leaders to managerial positions. Leadership qualities that have been demonstrated as union leaders are incorporated into performance appraisal for selecting future managers.

Fourth, the financial structure of Japanese firms makes it easier for management to elevate employees as major stakeholders, with greater importance than stockholders. Because Japanese firms heavily rely on debt financing (bank loans) and interlocking equity ownership by member companies of a business group, outside stockholders have only nominal influence on managerial decisions. Furthermore, SCAF destroyed the Japanese *zaibatsu* system in which business firms were owned and managed by individual entrepreneurs or financial cliques. As business ownership and management were separated, management (composed of professional managers) was able to pursue long-term growth, employment stability, and labor cooperation that would ensure their own interest (see Chapter 3).

Finally, Japanese society as whole promotes labor peace and harmony. It is culturally adverse to the concepts of "bargaining" and "grievance." The term "bargaining" implies cunning, guile, and bad faith; "grievance" implies failures or defects of the system (Taira, 1993). The society also has been capable of creating a tripartite body composed of high-level government, business, and labor leaders to consul and guide the nation's industrial relations. This body annually debates issues related to consumer prices, wage increases, bankruptcy rates, unemployment rates, corporate profits, and so on. These debates often yield a set of general guidelines related to these issues, acceptable to the concerned parties.

Would Japanese workers have gained more if they had developed strong and militant unions? The answer is probably no. By maintaining a cooperative relationship with management, they have gained more economically than their counterparts in the United Sates (Marshall, 1987). The cooperative relationship between labor and management does not mean that unions are becoming subservient to management. Japanese employers are aware of the consequences of violent labor-management relations and thus take proactive stands to avoid them. Progressive human resource management has been adopted by Japanese employers as a defensive mechanism in response to the violent labor unrest experienced just after World War II. Without this painful experience, the rights of Japanese workers might not have been granted.

The lessons that the Korean labor movement can learn from the Japanese experience is that the presence or threat of strong unions is essential to the enhancement of workers' rights. However, employers can preempt the resurgence of strong unionism by adopting progressive human resource management strategies. Since Koreans share many cultural similarities with the Japanese, the Japanese-style cooperative labor-management system would seem preferable. However, a major difference is that most Korean firms are owned and managed by individual entrepreneurs or their families, and thus workers' interests can not be elevated to the level of stockholders. The inherent conflict between workers and stockholders will continue to become an obstacle for harmonious labor-management relations.

8.5.3 Industrial Relations in Germany

German industrial relations are characterized by a pattern of "cooperative conflict resolution" within the corporate governance structure of codetermination (Streeck, 1993; Kochan, 1994). Under the Works Constitution Act of 1972, works councils are created in German firms. These councils are given the right to consult and participate in decision-making processes involving such matters as employee training, layoffs, health and safety, technological change, and others. Works councils are also charged with the responsibility of supervising the implementations of industrial agreements, but they are barred from negotiating on matters that have already been negotiated. Works council members are elected from rank-and-file employees regardless of their union membership. However, about 80 percent of works council members are elected from candidates endorsed by German Trade Union Federation (DGB) (Streeck, 1993). Consequently, works councils have become the centers of the German labor movement in the workplace.

Workers are also represented at the supervisory boards of German firms, which are high-level decision-making bodies. One of the supervisory board's functions is to appoint a top management team, including president, vice presidents, and a personnel director. Most decisions made by supervisory boards are taken unanimously. However, in the case of a split vote, the chairman who represents the shareholders' interests casts the deciding vote. Nevertheless, since workers occupy 50 percent of the board's seats, they have strong voices in the corporate governance of German firms, characterizing it as a "system of codetermination."

While labor-management cooperation is achieved internally through a system of codetermination, actual collective bargaining activities take place largely outside the firm at the industry level, either nationwide or regionally. Regional bargaining sessions are attended by the representatives of industrial unions and corresponding employers associations, who work closely with their national organizations. On the union side, the German Trade Union Federation (DGB) is the most dominant national labor center. Others include German Staff Union (DAG) and the German Association of Civil Servants. On the employer side is the Federation of German Employers Associations (BDA). Agreements reached at the industrial and regional level are generally honored by individual firms.

The government also plays an important role in shaping the characteristics of the nation's industrial relations. The government provides labor exchange services, administers unemployment insurance, and finances training programs. The government's labor-related services are administered by the Labor Administration (BA), and the representatives of trade unions, employers associations, and government officials sit on the BA's national decision-making bodies. Through this labor-business-government partnership, cooperative labor-management relations are maintained.

If satisfactory industrial agreements are not achieved, labor strikes can be called only by the national executive of industrial unions. The number of actual strikes is small because the partnership between labor, business, and government has been productive and costs of labor strikes would be high for workers. By law, unions have to pay strike benefits at the rate of two-thirds of take-home pay. Strikes in conjunction with industry-wide settlements tend to be lengthy and costly. To add to the pain of striking, employers associations impose "retaliatory lockouts" in a region where the union has taken a selective strike. Consequently, unions will not strike unless a large strike fund has been accumulated. If they decide to strike, efforts will be focused on a limited number of companies which would give them a maximum impact (Streeck, 1993).

Cooperative labor-management relations in Germany have helped to create and maintain the world's most productive economy. Germany continues to be the world's largest exporters of manufactured goods, and its workers enjoy the world's highest standards of living. The partnership between labor, business, and government has made it possible for them to pursue high product quality, high wages, and efficient service strategies in high value-added industries. The unique feature of industrial relations in Germany, however, has created the problem of high unemployment. As the economy focuses on high value-added industries with high-skilled workers, job opportunities for others have dwindled. During the first-half of the 1990s, the unemployment rate was more than ten percent, higher than that of the U.S., Japan, and Korea.

Can or should Korea emulate the German model of industrial relations? A labor-business-government partnership is certainly desirable for developing a coherent set of industrial relations strategies that are acceptable to the concerned parties. The creation of an informal tripartite body that can productively debate various issues such as wages, profits, unemployment, industrial competitive, labor-management relations, and others in an interconnected manner is in order. However, the pursuit of high wage strategies in high value-added industries can cause a severe problem for the Korea economy, which is saddled with high population density.

8.5.4 Implications for Korean Labor Relations

The industrial relations systems of these three countries differ in their structures and collective bargaining processes. However, they share several characteristics that are common to all advanced industrial societies (Kochan, 1994). First, labor-management relations in all advanced nations are based on the fundamental rights of workers to organize, bargain, and strike. Within this framework, workers have the right to join or not join an union, and if they want to join, they have the right to join a union of their choice. Second, the effectiveness of these industrial relation systems is evaluated against the impacts they have on the twin goals of industrial societies--equity and efficiency. The equity issue is concerned with how well the fruit of labor is distributed; and the efficiency issue deals with labor productivity and economic performance. Finally, in all these examples, labor and management frequently found and still find themselves in conflict situations. However, they have developed an effective mechanism for conflict resolution--through the market system, progressive human resource management, or a cooperative mechanism. In the case of the U.S., the marketplace moderates the balance of power between labor and management. In Japan and Germany, such a balance is achieved through cooperation between labor and management. The key to this conflict resolution effort is to achieve a balance between the issues of equity and efficiency. Achieving the same kind of balance should be the standard against which Korean industrial relations are to be evaluated.

Judging against this standard, Korean industrial relations are considered to be in an early stage of development. Prior to 1987, Korea's economic growth had been achieved at the expense of workers' welfare (the equity issue). Under the "growth first, distribution later" policy, the government suppressed the workers' basic rights and their demands for higher wages. Even after the political democratization and labor movement liberalization in 1987, the government continued to suppress union activities associated with *Chunnohyup* (Korean Trade Union Congress) and *Chunkyocho* (Korean Teachers' Union). Fortunately, Korea has joined the ranks of advanced nations in granting the workers' basic rights to organize or join any union and freely participate in collective bargaining and action. It is now the workers' turn to function responsibly in the new framework in labor-management relations.

Regarding the issue of efficiency, the military-dominated governments prior to 1987 achieved remarkable success in disciplining and influencing all sectors of the economy, including business and labor, in their efforts to industrialize the nation. Ironically their success stimulated the growth of the middle class, which in turn fought for political democratization as well as labor movement liberalization. Although the labor movement is not totally free in the new political environment, workers mustered enough power to force business and government to increase their wages and improve their working conditions. In fact, increased wages surpassed increases in productivity to the extent that the growth of Korean economy stalled somewhat in the early 1990s (the efficiency issue). The Korean economy recovered from this setback in the mid-1990s primarily due to the over-valued Japanese yen, but it would encounter a setback in the second-half of the 1990s unless increases in wages are substantially moderated. Although workers have moderated their demands for higher wages, the pressure for improving labor productivity has not been resolved.

What all this implies is that Korea needs to find an effective way of resolving labor-management conflicts. At the moment, the task of conflict resolution is left to the outcome of power struggle between labor and management. When labor and management engage in continuous power struggles, much needed cooperation is hard to achieve. When employers have the upper-hand, employees' well-being is threatened. Conversely, when unions are disproportionally strong, wages outpace labor productivity, causing business to falter. An alternative is to develop a corporative body that seeks a balance between the conflicting demands of labor, business, and government (general public). The industrial relations systems in Japan and Germany have demonstrated how such corporatism can be developed. Additionally, the Japanese have demonstrated the importance of practicing progressive human resource management in keeping labor peace. Koreans certainly should emulate some of the Japanese labor management practices and benefit from their experience.

8.6 Summary

Labor-management relations in Korea have been characterized as confrontational. Unlike labor movements in other industrial nations, which started and continued as economic entities seeking economic gains for labor, the labor movement in Korea started as an anti-colonial movement during the Japanese occupation of Korea (1910-1945) and was maintained as a political tool in the aftermath of World War II and during the first Republic (1945-1961). Even during the period of substantial economic growth (1961-1987), labor became a tool for economic growth. The labor movement was suppressed by the military-dominated governments for the sake of maintaining labor peace and low production costs.

The political, economic, and social situation has changed since the political reform process, started in the summer of 1987. With political reform came the liberalization of the labor movement. This opened the flood gate for labor's demands for higher wages and improved working conditions. The number of labor disputes increased from less than 300 in 1986 to more than 3,600 in 1987. Workers' wages doubled during the first four years after the political reform process started, making them the second highest in Asia. Working hours were reduced from 54 to 49 hours per week during that period. Labor unrest during this period was to a large extent due to the lack of direct collective bargaining experience without government intervention.

Labor-management relations have gained some stability since the installment of a civilian-dominated government in 1993. The new government has been more sympathetic to the plight of workers but even-handed in dealing with labor-related problems. It has aimed at achieving the twin goals of achieving equity and efficiency, but it has been lacking in developing an industrial relations system to this end. Korean labor-management relations are at crossroads. It is difficult to foresee whether they will adopt the cooperative mode of the Japanese, the German system, or the confrontational mode of the Americans.

Korean labor-management relations are still confrontational in nature. The balance of power between labor and management is moderated by market forces. What is needed for now and in the future is the creation of a cooperative mechanism that can bring labor, business, and government together to develop a coherent set of industrial relations policies aimed at achieving twin goals--equity and efficiency. Such a mechanism requires the development of trust by sharing gains or pains among the concerned parties; it must be a mechanism different from the old system that imposed sacrifice on labor. This system, if properly instituted and managed, is likely to minimize the incidents of labor disputes.

References

Business Korea. (1994): "Labor-Management Wage Negotiations: Unions Focus on Improving Employee Benefits," 11(9):34-35.

Business Korea. (1995): "Korea-Japan Rivalry: A Different Kind of War," 12(8):18-20.

Business Week. (1995): "Korea: A Cover Story," July 31:56-63.

Chung, K.H. (1988): "Labor-Management Relations in Korea: In Comparison with Industrial Relations in the United States," *KRC Quarterly*, 1(3):1-4.

Chung, K.H. and Lie, H.K. (1989): "Labor Management Relations in Korea," in K.H. Chung and H.C. Lee (eds.), *Korean Managerial Dynamics*. New York: Praeger, pp. 217-231.

Craver, C.B. (1993): "The American Labor Movement in the Year 2000," *Business Horizons*, 36(6):64-69.

Federation of Korean Trade Union (1979): *History of Korea Labor Union Movement*. Seoul: Federation of Korea Trade Union.

International Monetary Fund (IMF)(various years): *International Financial Statistics*. Washington, DC: International Monetary Fund.

Kim, C.S. (1995): "Korea's Labor Legislation: Past and Present," *Korea Focus*, 3(3):78-84.

Kim, I.J. (1985): "Korea's Trade Union Movement," in K.S. Kim and H.C. Park (eds.), *Korea's Trade Union Movement Theory*. Seoul: Miraesa, pp. 13-112.

Kim, S.K. (1994): "Korean Labor-Management Relations," in L.J. Cho and Y.H. Kim (eds.), *Korea's Political Economy: An Institutional Perspective*. Boulder, CO: Westview Press, pp. 623-661.

Kim, T. (1990): *Industrial Relations and Collective Bargaining in Korea: Recent Developments*. Seoul: Korea Labor Institute.

Kochan, T.A. (1994): "Industrial Relations and Human Resource Policy in Korea: Options for Continued Reform," in L.J. Cho and Y.H. Kim (eds.), *Korea's Political Economy*. Boulder, CO: Westview Press, pp. 663-697.

Korea Labor Institute (1991): *Quarterly Labor Review*, 1(4):42-65.

Leap, T.L. (1991): *Collective Bargaining and Labor Relations*. New York: Macmillan.

Lee, J.T. (1988): "Labor Politics and Industrial Relations in Korea," *Journal of East and West Studies*, 17(2):17-30.

Lee, M.B. (1993): "Korea," in M. Rothman, D.R. Briscoe, and R.C.D. Nacamulli, (eds.), *Industrial Relations Around the World*. Berlin, New York: Walter de Gruyter, pp. 245-269.

Lee, Y.H. (1989): *Industrial Relations and Trade Union Movement*. Seoul: Younghak Press.

Marshall, R. (1987): *Unheated Voices*. New York: Basic Books.

McMillan, C.J. (1996): *The Japanese Industrial System*. Third Revised Edition. Berlin, New York: Walter de Gruyter.

Ministry of Labor (various years): *Labor Statistical Unheard*. Seoul: Ministry of Labor, Republic of Korea.

National Statistical Office (1994a): *Korea Statistical Yearbook*. Seoul: National Statistical Office, Republic of Korea.

National Statistical Office (1994b): *Major Statistics of Foreign Economy*. Seoul: National Statistical Office, Republic of Korea.

Ogle, G. (1981): "South Korea," in A.A. Blum (ed.), *International Handbook of Industrial Relations: Contemporary Developments and Research*. Westport, CT: Greenwood, pp.499-514.

Park, Y.B. and Lee, B.N. (1994): *Economic Development, Globalization Practices in Industrial Relations and Human Resource Management in Korea*. Seoul: Korea Labor Institute.

Park, Y.K. (1979): *Labor and Industrial Relations in Korea*. Seoul: Seogang University Press.

Sohn, J.A. (1994): "New Direction for Labor Union: Older, But Wiser," *Business Korea*, 12(1):24-26.

Sohn, J.A. (1995): "Korea-Japan Rivalry: A Different Kind of War," *Business Korea*, 12(8):18-20.

Taira, K. (1993): "Japan," in M. Rothman, D.R. Briscoe, and R.C.D. Nacamulli (eds.), *Industrial Relations Around the World*. Berlin, New York: Walter de Gruyter, pp. 217-234.

Streeck, W. (1993): "The Republic of Germany," in M. Rothman, D.R. Briscoe, and R.C.D. Nacamulli (eds.), *Industrial Relations Around the World*. Berlin, New York: Walter de Gruyter, pp. 127-150.

Chapter 9
Corporate Transformation

9.1 Introduction

New Year's Day is a special day for all Koreans. On New Year's Day, Koreans pay respect to their ancestors, elders in the family and those holding a higher status. They exchange well wishes among friends and acquaintances. It is also a day of reflection on the past and resolution for the future. In business, Korean employees pay respect to their employers and superiors, and exchange well wishes among peers and associates. They also listen to the Chief Executive Officer's address on major goals and policies, and together they affirm their resolution and unity to achieve the new year's objectives.

Traditionally, the new year's resolution focused on meeting growth targets in sales, exports, growth rate, and market share. Recently, however, there have been significant changes in their new year's resolution. CEOs of Korean *chaebols* no longer emphasize growth targets in their new year's addresses. Instead, their focus has been on corporate transformation and survival. Global competition, competitive advantage, cultural and technological transformation, becoming a "super first-class" business, innovation, quality, customer satisfaction, and employee empowerment have become the main thrust of their addresses. Even CEOs of non-*chaebol* companies are addressing issues related to corporate transformation in order to strengthen their competitive capabilities. This chapter discusses issues related to corporate transformation in Korean businesses: corporate restructuring, corporate cultural change, and transformation in human resource management.

9.2 Restructuring Korean *Chaebols*

The globalization of the world economy has made a tremendous impact on Korean businesses in recent years. Korean firms grew rapidly during the past several decades under a sheltered environment: the domestic market was protected from foreign competition; exports were fostered by the government; and the labor movement was suppressed to give Korean businesses a competitive advantage in the world market. However, the globalization of the world economy has changed all of this. The home market is now open to foreign competition; rapid increase in wages and changing work ethics of Korean employees have eroded the competitive edge of Korean firms in the international market; and the government no longer provides financial support for Korean businesses. These environmental changes have led to a restructuring of Korean businesses.

The growth strategy of Korean businesses in the past was diversification (see Chapter 4). A study of Korean by Jung (1991) revealed that 73 percent of *Chaebols* were single-product or dominant product companies in the mid-1970s. Only 27 percent were diversified, related or unrelated. However, in the mid-1980s, the proportion of single or dominant product *chaebols* declined to 42 percent, while the proportion of *chaebols* with related and unrelated diversification increased to 58 percent. The proportion of *chaebol* groups with related or unrelated diversification further increased to 71 percent toward the end of 1980s. The study further showed that larger *chaebols* tended to follow a strategy of unrelated diversification. Seven of the ten largest and 15 of the 30 largest *chaebols* had followed a strategy of unrelated diversification.

It was pointed out in Chapter 4 that government economic development policies favoring domestic market protection, financial subsidies, and low-cost labor were conducive for *chaebols* to expand their businesses domestically through diversification, especially through unrelated one. However, the changing business climate in the 1990s, favoring free market competition, forced Korean firms to restructure their businesses. They then had to focus their resources on a few business areas and build competitive capabilities. Even then, they were not sure of surviving in the fierce global competition. The following examples illustrate the extent to which Korean firms have been restructuring.

9.2.1 LG Group

The LG (Lucky Goldstar) Group started in 1947 as Lucky Chemical, a cosmetic producer. Bando Trading was added in 1953 to engage in international trading, Goldstar to manufacture electric/home appliance products in 1959, and Honam Oil Refineries in 1965. These additions resulted in LG's rapid growth. In addition to chemicals, trading, and electric products, LG diversified into electronics, communication, construction, distribution, finance, insurance, information and other services. The Group was known as Lucky-

Goldstar until 1995, when LG was formally adopted as the new name to under score its corporate transformational effort.

By 1987, LG Group had over fifty corporations and joint venture firms and grown into the third largest *chaebol* group after Samsung and Hyundai. Korean businesses at that time prospered under the "three-low economy" (low oil prices, low interest rates, and low exchange rates for Korean *won*). LG was growing at a 20 percent rate annually toward $15 billion in sales. LG's CEO staff thought it was an opportune time for LG to venture into new businesses such as automobile, aerospace, and bioengineering, and presented a strategic plan for such diversification.

The proposed strategic plan in 1987 made good strategic sense. Not only were the automobile, aerospace, high-tech materials, and life sciences considered to be high-growth industries in Korea, but the also complemented the Group's existing businesses. More importantly, LG had the resources to launch new ventures. Diversification into new industries was not a new idea. There had been many talks among executives about entering new businesses before, and many executives believed that the Group should have pursued a growth strategy through diversification more vigorously. Chairman C.K. Koo was generally in agreement with his staff on many strategic decisions involving business diversification during his 17 year tenure. But, unlike in his previous decisions, Chairman Koo was not really sure whether LG could succeed in the new businesses under the changing business environment. Although the Korean economy was prospering at the time, Chairman Koo saw the wave of free trade and open competition, which could impose serious challenge on Korean businesses. Growth strategy had been generally successful at LG, but it had also brought many overlaps in business and product lines, making coherent strategic decisions increasingly difficult. LG's resources were thinly stretched. Past success made LG managers complacent. Rapid growth had been achieved not through open competition but through government protection.

Under the new environment, Chairman Koo feared, LG's existing businesses, let alone the new businesses in automobiles or any others, would not survive the open global competition (Lee, 1994). He felt an urgent need to streamline existing businesses and strengthen their basic competitive capabilities before attempting any diversification into new businesses. He directed his staff to plan for corporate transformation in order to meet the challenge of the forthcoming new global environment. In December 1987, a "Vision Team" was formed to lead LG's corporate transformation, and Chairman Koo himself assumed the Team Leadership. McKinsey and Company was brought in as a consultant. They then began the LG's epoch-making corporate transformation involving business restructuring, new values and strategies, and changes in human resource management.

LG has restructured 41 of its 50 group companies into 21 Culture Units (CU) based on common product lines and/or technologies. Seven electronics firms were restructured and put under the management of a single CU, LG Electronics; six chemical firms into another CU, LG Chemicals; five energy firms into Honam Oil CU). CU presidents were selected on the basis of ability, and are empowered with complete authority (Nakarmi, 1994). Most people in the owner family have been relieved of major responsibilities at the top executive levels, and none of the 21 CU presidents are owner family members (*Korean Economic Daily News*, February 28, 1995, p. 8). The CU system has streamlined complicated product lines, eliminating duplications in products and manpower. The system is expected to increase the effectiveness of strategic management in each CU and further contribute to the strengthening of its competitiveness.

9.2.2 Samsung Group

Samsung's corporate transformation was formally launched in 1993. But the seed for the idea was sown in the mind of Chairman K.H. Lee when he took over the Group in 1987 upon the passing of his father and Samsung's founder, B.C. Lee. Like Chairman Koo of LG, Chairman Lee was apprehensive of the coming trends in deregulation and free trade. He felt that, in order to grow continuously under open global competition, Samsung should be managed as a world-class business. In order to meet this challenge, he felt the need for corporate restructuring and managerial transformation.

As soon as he took over the group, he broke away from its centralized, bureaucratic, control-oriented, and inward-looking management style. To replace the old managerial orientation, he initiated a managerial revolution, called *New Management*, by emphasizing decentralization, innovativeness, globalization, and outward-looking management. He drastically expanded R&D activities, promoted technological orientation among employees, strengthened overseas subsidiaries, and launched a 5-year program to develop 2,000 international area specialists.

However, Chairman Lee was not content with the pace of transformation under the "New Management." In June 1993, while in Frankfurt, Germany, Chairman Lee declared a new *Quality Management* program, as a new stepped-up campaign for management revolution that would transform Samsung into a "super first-class" business. During the next two months, he summoned 850 senior executives to Frankfurt, London, and Osaka, and held retreats on quality management in groups of 20 to 40 executives for a total of 250 hours (Nakarmi and Neff, 1994). The foreign setting was particularly effective for him to point out to his top managers how poorly Samsung products were positioned in the world market. He termed the situation a "crisis," and proclaimed "quality-first management" even at the expense of product quantity. He told his 180,000 Samsung employees to change their ways of thinking about their products, customers, competition, morality, social responsibility, and behavior (*Economist*, March 25, 1995, p. 79). Thus, Samsung's vigorous campaign for Quality Management began.

Samsung has restructured its 50 group companies into 24 companies in six major industrial areas including electronics, machineries, chemicals, and finance/insurance services. Ten companies were merged or consolidated and 16 companies were divested or separated out of the Group. This restructuring defined the core business areas in which Samsung's future strategies are going to be focused. Each of the core businesses is a sectoral group to which managerial responsibility and authority are completely delegated. Overseas subsidiaries are also restructured into five regional organizations with greater autonomy. This strategy of focusing on core businesses and decentralized management of domestic and overseas operations was made possible by restructuring and is expected to help Samsung strengthen its competitive capabilities.

9.2.3 Hyundai Group

Hyundai also has undertaken comprehensive restructuring of its businesses. It reduced the number of companies from 50 to 23 in 6 core businesses: automobile, heavy industries (including shipbuilding), electronics, construction, chemicals, and machineries. In the process, 11 companies were consolidated or merged, 6 companies were divested, and 10 companies would be separated out of the Group. This restructuring promoted Hyundai's specializations in the core businesses, each of which function as an autonomous mini-group, ultimately reinforcing Hyundai's competitiveness. Hyundai also planed to make more company shares available to public investors and reduce the Chung family's controlling shares from the current 60 percent to less than 40 percent by 1997 (*Korean Economic Dail News*, January 26, 1995, p. 3).

Many other Korean businesses have launched similar campaigns for corporate transformation in recent years. They all have the common objective of strengthening their competitiveness in order to become a world-class company in the increasingly competitive global market. They are putting an end to the "octopus" style expansion and indiscriminate diversifications, which many Korean *chaebols* had followed during decades of the protected market environment. They are reviewing their competitive positions in the world market and initiating new strategies and corporate transformation schemes in order to strengthen their competitive capabilities.

Korean *chaebols* are pursuing several common objective through business restructuring. First, they are identifying the core businesses to which they are committing their resources. The core businesses are generally in high growth, high-tech, and high value-added areas. Second, product lines and related technologies are realigned through consolidation to form appropriate core business groups (or mini-groups), making integrated and synergistic strategies possible. Also, through restructuring, declining businesses are divested, while prospective businesses unfit for the core businesses are separated out of the group so that they can grow faster on their own. Third, core business units enable Korean *chaebols* to empower the managers and decentralize management. Finally, the ultimate objective of Korean *chaebols* in business restructuring is of course to strengthen their overall competitiveness and to grow toward becoming "world-class super" businesses.

Business restructuring makes sense to over-extended Korean *chaebols*, but it is easier to plan than to execute. There are not many buyers who are interested in declining businesses and it takes more than a strategic plan to exclude profitable businesses from the group simply because they do not belong to core businesses. Furthermore, core business units can not increase their competitiveness unless *chaebols* change their corporate culture and their management styles and practices. This is the real challenge and task that Korean *chaebols* are confronted with in corporate transformation.

9.3 Changing Corporate Culture

Corporate transformation involves not only structural changes in business and organization, but also changes in the organizational culture and management style. In Korean businesses, which run typically on a top-down management style, restructuring businesses and designing a new organizational structure are relatively easy. However, transforming the organization into a new culture with changes in employee values, attitude, behavior, and management style necessary for high performance is relatively difficult and time-consuming. Many Korean businesses have initiated corporate transformation. This section looks at the cultural changes attempted by Korean businesses.

It is generally believed that business environment, corporate culture, organizational, and organizational performance are closely related. According to Chandler, business firms pursue strategies that are consistent with the business environment and that develop appropriate organizational culture and structure. And then they adopt management practices that best implement the strategies (Chandler, 1962). To be effective, business firms normally need to achieve organizational fits between various internal and external forces that influence organizational performance. Thus, it is generally understood that the better the fit among the environment, strategy, structure and managerial behavior, the higher the business performance will be (Exhibit 9.1).

Exhibit 9.1: Enviroment, Strategy, and Structure

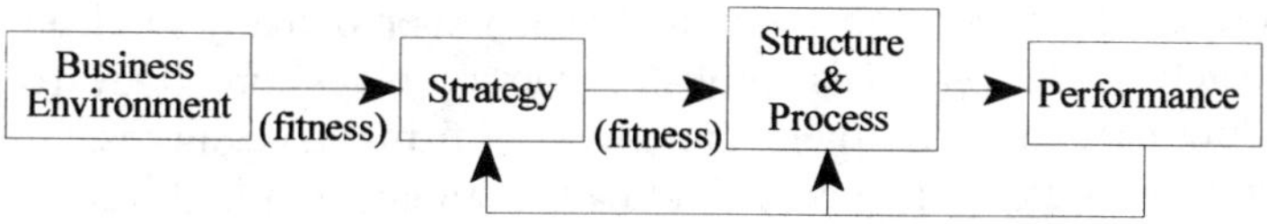

Kotter and Haskett (1991) found that there is a positive relationship between corporate culture and performance. In their extensive research on the corporate cultures of over 200 business firms, they found that the corporate culture that contribute to organizational performance is the one that best fits to a firm's business environment, adapts well to environmental changes, and is also strong in the sense that core values are deeply instilled in employees' value systems. A strong corporate culture that meets the needs of customers, employees, and shareholders is considered to be a desirable cultural trait.

High performance is usually associated with strong corporate culture. However, strong corporate culture becomes at times an obstacle to the cultural adaptation required in a rapidly changing environment. IBM, for instance, had a long-standing corporate culture that favored mainframe computers. Moreover, its centralized and hierarchical structure encouraged conservative norms and values, making its managers averse to risk taking. As a result, IBM managers were unable to see the changing demands in the market for PCs. GM's culture, built around the big car and hierarchical structure, had made GM less adaptive in meeting the market's needs for small cars. Xerox's culture, based on high-speed/high-volume copying machine, had made Xerox insensitive to changing demands in the marketplace (Keller, 1989: Carroll, 1993; Kearns and Nadler, 1992). These companies suffered drastic declines in their performances and they all had to go through a painful process of downsizing and restructuring.

Culturally, many Korean firms are in a similar situation. Korean businesses have achieved a spectacular growth since the 1960's, and in the process, they have developed strong corporate cultures. These cultures favored corporate growth through diversification and fit the past business environment characterized by a closed home market and strong governmental support for business. As a result, many Korean firms now find it difficult to abandon their growth-oriented strategy through diversification. Only after being faced with serious threat of foreign competition are they now looking toward corporate transformation.

9.4 New Value Orientations

For the past three decades, Korean firms have encountered many environmental changes such as the oil crisis, global economic recession, trade restrictions by trading partners and others. But, Korean firms have successfully adapted themselves to these challenges and have maintained a high rate of growth. Korean firms warded off these challenges by creating locational advantages through domestic market protection, government financial support, low-cost labor, and economies of scale. In the 1990s, Korean firms have been faced with new kinds of challenges. The worldwide globalization movement has removed much of Korea's locational advantages. As a result, the traditional remedies are no longer appropriate in the new open global market. The only remedy that will work in this new age of globalization is for Korean firms to gain competitive advantages through technological innovation and globalization. This new business environment requires Koreans to reorient themselves in dealing with products, customers, employees, global market, and so forth. Let us examine the new value orientations required from the Korean employees in the new global environment (Exhibit 9.2).

Exhibit 9.2: Old and New Values

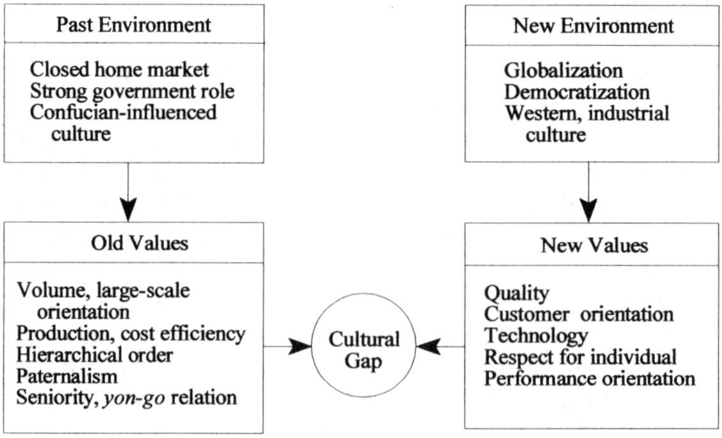

9.4.1 Quality Orientation

The new value orientation that many Koreans feel is most needed in their businesses is quality. The success of Korean businesses in the past was achieved mainly through exports of low-price and low-technology products. Hence, quality was not important. Economies of scale, efficient production in large quantities, and meeting the delivery schedule of overseas buyers were more important. Although Korean businesses began to emphasize quality as they moved into high-tech industries in recent years, they could not shake off their preoccupation with the large volume production deeply rooted in their growth strategy. Chairman K.H. Lee of Samsung calls the volume-oriented mindset a "Samsung disease," saying, "some 1,000 Samsung employees are kept busy repairing 20,000 defective products annually produced by 30,000 other Samsung workers." He further says, "you can find no comparable inefficiency in the world ... making defective products is cancerous and a criminal act on the part of management" (Kraar, 1994, p. 156).

The lack of concern for quality is not only an issue in Korean businesses, but also a social and cultural issue for all Koreans. In October 1994, the Sungsoo Grand Bridge, a major bridge over the Han River in Seoul, collapsed taking 32 lives. The bridge was less than six years old. The main cause for the collapse of the bridge was defective workmanship, the result of rushing to meet construction deadline. In June 1995, the Sampoong Department Store, a major 5-story store (less than 5 years old) located in a well-to-do residential area in Seoul collapsed taking 458 lives and injuring a thousand people. The cause was again defective workmanship. There are also numerous other incidents such as gas line explosions, a ferry boat sinking, all caused by defective workmanship and rushing the work schedule.

Such major disasters, unthinkable in a nation with $10,000 per capita annual income, have awakened the Korean people and stirred up a national concern for quality. They realize that they have placed too much emphasis on quantitative achievements in the past--high growth, expansion in scale, efficiency in large-volume production, quick completion of work, and so on. The volume-oriented mindset and work habits have also undermined the competitiveness of Korean firms in the global open market. In order to combat such a mindset, quality now has become the new value orientation most emphasized by many Korean firms in recent years.

9.4.2 Technology Orientation

In recent years, technological orientation has become an important cultural transformation in Korean businesses. Korean firms have relatively short histories compared with businesses in advanced countries. Only a few of the largest *chaebols* like Samsung and Hyundai were established before 1945 when Korea was liberated from Japanese annexation, and most *chaebol* groups began their business in and after the 1950s. As latecomers in the process of industrialization, they did not have to develop their own technologies. They could acquire the needed technologies from advanced countries at fractional costs of developing their own technologies (Moskowitz, 1989). Because Korean firms initially depended heavily on the development of low-tech industries, there were many firms in advanced countries which were willing to extend helping hands.

However, as Korean firms move up the technological ladder, it is becoming increasingly difficult to import foreign technologies. Firms in advanced countries are reluctant to share their technologies with Korean firms for fear of a boomerang effect. As a result, Korean firms have become aware of the urgent need for developing their own technologies. To this end, as noted in Chapter 5, Korean firms have drastically increased R&D activities, set up research laboratories and product development centers, increased recruitment activities for scientists and engineers around the world, and promoted more technical personnel to managerial and executive positions in recent years. Thus, Korean firms are not only investing heavily in R&D in order to build their own technological capabilities, but are also creating the organizational climate necessary for heightening the awareness of technological transformation.

The case of the automobile industry illustrates the urgent need for technological transformation. Korea's auto industry is now the world's fifth largest. Yet, Korean cars have been positioned in the global market as cheap small cars. In order to change this cheap car image, Korean automakers must establish a new image by upgrading their product lines and quality. To this end, Hyundai currently spends nearly 7 percent of its gross sales on R&D and has created research centers not only in Korea but also in Japan and Germany for new product development and information gathering. Daewoo and Kia are also gearing up their R&D activities by setting up research centers at home and abroad.

9.4.3 Customer Orientation

Another value that Korean firms stress now is customer satisfaction. Customer satisfaction is most basic to business success in advanced economies, but Korean firms have achieved success without paying much attention to customers. The domestic market protection measures helped Korean firms to monopolize the home market. The OEM (original equipment manufacturer) status of Korean firms shielded Korean firms from direct contact with foreign consumers. Their success came from fulfilling large orders for overseas OEM buyers. These conditions all contributed to the lack of concern for customer satisfaction by Korean firms.

The home market is now open to foreign competition, the price advantage that Korean businesses have long enjoyed in the world's OEM market no longer exists, and an increasing number of overseas buyers are now attracted to China, Indonesia, and Thailand. As foreign MNCs invade Korean markets and overseas OEM buyers leave Korea, Korean firms now have to compete directly with foreign MNCs to woo customers in their domestic and foreign markets. As a result, Korean managers are faced with the daunting challenge of achieving customer satisfaction in product quality, price, and after-sale services. Hence, customer orientation is becoming increasingly important for Korean managers.

The changing emphasis in managerial training illustrates the increasing importance of customer orientation in Korea. In the past, managerial training in Korea focused on such topics as benchmarking, reengineering, strategic planning, human resource management, organizational change, and so forth. But now, many Korean companies include consumer behavior, relational marketing, market positioning, and global marketing strategy as part of their training programs. Additionally, their overseas training programs include industry tours with companies, such as Walt Disney and P&G, that are considered to be the best in achieving costumer satisfaction.

9.4.4 Individual Orientation

As explained in Chapter 6, the most dominant values in Korean business firms has been *inhwa* (harmony). Under the influence of Confucian culture, *inhwa* in Korean firms was built on employee's loyalty, their respect for authority and hierarchical order, and employer's paternalism and benevolence to employees. *Inhwa* along with the strong work ethic of Korean employees significantly contributed to the success of Korean firms. However, as Korean firms have advanced into high-tech industries in recent years, *inhwa* as a corporate value has not only become ineffective but has also bred complacency and an inward-looking attitude among employees.

LG is one of many Korean *chaebols* which are shifting its emphasis from the traditional value *inhwa* to new values more suited to the highly competitive global business environment. At LG, individualism that promotes creativity and personal initiative is now respected as a desired value. This new value recognizes individual differences in personality and ability, individual contribution to organizational success, and one's desire for self-actualization on the job. Individualism also stresses managerial responsibility for developing individual potential, giving employees opportunities to utilize their abilities and creativity, and rewarding employees commensurate to their contributions (Lee, 1994). Samsung is also revising its concept of the "Samsung man" with new emphasis on creativity, outward-looking attitude, and high moral character. Thus, the traditional *inhwa,* with its high respect for authority and hierarchical order, is giving way to new values of individual ability, creativity, autonomy, and personal development.

9.4.5 Performance Orientation

Influenced by Confucian culture, Korean firms have practiced relation-based and seniority-based managerial systems. Under these systems, promotion and pay are primarily based on seniority and personal relations rather than on performance. However, the democratization in Korean society and increasing global competition in recent years are making Korean people and Korean businesses less tolerant of seniority-based management practices. Many Korean firms now place greater emphasis on ability and performance than on seniority or personal relations, especially at upper management levels. And, the practice of performance-based promotions is now spreading rapidly to the middle management levels.

Performance-based reward systems are also putting pressure on the existing owner-manager system. In owner-managed companies, key positions are traditionally occupied by owners, their family members and friends. The new performance-based reward system calls for an end to this owner-dominated managerial system and movement toward a professional management system. LG is one of the *chaebols* making vigorous attempts to professionalize its management system. As discussed earlier, LG has relieved many senior owner-family executives from major responsibilities and appointed professional managers to head all 21 Culture Units with complete delegation of authority.

9.5 Managing Corporate Transformation

The orientation toward new values stressed by Korean firms is not different from that pursued by successful MNCs around the world. The problem for Korean firms, however, is that these new value orientations are drastically different from traditional Korean culture and management practices. As a result, Korean firms find it difficult to succeed in cultural and subsequent corporate transformation. The strong corporate culture built around authoritarianism, nationalism, hierarchical rigidity, and the bigger-the-better mentality has become a major obstacle to successful cultural transformation. In order to overcome this difficulty, Korean firms have carefully adopted a planned change strategy: creating a sense of urgency, communicating a vision, facilitating change, and reinforcing new behaviors (Bennis and Manus, 1985; Kanter et al., 1992).

9.5.1 Creating Sense of Urgency

The second half of the 1980s was politically unstable years for Korea, but the economy still expanded at an average rate of ten percent per year. The political instability paved the way for political reform in Korea, which in turn stimulated managerial reform in Korean businesses. Because the political reform called for an end to the symbiotic relationship between business and government, Korean firms could no longer expect almost unlimited support from government. Furthermore, the move toward global free trade threatened measures that protected the domestic market. That meant that Koreans firms had to compete with MNCs in their domestic and international markets on their own competitive strengths.

Faced with such a grim reality, Korean CEOs felt the need for transforming their companies in order to become more competitive globally. Unless they become more competitive, they felt that their survival was at stake. In response to this challenge, Korean *chaebols* set ambitious goals of becoming "world-class companies," "first-class businesses," and "super global companies" for themselves and launched major transformational efforts. The CEOs of major Korean *chaebol* groups publicly expressed their desires in their addresses to employees and in their annual reports.

Such announcements were, however, largely ignored by their employees initially. Employees did not share the same sense of urgency because the economy had been expanding at a high rate and the rate of employment remained high. As a result, any efforts to transform Korean firms failed to produce results. For example, Samsung's New Management Program, initiated in 1987, failed to bring about the needed change. LG's change efforts also were met with lukewarm responses by its employees. Similar experiences were shared by other business groups.

The situation has changed in the first half of the 1990s. During this period, the Korean economy grew slower than in the past; its exports declined substantially in comparison with its imports; and Korean firms were losing international market shares to foreign MNCs in almost all industrial categories. Not only were low-tech industries moving out of country but mid-tech as well as high-tech industries were also experiencing setbacks. For example, major Korean business groups built large plants to manufacture PCs, but none could maintain their international market share. Consumer electronics such as televisions and VCRs fared a similar fate. Hyundai's car exports to the U.S. dropped to 100,000 units in 1995 from its peak of 200,000 in the earlier years. The promising DRAM semiconductors built by Samsung were also experiencing a setback in the mid-1990s.

Seizing the opportunity, Korean CEOs reasserted themselves in creating a sense of urgency and in communicating the need for corporate trans-formation. For example, Samsung's Chairman K.H. Lee summoned his top level executives to overseas locations such as Frankfurt and Los Angeles to implement his Quality Management Program. At these meetings, he impressed on them that their products were poorly positioned in international markets and that they could not survive the global competition without quality revolution. Other Korean *chaebols* such Hyundai, LG, Daewoo, Sunkyong, and Ssangyong also called their employees' attention to the threat from global competition and have urged them toward corporate transformation.

9.5.2 Communicating the Vision

Creating a sense of urgency is not enough to bring about the needed change. Unless employees are given an opportunity to direct their energies, the sense of urgency will only frustrate them. This opportunity starts with the knowledge of where their energies need to be directed and what outcomes they can expect. CEOs can communicate such direction in the form of vision or strategic intent. Strategic intent or vision refers to what a firm ultimately wants to be in the future. More specifically, it is an obsession with winning at all levels of an organization to create a set of sustainable competitive advantages over a long period of time in search for global leadership (Hamel and Prahalad, 1989).

Samsung Business Group, for instance, wants to become a "the world's first-class super global company." Like Jack Welch of GE, Samsung's Chairman Lee believes that only the world's first-class companies will survive in the open global market because they will dominate the global market share (Ticky and Sherman, 1994). A vision or strategic intent describes aspirations for the future without being too specific to be embroiled in details. To be effective, however, visions or strategic intents must be inspirational and have emotional appeal that goes beyond the normal carrots and sticks (Beck, 1987; Keichel, 1989; Tregoe, 1990). It is not unusual to see a CEO's vision stated in forms of "becoming the best," "first-class," or "super company." Such a vision has both practical and emotional appeal.

In communicating a vision, one has to be persistent and use all forms of communication channels: written communiques, oral presentations, and actions. First, a vision can be translated into a firm's mission statement or published in newsletters or books. Second, the CEO can use the New Year forum and the company's annual meeting with employees to address his or her vision for the future. Finally, the CEO must convey his or her vision through actions because actions often speak louder than words (Sohn, 1993). For example, whenever a defect is found in Samsung products, the plant is stopped immediately until the problem is identified and solved. Also, to communicate the importance of organizational change, Samsung has changed some human resource management practices in hiring and rewarding employees. This point will be further elaborated on later.

9.5.3 Facilitating Change Process

Most change efforts in Korean firms are initiated by CEOs. But in a few cases, such efforts are made through employee participation. LG's Vision Team, which leads the Group's corporate transformation efforts, is composed of the members from the low, middle, and top management levels, thus incorporating the views and opinions from all hierarchical levels into the programs for change. Ssangyong's Culture Team leads and coordinates the Group's cultural transformation activities, but allows maximum autonomy at each subsidiary company level. Employee participation naturally slows down the pace and speed of change, but the change effected may be more permanent.

Another change strategy that Korean businesses are applying to their corporate transformation is the retaining of services of world renown consulting firms. McKinsey, Boston Consulting Group, Ernst and Young, Cooper Lybrand, and Japan Excel Management Consulting are some of the consulting firms helping the transformation efforts in Korean firms. The fact that most consulting firms retained by Korean businesses are U.S. based has some implications for the general direction of change that Korean businesses are pursuing.

Corporate transformation is a complex and difficult process, which normally takes a long time. Large Korean firms retain experienced consulting services with international reputations to ensure a successful corporate transformation. Furthermore, retaining such consulting is an effective way for management to communicate employees about its strong commitment to the change, to earn employees' trust and confidence in the change, and to elicit their active participation and cooperation in the implementation of change.

9.5.4 Education and Training

Education and training play an important role in facilitating organizational change. Korean *chaebols* have been drastically increasing their education and training expenditures for the past three years. As noted in Chapter 7, Korean firms have begun emphasizing in their employee education and training programs the instillation of the new values, the teaching of new skills for change (such as re-engineering, benchmarking, and quality improvement), and the development of the basic skills that are prerequisites for global managers (such as foreign language skill, in-house MBA program and overseas training).

Employee education and training are especially important in the corporate transformation of Korean businesses because of the life-time employment practices typically found in Korean firms. In Western societies, which rely on the labor market perspective, employees are hired and replaced as situations dictate. In contrast, in Oriental societies, workers are considered to be a capital that needs to be invested and cultivated (McMillan, 1996). Because heavy investment is made in employee education and training, Korean firms are reluctant to lay off employees. If an organizational downsizing is to be achieved, it is usually done through natural attrition.

In addition to education and training, a variety of modern change methods and intervention techniques of organizational development are actively utilized. Process re-engineering, competitive benchmarking, total quality management, team management, and organizational restructuring are widely utilized in Korean businesses, in some cases with the help of outside consultants. In Ssangyong, for example, some 600 low to middle level managers are trained to serve as change agents in their work units in order to facilitate the cultural transformation (Lee, 1994, pp. 294-295).

9.5.5 Reinforcing New Values

Efforts toward change will be successful only when newly acquired behaviors are reinforced. To this end, Korean firms have adopted new human resource management practices that reinforce newly instilled value orientations. For example, in hiring college graduates, the traditional education-based selection process is being replaced with an assessment-based selection systems. In employee evaluation, new values such as quality, creativity, and teamwork are increasingly being emphasized. And, in promotion and compensation, ability and performance are gradually replacing seniority and experience as important components of performance evaluation.

The Samsung case illustrates how a firm changes its human resource management practices to reinforce new value orientations. When Samsung CEO Lee initiated the Quality Management Program in 1993, he told his employees to "change everything but your wives and children." His words reflected how strongly he was determined to change Samsung's corporate culture. He then decreed that office hours would be from 7:00 am to 4:00 pm, and he personally checked to make sure that they would not stay in their offices after 4 o'clock. Samsung employees had often stayed in their offices as late as 10 pm. But the change in working hours forced them to increase the quality and efficiency of their work. More importantly, the decree sent a strong message to Samsung employees that everything would be done differently.

Samsung also changed its hiring practices from the traditional system based on education to one that is based on ability assessment. In the past, job applicants were primarily evaluated on the basis of their performance on written examinations. In the new system, job applicants are now evaluated on the basis of their ability to handle simulated job situations, in depth personal interviews, and specific job-related knowledge. While the majority of Korean firms still maintain written examinations, their focus has changed considerably. For example, Samsung tests job applicants on their foreign language skills and technological competence (*Business Korea,* 1994, pp. 22-23).

9.6 Transformational Challenges

While changes in education and training, organizational development interventions, and new practices in human resource management practices reinforce new values and facilitate the cultural transformation in Korean businesses, these changes face some resistance. A recent survey by the Korean

Productivity Center found that 36 percent of employees expressed a positive attitude toward change, 37 percent expressed indifference, and 24 percent responded negatively (*Korean Economic Daily News*, February 2, 1995, p. 9). While the younger generation favors changes, the older generation of mostly middle and upper level managers seem to resist changes and have become passive in many Korean firms. There are several forces that challenge corporate transformation.

First, many managerial practices that Korean businesses have recently introduced are relatively new and have yet to be validated. For example, the concept of performance-based evaluation systems is still vague; assessment methods are not yet systematically designed and validated. Korean firms generally lack an objective performance evaluation system to assess the abilities of employees and measure their performance. The old system is seniority based, and the new one has yet to be tried and tested. This means that the new practices in human resource management may experience a long period of trial and error before being stabilized.

Second, transformational efforts by Korean firms face some organizational and cultural inertia. Many Korean CEOs feel the need for corporate transformation. They feel that unless Korean firms break away from a preoccupation with large-volume and large scale operations and shake off the centralized and bureaucratic style of management, these firms will not survive global competition, let alone become "super first-class" businesses. But such changes require a fundamental change in the mindset and the value systems of Korean employees as well as employers. They also require a complete departure from past ways of thinking and behaving. Therefore, change will take more than a strong determination on the part of chief executive. The problem, however, is that while Korean employees and employers generally favor the new values and recognize a need for change, they also want to preserve traditional harmony-oriented culture in their organizations.

As discussed in Chapter 6, rapid economic development and the social changes in Korea have caused conflict between the Confucian-influenced traditional values and the Western-influenced new values. Although the vast majority of Korean employees desire a performance-based reward system, they still generally accept the validity of traditional education and seniority. Additionally, while they support individual creativity and autonomy, they want to preserve traditional paternalism. The conflict or mixture of the traditional and new values certainly make cultural transformation difficult in Korean business firms.

Finally, while the Korean economy has experienced setbacks in recent years, it is still growing at a respectable growth rate. Such economic growth makes it difficult for Korean firms to stay focused on corporate transformation for a long period of time. Moreover, continuous growth makes Korean employees skeptical about the need for a major organizational change. Koreans have achieved many economic miracles amidst formidable international competition; this success may lead them to be complacent. Until workers experience economic setbacks affecting their jobs and incomes, they may not actively support major organizational change efforts.

In any case, the corporate transformation in Korean firms is expected to take a long time. Although the transformation efforts are supported by the strong leadership of top management, the corporate culture that has existed for the past 30 years is too strong to be readily changed and adapted to a new environment. The reconciliation between the old and new values will take time. While there are many new compelling forces evident in the high value placed by Korean employees on individual ability, creativity, and autonomy, there are also strong divergent forces that support the preservation of the traditional harmony-based, seniority-based, and paternalistic culture.

Koreans believe that corporate transformation is an absolute necessity not only for Korean firms to survive in the global competition and to become a world's class business but also for the nation to move into the ranks of advanced countries. In the midst of conflicting values, Korean businesses are confronted with a difficult task of achieving successful corporate transformation. But, Korean businesses have achieved many miracles which seemed impossible in the past. Corporate transformation may take a long time to accomplish, depending on the threats from global competition. Ultimately, the external threats they feel will lead Korean firms to successful cultural transformation.

9.7 Summary

This chapter has discussed the corporate transformation that many Korean *chaebols* have undertaken in recent years. Korean businesses developed a strong corporate culture, characterized by the high value placed on economies of scale, efficient volume production, centralized control, and hierarchical order. All of these contributed enormously to the high growth experienced in past decades. However, drastic changes in the business environment have made the strong corporate culture no longer effective under the new environment. This necessitated changes in the shared values, corporate strategies, and management practices.

The corporate transformation of Korean *chaebols* is primarily concerned with restructuring businesses and developing a new corporate culture so that it is comparable with the new business environment. In business restructuring, the large *chaebols* are consolidating their over-extended businesses into a few core business areas in order to increase their specialization and ultimately to strengthen their competitiveness. Developing a new corporate culture involves instilling new value orientations such as quality, customer satisfaction, respect for the individual, and performance orientation. These values are considered to be the basic success factors in Western businesses. However, these value orientations are relatively new for many Korean businesses, as a result of operating in a closed home market. A successful transformation requires a complete re-orientation of the values and a way of thinking on the parts of Korean employers as wells as employees.

Conscientious efforts are being made by Korean firms to bring about major organizational changes. In many organizations, CEOs are leading the change efforts. They not only preach the need for changes but also are actively involved in implementation processes. Employee education and training have been re-designed to instill new values. Many changes have been made in human resource management to reinforce the new values (assessment techniques and performance-based reward systems). Various modern management tools of change are actively being utilized to improve organizational performance (reengineering, benchmarking, and quality control). Additionally, many intervention techniques in organizational development are being applied to facilitate the cultural transformation (employee participation and behavioral modification).

Corporate transformation is critical not only to the continued growth of Korean businesses faced with open global competition, but also to their long-run objective of becoming world-class businesses. Therefore, corporate transformation is being carried out with strong determination of top management in many Korean firms. While there are many converging forces from recent cultural development which support the cultural transformation, there are also traditional values deeply ingrained in the Korean culture which resist the change. The conflict between new and old values will certainly slow down the process of cultural transformation, but the strong determination and leadership from top management along with the "an do" spirit of Korean people will ultimately lead to a successful transformation.

References

Beck, R.N. (1987): "Vision, Values, and Strategies: Changing Attitudes and Culture," *Academy of Management Executive*, 1(1):33-41.

Bennis, W. and Manus, B. (1985): *Leaders: The Strategies for Taking Charge*. New York: Harper and Row.

Carroll, P. (1993): *Big Blue: the Unmaking of IBM*. New York: Crown Publishers.

Chandler, A.D. (1962): *Strategy and Structure*. Cambridge, Mass.: M.I.T. Press.

Hamel, G. and Prahalad, C.K. (1989): "Strategic Intent," *Harvard Business Review*, 67(3):63-76.

Jung, K.H. (1991): *Diversification Strategy and International Competitiveness of Korean Businesses*. Seoul: Korea Economic Research Institute.

Kanter, R.M., Stein, B.A., and Jick, T. (1992): *The Challenge of Organizational Change: How Companies Experience It and Leaders Guide It*. New York: Free Press.

Kearns, D.K. and Nadler, A. (1992): *Prophets in the Dark*. New York: Harper Business.

Kiechel, W. (1989): "A Hard Look at Executive Vision," *Fortune*, 120(9):207-211.

Keller, K. (1989): *Rude Awakening*. New York: William Morrow.

Kotter, J.P. and Haskett, J.L. (1991): *Corporate Cultures and Performance*. New York: Free Press.

Kraar, L. (1994): "Korea Goes for Quality," *Fortune*, 129(8):153-159.

Lee, H.C. (1994): *Corporate Transformation of Korean Businesses*. Seoul: Bupmoonsa.

Moskowitz, K. (1989): "Ownership and Management of Korean firms," in K.H. Chung and H.C. Lee (eds.), *Korean Managerial Dynamics*. New York: Praeger, pp. 65-78.

Nakarmi, L. (1994): "Gold Star Is Burning Bright", *Business Week,* September 26,:129-130.

Nakarmi, L. and Neff, R. (1994): "Samsung's Radical Shakeup," *Business Week,* February 28:74-76.

McMillan, C.J. (1996): *The Japanese Industrial System.* Third Revised Edition. Berlin, New York: Walter de Gruyter.

Sohn, J.A. (1993): "Samsung Group: Embracing Breathtaking Changes," *Business Korea*, 11(2):15-19.

Ticky, N.M. and Sherman, S. (1994): *Control Your Destiny or Someone Else Will*. New York: Harper Business.

Tregoe, B.B., Zimmerman, J.W., Smith, R.A., and Tobia, P.M. (1990): "Implementing the Vision: The Lessons Learned," *Planning Review*, 18(1):39-44, 48.

Chapter 10
Korea's Challenge: Moving Up the Ladder?

10.1 Introduction

At the rime of this writing, the following seven stories dominated Korea's business news:

(1) achieving the per capita GNP of more than $10,000;
(2) gaining membership of the OECD;
(3) the trial of two former presidents for taking bribes;
(4) declining international competitiveness;
(5) the general labor strike;
(6) the collapse of the Hanbo business group;
(7) the plight of the North Korean economy.

These stories collectively and independently tell the major accomplishments of the Korean industrial system over the past three decades but at the same time they expose the major weaknesses of the Korean industrial system. How well Korea deals with such problems will determine the future of the Korean economy and its position in the world's economic affairs. If Korea reforms its industrial system to effectively overcome the system's weaknesses and adopt the behavioral standards of the advanced nations, it will have a chance to move up the economic developmental ladder and join the ranks of advanced nations (Exhibit 10.1). If it fails to reform, Korea's economy will remain a developing economy or it may even move back down a notch in the developmental ladder. This concluding chapter deals with the changing nature of the Korean industrial system and the challenges that lie ahead for the Korean economy.

Exhibit 10.1: Economic Development Ladder

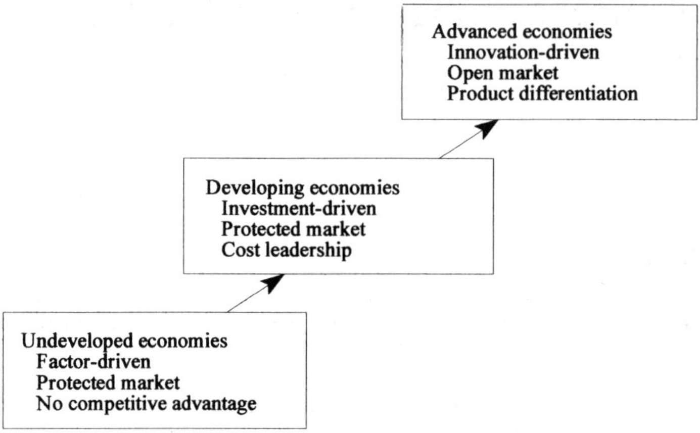

10.2 Korean Economy at Crossroads

During the past three decades, Korea has transformed its economy from agrarian to industrial. It has achieved its economic success by investing heavily in human resources and production systems. Unlike other developing economies in Asia such as Hong Kong, Taiwan, and Singapore, which gained competitive advantage through a factor-driven strategy, Korea gained its competitive advantage by pursuing an investment-driven strategy (Porter, 1990, pp. 685-690). Korean firms have aggressively invested in large scale production systems and in modern process technology. As a result, Korea has emerged as an economic power. It is now the world's thirteenth largest economy in terms of GNP and the tenth largest trading nation. It is now a member of OECD, a precursor to joining the ranks of advanced economies.

While celebrating the milestone of achieving a level of $10,000 per capita income and gaining OECD membership, Koreans feel uneasy about the future of their economy. After a 30-year of almost uninterrupted annual growth rate of 9 percent, the Korean economy is expected to grow at a moderate rate (around 5 percent) for most of the second-half of the 1990s. The once powerful export machine is also showing signs of strain. Korea now imports more than exports. In 1996, the trade deficit amounted to more than $20 billion, and it is expected to increase in the coming years. In the 1980s, Korea ranked highest in the world in international competitiveness. But in 1997 it is ranked thirty-first among industrial nations.

In order to gain international competitiveness, the Korean government in the past supplemented its investment-driven strategy with protection of domestic markets, low-cost labor, and financial incentives. When the economy was relatively small, the combination of state-supported, investment-driven, and low factor-cost strategies worked for Korea. But as the economy has grown larger, Korea can no longer depend on such strategies to gain competitive advantage. The economy has become too big and complex to be supported by the government. As the economy prospers, workers demand higher wages, pushing up labor costs substantially. Trading partners have demanded the removal of domestic market protection and the creation of a level-playing field for them. Furthermore, Korea's investment-driven strategy has been imitated by other nations, eroding its competitive advantage (Barney, 1997, pp. 210-215).

Sandwiched between newly developing countries (NICs) and advanced nations, Korea now competes on both ends. It competes with NICs on maintaining cost leadership, while it struggles to catch up with advanced nations on product quality and innovation.

Korea has already lost cost leadership to NICs in such labor-intensive industries as food, footwear, and textiles. This list is likely to increase. Since Korea cannot count on low factor-cost strategies, it has no choice but to compete with advanced nations on product quality, product innovation, and process innovation. This means Korea has to pursue an innovation-driven competition strategy.

Korean firms have made majors investments in large scale production systems, in developing human resources, and in improving their own product quality. They are also making vigorous efforts to globalize their operations not only by establishing global brand names and expanding international marketing channels but also by setting up production sites overseas. And yet, their main strategy is to compete on price rather than on product quality and differentiation; Korea is lagging behind advanced nations in product development and process innovation.

If Korea wants to move up the economic development ladder, it has to go beyond relying on an investment-driven strategy. But the transition to an innovation-driven economy would require different kinds of corporate strategies, managerial practices, and cultural orientation than the ones that Koreans are familiar with. Koreans' obsession with bigness, strong nationalism, cultural conformity, authoritarianism, and foreign technology dependency were compatible with the investment-driven strategy of the past. But these values are less conducive for developing an innovation-driven economy. The development of an innovation-driven economy calls for individual initiative, creativity, pattern-breaking nonconformity, diversity, global awareness, and other nontraditional behavior.

Exhibit 10.2 illustrates the international competitiveness cycle for Korean businesses. In the 1970s and 1980s, Korea gained its international competitiveness by economies of scale and low factor costs. Then in the late 1980s and the first half of the 1990s, economic prosperity caused factor costs to arise and fostered complacence among the populace, which in turn lowered the Korea's ability to compete in the global market. If Korea wants to regain its international competitiveness and achieve the transition to an innovation-driven economy, major changes must occur at corporate, industrial, and societal levels. If Korea is successful in bringing about these changes, it should be able to regain its international competitive in around year 2000 and prepare to move up the economic ladder.

Exhibit 10.2: International Competitiviness Cycle

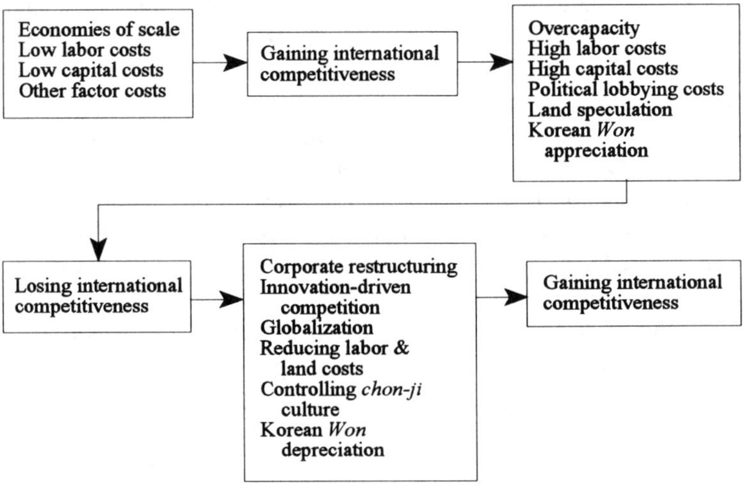

10.3 Corporate Restructuring

Korean firms need to restructure their businesses in order to focus their resources on a few selected businesses that can create synergy and give them sustainable competitive advantages. Corporate restructuring is also needed to achieve minimum efficiency scale (MES) for global competition. Korean *chaebol* groups are large in size but individual firms within a *chaebol* are too small to compete in such global industries as automobiles and tires. But not all industries require large scale economies. Firms in emerging industries will be better off if they are small, flexible, and independent in order to adapt to fast changing technological developments.

10.3.1 Core Competencies

Korean *chaebols* need to streamline their far-flung businesses and focus their resources on a few selected businesses that can create synergy and give them competitive advantage. Because their resources are widely spread among a variety of businesses, they have not developed the core competencies that can give them competitive advantage. As a result, they are producing and marketing mid-range quality goods at mid-range prices (Clifford, 1994, p. 335). As Porter (1985) argued, the "stuck in the middle" strategy does not give a firm competitive advantage. A firm that is stuck in the middle is at a disadvantage because the cost leader or the product differentiator is better positioned to compete in any market segment.

According to Porter (1985), a firm that is stuck in the middle will make profits only if other competitors are in the same situation, or if the industry structure is favorable enough to tolerate mediocre performers. When the Korean domestic markets were protected from foreign competition, mediocre performers were tolerated. As global competition increases and the domestic market protection is being removed, only those firms that can compete in both quality and price will survive and emerge as industry leaders. Such a competitive environment may tolerate cost leaders and product differentiators but not mid-range performers. Many mid-range performers still exist in Korea; this suggests that the Korean market is not fully opened to foreign competition.

Even if the industrial structure tolerates mid-range performers, Korean firms will not be able to maintain a mid-range pricing strategy. Increasing factor costs such as labor, capital, land, and political lobbying will make it harder for Korean firms to maintain mid-range prices. As a result, Korean firms will be forced to produce and sell mid-range goods at high prices. Just to sustain the current level of economic growth, Korean firms have to control factor costs and/or improve product quality substantially. Failure to do so means losing the opportunity to regain its international competitiveness.

10.3.2 Minimum Efficiency Scale

To be competitive in global industries, a firm must maintain the minimum efficiency scale (MES). For example, in the automobile industry, the MES is estimated to be more than one million cars a year in order to cover the production, R&D, and marketing expenses. Korea currently produces a little over two million vehicles a year. That means Korea should have not more than two automakers if the MES is taken into account. As of now, Korea has four automakers (Hyundai, Daewoo, Kia, and Ssangyong) and one is on the way (Samsung). Keep it mind that the U.S., the world's largest automobile market, has only three automakers--GM, Ford, and Chrysler.

Understandably, Korean automakers plan to increase their production capacities to six million cars a year by the end of this decade in order to meet the MES requirement. But the questions that need to be raised are the sources of funds for expansion and the marketability of Korean cars. Korean capital markets have not been sufficiently developed to supply the needed funds, and they are also lagging behind the world's leading automakers in product development and innovation. What is possible, however, is that Korean *chaebols* divest unprofitable businesses as well as businesses that are unrelated to their core technologies. Proceeds then can be used to increase the MES for the remaining core business units and to support R&D activities needed to improve the quality and marketability of their products.

10.3.3 Small Independent Companies

Not all industries require large scale production facilities. In emerging and growing industries such as bioengineering and electronics, whose products and production technology are still evolving, operational flexibility rather than fixed size would be more important. Let us take personal computers as an example. In the 1980s, Korean business groups heavily invested in large scale personal computer manufacturing facilities, but none could achieve international competitiveness. In this industry, Taiwanese computer manufacturers with smaller scales of operations have done better than Korean manufacturers by quickly introducing new product design and cutting production times. Because products and their design change quickly, they tend to maintain smaller manufacturing facilities.

Korean industries are dominated by large bureaucratic firms. There are not many small independent companies in Korea that can start and promote creative and innovative technologies. In the U.S. and Europe, small independent technologically-oriented companies focus their energies and resources on cutting-edge technologies or specialty products in order to gain a competitive advantage. Some of these small companies dominate the global market. In Japan, large bureaucratic firms promote creativity and innovation through intraprepreneurial group activities (entrepreneurs within a large organization) supported with substantial R&D budgets.

Korea too has small independent companies that are globally-oriented. Taeil Media (hard-disk driver), Komeron (meaurement instruments), and Korea Steel Pipe (steel pipes) are just a few examples. But the numbers are few in comparison with other industrial nations. Korea has yet to invest more in developing small independent technologically-oriented companies and intrapreneurial work groups within large companies to develop creative and innovative new products.

10.4 Industrial Restructuring

In addition to corporate restructuring, Korea needs reforms in the nation's industrial structure. The most urgent structural reforms at this juncture are:

(1) developing high value-added supporting industries (especially technology-based small and medium industries);
(2) increasing R&D expenditures;
(3) overhauling the financial institutions;
(4) improving labor-management relations;
(5) social overheads investment.

10.4.1 High Value-Added Industries

The Korean industry is built on large end-user goods manufacturing. Small and medium-size industries that produce technologically sophisticated intermediate goods, information processing products, and specialty products are not well developed. As a result, large Korean firms are depending on foreign suppliers of parts, subcomponents, and specialty goods. These imported products tend to be high value-added goods, requiring substantial outflows of foreign exchange. Furthermore, the dependency on foreign suppliers of high value-added parts makes Korean firms vulnerable in timely delivery and in maintaining cost leadership.

If Korean industries want to catch-up with those of the leading nations, they need to develop a large number of independent companies that can focus their resources on developing high value-added intermediate goods and specialty products. The government can play an important role in developing such industries by removing cumbersome regulation and providing needed funds. Although the government has a pronounced policy of supporting small and medium-sized industries, Korea is still considered to be one of the highly regulated economies in the world (Holmes and Kirkpatrick, 1996).

Large Korean firms have their own suppliers of relatively low to mid-tech parts, machinery, and equipment. The problem is that because their sales are guaranteed and exclusive, there is no incentive for them to be innovative. Independent firms are more likely to foster innovation in order to survive in a competitive market. Large Korean firms, rather than depending on foreign suppliers for their high-tech and high value-added parts, should encourage Korean small independent companies to develop such high-value-added parts.

10.4.2 R&D Expenditures

Korean firms are making major investments in high-tech industries such as consumer electronics, telecommunications, memory chips, and semiconductors. And yet, their level of spending on R&D is behind that of leading industrial nations. Korea currently spends about 2.7 percent of its GNP on R&D activities, compared to about 2.8 percent for Japan and the U.S.A. When the size of the economies are taken into account, Korea's R&D expenditures are minuscule compared to those of the leading nations. Korea needs to at least double its R&D expenditures in the coming years just to be in the technological contest.

To be effective, R&D efforts should be focused on a few selected industries in which Korea has some competitive advantage. Even the industrial nations such as the U.S. and Japan do not have the luxury of pursuing a wide range of technological innovation. Consequently, they focus their R&D efforts on selected industries. The need for focusing on a few strategic industries should be evidentally clear for countries such as Korea in which R&D expenditures are only a fraction of those of the leading nations. Also, R&D efforts should be focused on adapting technology for commercial uses that include product development, product innovation, and process engineering.

10.4.3 Efficient Capital Markets

The collapse of the Hanbo Business Group in January 1997 illustrates the serious weaknesses in Korean financial institutions. (Another business group Sammi failed in March 1997). The Hanbo used to be the fourteenth largest business group in Korea. Its largest steel company declared bankruptcy in January 1997 and left $6 billion in debt. Korea has had its share of bankruptcies, but this was by far the largest corporate bankruptcy in Korean history (Clifford and Lim, 1997; *Hankook Ilbo*, February 4, 1997, p. 1).

There are many things that are unusual about this corporate collapse. Let us look at just a few.

First, the company was able to borrow $6 billion on a very limited owner's equity of an estimated $200 million. The debt-to-equity ratio of 30:1 was way beyond any one's comprehension in any industrial society. Second, the steel industry is an overcrowded mature industry. And yet, more than 60 lending institutions were willing to pour money into such an unpromising industry with little collateral. Third, the steel making technology that the company adopted was not a widely-used technology; the government nevertheless approved the venture. Adoption of this technology had been previously rejected. Fourth, the central bank is injecting an additional $7.1 billion into the financial system to avoid major economic disruption. Fifth, in order to complete the Hanbo Steel Mill, additional investments will be required. Because of cost overruns, the mill is not likely to turn any profit. Is the government planning to rescue the failing firm?

Sixth, Hanbo's discretionary funds were speculated to be somewhere between $600 million to $2.5 billion; its management has been accused of using these funds to pay off bank officials, to bribe government officials and politicians, and for personal use (*Hankook Ilbo*, February 4, 1997, pp. 1 and 3). How can such a huge amount of money be disguised as discretionary expenses for several years without being exposed? Finally, more than 60 bankers, government officials, and politicians were allegedly involved in securing the loans for Hanbo and/or receiving loan commissions, political contributions, and/or bribes from Hanbo's management. What business do politicians have in bank loans? In order to understand the mysteries associated with Hanbo's collapse, one has to understand the Korean *chon-ji* "gift-giving" culture, the symbiotic relationship between business and government, and the political lobbying practice in Korea. These points will be elaborated on later.

What this episode has demonstrated is that the Korean banking and financial systems have yet to be developed to gain respectability and to function as vital economic institutions. During the military-dominated political regimes, Korean banks were under the control of the government and were used as a means to mobilize the nation's resources to achieve the nation's economic development plans. Loans were made to firms on the basis of political connections, called "policy loans," rather than cash flow projections and sufficient collaterals. As a result, Korean banks are stuck with unproductive loans.

The civilian government under President Kim Young Sam has made an attempt to free these banks from government control but it has a long way to go to achieve its goal. In order to make another attempt to rationalize the Korean banking systems, President Kim created a presidential committee to overhaul Korea's financial institutions, just a few days earlier the announcement of the Hanbo's collapse (*Hankook Ilbo*, January 8, 1997, p. 1). What Korean financial institutions need most at this juncture is to free themselves from political influence and to develop efficient capital markets which can allocate funds for promising industries. Korean interest rates have been the highest among any industrial nations; this hinders the development of competitive industries. Creation of efficient capital markets is badly needed in order to lower the costs of capital for Korean firms.

In the absence of efficient domestic capital markets, the government recently freed Korean banks and industries to tap foreign capital in order to meet funding needs and to reduce the cost of capital (Kim, 1997; *Hankook Ilbo*, March 15, 1997, p. 8). It is an welcome move for Korean industries, but it can be a threat to Korean financial institutions. This financial reform will undoubtedly stimulate Korean banks and other financial institutions to reform themselves to be competitive.

10.4.4 Wage and Productivity

The widespread general labor dispute and strike, which started in the closing days in 1996 and continued in early 1997, demonstrated an urgent need for improving labor-management relations in Korea. Labor-management relations in Korea never have been able to strike a proper balance in meeting the needs of businesses and employees. In the past decades, labor was used as a strategic weapon in gaining Korea's low cost advantage in the international market. Labor's rights to organize, negotiate, and take collective action were denied and worker wages were arbitrarily set low under the policy of "growth first and distribution later." Since political reform in 1987, the situation has reversed completely. Workers have not only gained their rights to organize, negotiate, and take collective action but have also received substantial annual pay increases irrespective of their productivity.

Faced with declining international competitiveness, in the late 1996, the government revised the labor law to legalize previously unlawful labor unions and to allow third party intervention in settling labor disputes. This new law was to give employers the right to lay off employees during economic downturns and to deny payment of wages for employees who are on strike. This revision met the standards of international labor laws. The labor unions and the opposition political parties, however, rejected the new law and demanded its abolition. When their demands were not met, the labor unions went on a nationwide general strike. Fearing a major disruption in the economy, the ruling party backed off from its original stand.

The revision of labor law once again debated at the national assembly; a new labor law was passed in March 1997. This newly passed labor law has not altered much from the previous one that was passed in December 1996. What made the situation different in March 1997 was the sense of economic urgency created by the Hanbo collapse and the widespread economic recession in the spring of 1997. Regardless of the status of the law, it will be extremely difficult for Korean firms to lay off employees because labor unions will vigorously object to any layoffs. Over the years, militant labor unions have demonstrated their capacity to force management to accept their demands and their willingness to destabilize the nation's economy in order to serve their interests. In order to avoid increasingly militant labor unions and higher wage demands, Korean firms are moving their operations overseas where wages and other factor costs are low.

This exodus of Korean firms will have two effects on the Korean economy. The first is to reduce employment opportunities for Korean workers. As firms are moving out of the country, there will be fewer jobs for Korean workers. And yet, Korean firms are forced to keep workers and even pay higher wages to maintain labor peace. As a result, Korean domestic firms are overstaffed and have become inefficient. This led to the loss of industrial competitiveness and has increased the chances of bankruptcy. The government often rescues failing firms in order to appease angry labor and to resurrect failing industries. But these measures only postpone the real problems--lack of productivity and managerial inefficiencies. As they are rescued, both managers and workers find no incentives to find solutions on their own.

Secondly, actual bankruptcies might have some positive effects on the economy. As bankruptcies put people (both managers and workers) out of work, they will have some moderating effect on wage increase. Until people see other people losing jobs, they will not feel the need for moderation. Furthermore, as factories move out of the country, the demand for land will be moderated too. This combined force of lowering wages and land costs will have a positive effect on the Korean economy. Solving problems through free market economic forces is a painful experience, but it is an effective way to deal with economic problems in a fundamental way.

10.4.5 Social Overheads Investment

While Korean policy makers were preoccupied with economic growth, they neglected the development of social overhead industries such as transportation, pollution controls and health care. As a result, the social overhead costs imposed on the nation's businesses is staggering. It is estimated that distribution costs (transportation, packaging, and warehouse) amount to 17 percent of total sales for Korean businesses, compared to about 11 percent for American and Japanese counterparts (*Hankook Ilbo*, January 9, 1197, p. 7). It sometimes costs more to transport goods within Korea than between Korea and the U.S.

The impact of poor infrastructure goes beyond the economic inefficiency; it has a negative consequence on the quality of life for the general population. As the economy expands, the people have more money to spend. In that sense, the quality of life has improved. But the increased consumption without the improvement of social overhead facilities tends to diminish the quality of life. For example, as more cars are dumped into streets, traffic jams have become a way of life in Korea. Cars are supposed to provide convenience, but they have become nuisance. Moreover, air-pollution generated from automobiles has become a major threat to public health.

Why do Koreans neglect the development of social overhead industries? Among various plausible reasons, the concept of wealth seems to be most significant. People in advance nations measure their wealth with what they personally possess along with what the society as a whole possesses. As a result, they have invested in such public goods as highways, parks, museums, and other facilities that the public can enjoy. In contrast, Koreans tend to measure wealth in terms of personal possessions; consequently they are less interested in investing in public possessions. As noted elsewhere, Koreans pay the lowest tax on real estate, compared to people in other industrial nations. If Koreans are interested in regaining international competitiveness and in moving up the economic ladder, they need to invest in social overhead industries.

10.5 Societal Change and Reform

There are three destructive elements in Korean society eroding the Korea's industrial competitiveness and its chance for moving up the economic ladder: the traditional *chon-ji* "gift-giving" culture, political corruption, and land speculation. These elements have been destroying Korea's international competitiveness. To cover gift-related costs, firms have to cut corners on projects, thus undermining safety standards. The collapses of the Sampung Department Store and Sungsu Bridge in recent years have proven this point. Gift-giving to government officials and politicians often takes the form of bribes and destroys the moral fabric of the nation. The rising costs of gratuities, bribes, and land costs are added to the costs of Korean products, eroding Korea's ability to compete in the global market. These costs also widen the gap between the "haves" and "have-nots," causing social injustice and unrest.

10.5.1 *Chon-ji* Culture

The practice of *chon-ji* (an envelope containing money) started as a societal virtue of exchanging gifts during new year holidays, August-harvest festivals, and Christmas holidays. This practice is also retained to celebrate someone's birthday, wedding, promotion, getting a job, and so on. It is also extended to show appreciation to someone who has done a favor. In the preindustrial period, a typical gift did not amount to more than a box of fruit, a sack of rice, some nice clothes, or a box of chocolate. But as the nation became prosperous, so did the size of a gift. As the magnitude of favors grew larger, so did the accompanying gratuity. For example, in the case of the Hanbo Business Group, bank presidents allegedly took gratuities ranging from $50,000 to $500,000, depending the size of loans (*Hankook Ilbo*, February 6, 1997, p. 5). The amount even grew larger when politicians were involved (*Hankook Ilbo*, February 6, 1997, p. 1).

Why do bank presidents take such a gratuity and risk their own careers? Common explanations are as follows: First, they consider the gratuity as an appreciation for their services. They hardly think of it as a bribe; they rather consider it as a gift of appreciation. In order to down play its significance, people even call it *dduck-gap*, translated as "cake money." Second, they need money to return favors to those people who put them into the positions. Third, their tenure tends to be short lasting one or two years. So while they are in such positions, they have to accumulate wealth large enough for retirement. If they can arrange just few large loans, they can easily achieve their retirement financial goals. Finally, even if they get caught, the financial benefits far exceed potential costs. They usually step down from their positions, which will occur regardless. In certain cases, some of them may go to jail, but not many serve long jail terms. As long as payoffs outweigh penalties, it will encourage rather than deter criminal gift-giving practices.

10.5.2 Political Corruption

The civilian government under the leadership of President Young Sam Kim took the initiative of dislodging government's close ties with business. President Kim himself declared that no political contributions will be received. And yet so many government officials and politicians are still taking bribes, often couched as political contributions. The Hanbo fiasco has demonstrated how serious political contributions or bribes can become. People close to President Kim (including his own son) and the head of the opposition party, politicians in influential positions, and government officials in economy-related ministries were allegedly involved in taking money from the Hanbo Business Group.

Two observations can be made as an explanation. First, government officials and political elites still have power to influence the banks in Korea. In the late 1980s, commercial banks were freed from government control. But the government still has some influence on commercial banks because the banks depend on government for mitigating the burden of unproductive loans. Another sources of influence come in the process of selecting bank presidents and in getting licenses and permits, and in handling government financial assets. For example, government officials and prominent politicians often serve on selection committees searching for new bank presidents. Monetary gifts for those people who may serve on such committees can be valuable investment that can pay off handsomely later, but such gifts are not considered to be bribes because there is no *quid pro quo* arrangement involved.

Second, politicians take money from businesses in order to get elected and to support their political activities. Once they are elected and strategically positioned, they may decide to return the favors. However, as long as there is no *quid pro quo* arrangement, there is no criminal liability. The line between political donations and bribes is so blurred that unsavory political lobbying can go on without being exposed. Additionally, there is no accounting systems to separate the boundary between political donations and "cake money." They all go to personal coffers; it is up to the receivers to decide their uses. Campaign financing and political donation laws must be clear on these matters and be open to the public so that the public and the court can judge the *quid pro quo* relationship.

The jail terms for two former presidents, bank presidents, and other government officials for taking bribes are the steps for the right direction. Congressional hearings on the Hanbo fiasco is also a welcome event. Public indictment and condemnation of such once powerful individuals show Koreans' determination to root out corruption and will undoubtedly deter such unsavory behaviors. What Korea needs now is to reform the systems in order to prevent such corruptions from reoccurring.

10.5.3 Land Speculation

Because Korea is densely populated and has little cultivatable land, the price of land is bound to increase. What exacerbates the situation is land speculation that involves such social elites including business executives, government officials, and politicians. Because they are in positions in which insiders' information regarding government's developmental projects can be traded, they have an unfair advantage over the general public in land speculation. It has been speculated that the upper ten percent of the population owns more than 75 percent of the land (SaKong, 1993).

Land ownership has become a major force dividing the nation into the rich and poor, causing a serious social class division. Land owners are the most conspicuous consumers who indulge most expensive foreign-made goods. Excessive unearned incomes give them purchasing power that is far beyond the reach of average wage earners, creating a sense of relative deprivation. This gives workers a justification for demanding higher wages and demoralize the nation's poor.

Escalation of land prices is dragging down the Korean economy. It adds to the costs of Korean products, making them less competitive in the international market. The cost of building a plant in Korea is ten times higher than that of the U.S. (*Hankook Ilbo*, January 14, 1997, p. 9). This is another reason why Korean firms move overseas. Land speculation is a serious national issue, but no one seems to have the power to do something about it. In the early years, President Kim's Administration took the initiative to curb land speculation by requiring real name-based land ownership systems. A real name-based ownership system would expose concentrated ownership of land; owners could be targeted for distribution or for heavy taxation. But the measure has never been fully materialized.

The government also can curb land speculation fever by taxing real estate, especially speculative land holdings. But the real property tax rate is the lowest among industrial nations (SaKong, 1993, p. 195; Korea Social Science Research Institute, 1993, p. 150). The tax systems have been revised several times to discourage land speculation, but these changes have not gone far enough to make any major dent in land speculation. Because the social power elites, who have the power to change the tax law, are the major beneficiaries of the current tax system, no significant change has been made.

Faced with an economic urgency, the government should make another attempt to moderate land speculation by increasing the tax rate on real estate. This will not only dampen land speculation but also produce some positive side effects. It will help to curb conspicuous consumption of expensive foreign-made goods by people with excessive unearned incomes.

Moreover, tax proceeds can be invested in social overheads to improve the quality of life for the general populace.

If land speculation is not moderated by changing tax systems, it will be eventually moderated by the forces in the free market economy. As Korean products become less competitive in the global market, the need for additional land space for commercial use will be minimized. For example, the exodus of Korean firms will have a moderating effect on land speculation. Such a phenomenon has already occurred in the Japanese economy. As Japanese companies relocate manufacturing facilities overseas and elderly farmers are abandoning their fields, demands for commercial land has gone down substantially. Commercial land price has dropped as much as 70 to 80 percent from its peak in 1991 (Holstein, 1997).

10.5.4 Hostile Northern Brothers

The need for social change and reform is even greater because Korea has yet to face the toughest challenge, the issue of reunification (Clifford, 1994, p. 335). The chronic shortage of food and the defection of North Korea's social and political elite signal the gradual disintegration of the oppressive society. While some, including the U.S. intelligence community, predict an imminent breakdown of the society, others such as northern defectors are more cautious about such a possibility. Life in North Korea is said to be unbearable; the Orwellian society has a way of keeping its people under control for a long time. What is clear to us is that such a society will come to an end sooner or later. When it does, it will be a tremendous burden for South Korea. The reunification cost is estimated to be somewhere between $500 billion and $1 trillion over a ten year period.

It is hoped that such an eventuality does not occur at a time when South Korea is struggling to deal with its own internal weaknesses. South Korea needs time to fix its own economic house in order and to prepare for reunification. It is suggested here that South Korea should build monetary reserves to pay for reunification costs. It may also serve South Korea's interests to help North Korea sustain its economic survivability at least until South Korea can effectively deal with the reunification issue. South Korea so far has done a remarkable job in keeping the north Korean hostility under control by not showing open hostility. Such a posture should continue.

10.6 The Last Word

Korea made a tremendous economic progress in the past three decades. It is at the threshold of moving up the economic ladder. However, whether or not Korea will make the transition to a more advanced economy depends on how its people deal with several major weaknesses that have surfaced in recent years: structural deficiencies in Korean industries, banking irregularities, political corruption, financial inefficiencies, land speculation, hostile labor-management relations, and hostile northern neighbors. The trial of two former presidents, the collapse of the Hanbo business group, the collapse of a fancy downtown department store building, the nationwide general labor strike, the exodus of Korean firms, and the north Korea's infiltration of the south by a submarine are the manifestations of these weaknesses.

No countries are immuned from labor unrest, political corruption, banking irregularities, and other problems. The difference between advanced and less-advanced nations is that advanced societies constantly reform their systems in order to prevent problems from reoccurring. Whereas less-advanced nations fail to reform their systems and thus allow problems to reoccur. Over the years, when unpleasant situations occurred, Koreans tended to replace law breakers without fundamentally reforming the systems.

The question now is: "Are the above incidents shocking enough for the Korean social and political elite and the general public to wake up and reform their society, its institutions, legal framework, and cultural norms to overcome Korea's internal weaknesses?" If the answer is yes, Korea will once again move up the economic developmental ladder and eventually join the ranks of advanced nations. If not, its future is not that bright. It is not the first time Koreans have faced such a formidable challenge. Koreans have survived many crises in the past. In fact, they have the tendency to rise up and meet challenges in the face of an urgent crisis. The political reform of 1987 was an example. The sense of urgency created by recent events might just stimulate Koreans to act and speed up the transformational process toward a more advanced society.

10.7 Epilogue

As of June 1997, two former presidents are in prison for taking bribes, and a son of the sitting president is arrested for bribery and tax evasion charges. These events reflect a shameful chapter of Korean history. But, at the same time, these events signal a new era in political economy in Korea. Political reforms are firmly taking place and the rule of law is taking hold. On the business front, three big businesses (Hanbo, Sammi, and Jinro) are either bankrupted or on the verge of bankruptcy. Other big businesses are taking notes of these events and undertaking restructuring of their own. The government's hands are less visible than they used to be. When they are visible, they demand a separation of management from ownership, hastening the separation process. Additionally, for the first time since the late 1980s, the increase in productivity outpaces that of wage increases. All in all, this is tough time for the Korean economy, but the much needed cultural, social, economic, political, and technological transformation processes are underway.

References

Barney, J.B. (1997): *Gaining and Sustaining Competitive Advantage*. Reading, MA: Addison-Wesley.

Butler, S. (1997): "Down, but Hardly Out," *U.S. News and World Report*, February 10:34-35.

Clifford, M.L. (1994): *Troubled Tiger: Businessmen, Bureaucrats, and Generals in South Korea*. Armonk, NY: M.E. Sharpe.

Clifford, M.L. and Lim, J. (1997): "Meltdown in Seoul: Hanbo's Fall Shakes the System," *Business Week*, February 10, 1997, pp. 50-51.

Holmes, K.R. and Kirkpatrick, M. (1996): "Freedom and Growth," *Wall Street Journal*, December 16:A-16.

Kim, C.T. (1997): "Financial reform: A Korean Big Bang," *Business Korea*, 14(2):64-65.

Korea Social Science Research Institute (1993): *Korean Economy*. Seoul: Yeiam Publishing.

Porter, M.E. (1984): *Competitive Advantage: Creating and Sustaining Superior Performance*. New York: Free Press.

Porter, M.E. (1990): *The Competitive Advantage of Nations*. New York: Free Press.

SaKong, Il. (1993): *Korean in the World Economy*. Washington, DC: Institute for International Economics.

Index